W9-BZG-378

Batos,

Bolillos,

Pochos, &

Pelados

Batos, Bolillos,

Class &

Culture

Pochos, **&** *Pelados*

on the

South

Texas

Border

Chad Richardson

 University of Texas Press   Austin

Copyright © 1999 by the University of Texas Press
All rights reserved
Printed in the United States of America
First edition, 1999

Requests for permission to reproduce material from this work should
be sent to Permissions, University of Texas Press, Box 7819, Austin,
TX 78713-7819.

⊗ The paper used in this publication meets the minimum requirements of American National Standard for Information Sciences—
Permanence of Paper for Printed Library Materials, ANSI Z39.48-1984.

Library of Congress Cataloging-in-Publication Data

Richardson, Chad, 1943–
    Batos, bolillos, pochos, and pelados : class and culture on the
South Texas border / Chad Richardson. — 1st ed.
        p.   cm.
    Includes bibliographical references and index.
    ISBN 0-292-77091-X (cloth). — ISBN 0-292-77090-1 (pbk.)
    1. Social classes—Texas.   2. Social classes—Mexican-American
Border Region.   3. Subculture—Texas.   4. Subculture—Mexican-
American Border Region.   5. Texas—Race relations.   6. Mexican-
American Border Region—Race relations.   7. Texas—Ethnic
relations.   8. Mexican-American Border Region—Ethnic relations.
I. Title.
HN79.T43S67   1999
305.5'09764—dc21   98-38365

Drawings by Noel Palmenez

Designed by LiMiTeD Edition Book Design, Linda Mae Tratechaud
Photographs by George McLemore

To the individuals
along this great
fault line we call
the border who
shared their lives.
They illuminated
ours in the process.

Contents

Figures

Tables

Preface

International borders often create unusual situations. Few situations are more unusual than the one on the southern end of the Texas-Mexico border. This region, frequently disputed territory in the past, has emerged as neither fully American nor fully Mexican.

Large numbers of Mexicans who cross with temporary permits become semipermanent residents of the border region. They, and thousands of Mexicans who cross illegally, often remain in the border zone because it is harder to get past the second checkpoint seventy miles to the north. For them, the United States starts at Falfurrias and other similar checkpoints.

By the same token, Mexico does not really start at the Río Bravo. Much U.S. industry has relocated to the maquila parks on the south bank of the Río Bravo. Americans generally cross the Mexican border zone with nothing more than a wave of the hand. Mexicans from the border zone, however, drive cars that cannot be taken into the interior of Mexico. Their quasi-Mexican status is formalized with tags proclaiming FRONT TAMPS (Tamaulipas, Border Zone). Mexico, in reality, starts at the secondary checkpoints twenty-two kilometers south of the river.

Sandwiched between these secondary checkpoints are, to borrow a term from Oscar Martínez, the core borderlands.[1] Inside this area, immigration and customs agents from both countries operate under laws somewhat different from those elsewhere in each country. Mexican citizens living in the core borderlands have legal exceptions and requirements not found elsewhere in Mexico. And citizens from either country can enter the core borderlands with fewer restrictions than those governing entry past the secondary checkpoints.

The South Texas borderlands are also different from other U.S.-Mexico border areas. Here, for example, Mexican Americans greatly outnumber Anglos. In addition, the Lower Rio Grande Valley is also the poorest stretch of borderlands, partly because it is home to the United States' largest farmworker population. Its impoverished colonias outnumber those found elsewhere along the two-thousand-mile border.

Mexicans from the lower Río Bravo core borderlands are also somewhat different from other Mexican borderlanders. Monterrey, Mexico's third-largest city and its industrial leader, for example, is only 150 miles to the west southwest. The power of its economy, the strength of its universities, and the independence of its newspapers have exerted a powerful influence on the culture and the economy of the downriver borderlands.

People from the core borderlands are also great innovators of culture. *Norteña* and *conjunto* music, for example, took the accordion from German immigrants, much like the Plains Indians took the horse from the Spaniards. Similarly, the Tejano culture of South Texas is more than a mixing of Mexican and American forms. In addition, "Tex-Mex" is more than just a combination of two languages. Many foods, customs, expressions, and the form of local speech and culture, are indicative of lively amalgamation.

The Lower Rio Grande Valley is also an exporter of culture. It is hard to find pockets of Chicano culture anywhere in the United States that do not trace some major roots back through the migrant streams to South Texas. And though Valley Anglos used to ridicule foods of Mexican origin, these same foods have become popular cuisine throughout the United States and even abroad. Fajitas, for example, were a local staple long before they became popular further north. Also, thanks to the wonders of science that have taken the bite out of Mexican jalapeños and chilis, salsa has replaced catsup as the number one condiment in the United States.

Valley culture, however, has an impact much greater than its influence on foods, language, and music. As Anglos, Mexicans, and Blacks interact with the predominantly Mexican American population, the culture of each group is affected. Newcomers to the area notice these nuances immediately. While some are greatly bothered by them, others come to feel a new sense of appreciation and belonging.

The sense of adaptability has both cultural and structural roots. Structurally, poverty requires innovation. When low-income housing became unavailable in Valley cities, for example, colonias developed almost overnight as a family-oriented response. Today, when Mexican women find it necessary to help support a family, becoming an undocumented maid in a border city produces one solution. When the homes of migrant farmworkers become increasingly threatened with vandalism, getting a dog or eliciting help from family and neighbors proves an affordable solution.

Mexican culture also encourages adaptability. Unlike Anglos, however, Mexicans tend to respond to needs and new situations by informal means. Less formal relations predominate over formal ones, and outcomes are assured more by personal obligation than by contract and formal systems. As a result, people of Mexican origin in the Valley tend to take the obligations associated with friendship and family very seriously.

This tendency toward responsiveness and warm interpersonal relations may help explain another puzzle of the South Texas border. How can so much diversity exist without serious and sustained conflict? Though Anglos dominated Hispanics in South Texas for generations, relatively harmonious relations characterize their interaction today when Anglos are a relatively small numerical minority. Though some Mexicans consider Mexican Americans "gringoized," and some Mexican Americans regard Mexicans as *mojados* ("wetbacks"), most individuals from both groups get along relatively well. Finally, though retired Winter Texans generally isolate themselves from local residents, they almost uniformly report very friendly treatment.

When I set out to write this book, I wanted a title that could represent the Valley's uniqueness and its diversity. *Batos, Bolillos, Pochos, and Pelados* seemed to fit. *Bato* to young Mexican Americans means "man," as in "Oye, bato" (Hey, man). It expresses in-group solidarity and epitomizes the sense of identity found among many South Texas Mexican Americans. *Bolillo* (white bread roll) and *pocho* (faded; off-colored), in contrast, are terms used to designate members of out-groups. The first indicates an Anglo and the second a Mexican American who is overly Americanized in speech and culture. In Mexico a *pelado* (one who is hairless) is someone suspected of criminal activity, possibly related to the practice of cutting the hair of Mexican prisoners. Along the border, however, it means someone disreputable, whether involved in criminal activity or not. These terms are not normally used around members of these groups except in gentle kidding. They are, however, part of local culture. Since the book is also about culture and intergroup relations, I felt these terms, each closely related to the border, were appropriate.

Though I do not say much in this volume about *pelados*, those to whom this term is often applied will be a major focus of a planned second volume. It will deal with, among other things, the criminal element along the border (car thieves, smugglers, coyotes, and youth gangs).

I hope that the research on which this book is based exemplifies border culture. Storytelling is an important part of the culture of South Texas, and the project was designed to let South Texas borderlanders collectively tell their own stories.

I trust the project also represents Valley culture in its effort to identify and build upon local strengths. The University of Texas–Pan American may lack some of the resources of larger universities, but its students (85 percent of whom are Mexican American) are intimately connected to the local community. Because of these connections, the students who interviewed the borderlanders were able to obtain accounts that more highly trained (or better paid) researchers would have missed.

I anticipate that this project will give something back to the interviewers and to the people they interviewed. Besides learning interviewing skills, many students gained a new appreciation for the sacrifices their parents and others have made. Alma, for example, learned for the first time of the discrimination her grandmother experienced growing up in South Texas in the 1920s and 1930s. "All the time I was growing up," she says, "I never knew about the discrimination and horrible treatment my family suffered in those times. After the interview, I asked her why she had never told us these stories. She told me she didn't want us to live with the hard feelings she had grown up with. Hearing about her life, though, made me feel deep respect for what she became in spite of those obstacles."

I also hope the people interviewed feel vindicated for sharing their stories. Leticia Núñez, a farmworker for her entire life, burst into tears when told the purpose of her interview. "She said she was glad I was doing the interviews," reports the young woman who conducted the interview, "because she wanted the community to know what migrant farmworkers suffer to put food on America's table."

It is our aim to tell the stories of the *batos, bolillos, pochos,* and other subcultures of South Texas not only with objectivity but also with respect and dignity. They have so much to teach us.

Acknowledgments

Many individuals have contributed to this work at various stages. In 1982 Dorey Schmidt and Hal Kopel helped me initiate the Borderlife Project with a grant from Ideas, Inc. From 1989 until 1992, Juanita Garza directed the project, gaining the collaboration of many talented individuals. At the time I again became director of Borderlife, in 1992, Cruz Torres came to the University of Texas–Pan American (UT–Pan American). She helped analyze and organize the research on migrant farmworkers and undocumented maids.

In 1994 a grant from the Texas Committee for the Humanities, then under the direction of Dr. Roberto Salmón, allowed us to develop a series of seminars to extend Borderlife into the public schools of the Lower Rio Grande Valley. The idea for this text arose from these seminars.

When I started writing, several colleagues provided invaluable reviews of the material. Dale McLemore, a mentor and friend since my graduate days at the University of Texas at Austin, provided thoughtful suggestions and timely encouragement. Dr. Hugh Miller, a longtime friend and a borderlands scholar, gave excellent reviews, especially related to historical aspects of the book. Jan Seale and Letitia Blalock edited the first manuscript.

Countless other friends and colleagues have provided assistance and made useful observations. Colleagues Al Nelson, Joseph Speilberg, James Aldridge, and Rudy Rocha gave helpful comments on key portions of the book. Rafael Sevilla and Joy Sevilla made suggestions from their reading of the early manuscript. Mary Rose, formerly of the UT–Pan American Computer Center, provided much needed assistance in coding and analyzing the survey research.

I am especially indebted to Theresa May, executive editor of the University of Texas

Press, who gave valuable encouragement for the project from the early stages of writing through the reviewing and editing. Her suggestions were always timely and valuable.

I must give the most important acknowledgment, however, to the student interviewers associated with the Borderlife Project. They collected the stories and interviewed most of the individuals whose stories and interview responses make up this work. Those who allowed their names to be used are credited in Appendix A. In addition, Sonia Saldaña, Norma Anzaldúa, Teresa Mendez, Eric Martinez, Sreelatha (Lata) Goburu, Elizabeth Castillo, and Marioli Villarreal helped organize the files and prepare the surveys for computer analysis.

Finally, I must add special thanks to my wife, Elizabeth, for her comments on the manuscript and for her encouragement in producing it. She and our children allowed me the quiet time needed to write. They also provided occasional respite from the writing and the sense of balance so essential to maintaining one's sanity in a project of this nature.

Batos,

Bolillos,

Pochos, &

Pelados

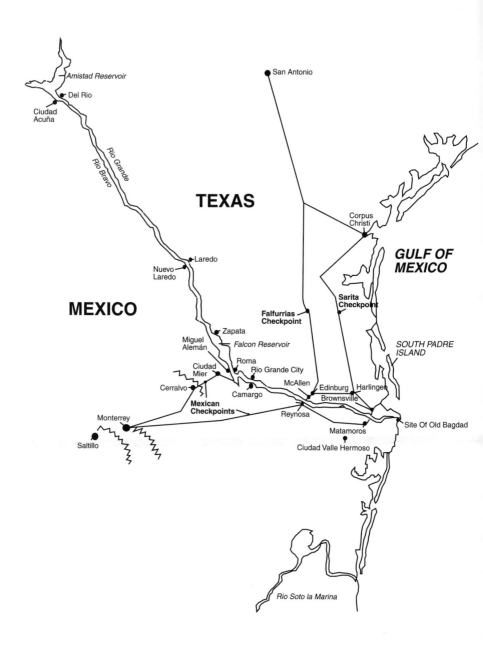

South Texas and Northern Mexico

The following is a list of the interview projects in this book, the number of respondents in each, the dates they were conducted, and the chapters in which the findings are discussed.

Borderlife Interview Projects

Exploratory Interviews

MIGRANT FARMWORKERS: 1,398 respondents, 1988–1993, Chapter 1

COLONIA RESIDENTS: 67 respondents, 1990–1994, Chapter 2

UNDOCUMENTED MAIDS: 432 respondents, 1991–1993, Chapter 3

EMPLOYERS OF UNDOCUMENTED MAIDS: 214 respondents, 1992–1993, Chapter 3

MAQUILA WORKERS: 75 respondents, 1992–1997, Chapter 4

MEXICAN STREET CHILDREN: 90 respondents, 1990–1997, Chapter 4

FORMER STUDENTS: 603 respondents, 1989–1994, Chapter 5

MEXICAN IMMIGRANTS: 270 respondents, 1988–1995, Chapter 6

ANGLO NEWCOMERS: 192 respondents, 1992–1996, Chapter 7

WINTER TEXANS: 288 respondents, 1994–1995, Chapter 7

VALLEY BLACKS: 85 respondents, 1994–1996, Chapter 8

Survey Interviews

MIGRANT FARMWORKERS: 260 respondents, 1993, Chapter 1

COLONIA RESIDENTS: 545 respondents, 1994, Chapter 2

UNDOCUMENTED MAIDS: 162 respondents, 1993, Chapter 3

EMPLOYERS OF UNDOCUMENTED MAIDS: 136 respondents, 1993, Chapter 3

FORMER STUDENTS: 243 respondents, 1994, Chapter 5

MEXICAN IMMIGRANTS: 324 respondents, 1995, Chapter 6
ANGLO NEWCOMERS: 224 respondents, 1996, Chapter 7
WINTER TEXANS: 326 respondents, 1995, Chapter 7
VALLEY BLACKS: 37 respondents, 1996, Chapter 8
MULTIETHNIC CULTURE: 532 respondents, 1996, Chapters 6, 7, 8

Introduction

Just north of Brownsville, a few miles from the Gulf of Mexico, are two historic battlefields. One is the site of the first battle of the war with Mexico. The other is the location of the last battle of the Civil War.

In 1846 war with Mexico began here when President James Polk, apparently to provoke a war, sent U.S. troops into this disputed territory, which Mexico also claimed. Mexico's response to the decision made in faraway Washington had its most direct impact on the border. And in 1865 the last battle of the Civil War was fought here six weeks after the war had officially ended at Appomattox. The commanders were simply so far removed from decision makers that they had not gotten the news.

Today, residents of the Texas-Mexico border are still the first affected and the last consulted when decisions are made in Washington, D.C., or Mexico, D.F. The NAFTA agreement, for example, has had its greatest impact on the border, though neither Washington nor Mexico City has paid much attention to sentiments and opinions of border residents. Similarly, the maquiladora industry produces strategic benefits for far-off economic and political centers. Border residents are left to manage the resulting stresses on their infrastructure with a small fraction of the economic resources created.

The same pattern was revealed when refugees from violence in Central America poured into the Lower Rio Grande Valley during the 1980s. U.S. involvement in Central America helped produce the flow of refugees, and federal decisions forced the refugees to remain in the Valley. Still, Washington showed little concern for the strain on scarce local resources that these decisions created. In a similar way, Supreme Court decisions have forced border schools to

South Texas—Definitely not Anywhere, USA
(photo courtesy of George C. McLemore).

educate the children of undocumented residents but have mandated no additional federal funds to do so.

The pattern is the same with drug enforcement, environmental contamination, trucking regulations, requirements for medical treatment, and a host of other issues. The border—the first affected and the last consulted—is a place of conflict created by decisions in far-off capitals.

Being the first affected and the last consulted, however, also creates a dynamic process that puts the border at the edge of social change. The growth of the Hispanic population of the United States, for example, is far advanced in the South Texas borderlands, where almost 90 percent of the population is of Mexican origin. The global community that is talked about in schools in the northern United States is forged on a daily basis on the streets and in the markets of the South Texas region.

Thus, "la frontera," the border, is more than a backwater of industrialization, just as border residents are more than victims of neglect and powerlessness. In actuality, they are innovators and problem solvers on the forefront of change. This cutting-edge aspect of the border is reflected in a second meaning of the Spanish term for the border: "la frontera" also means "frontier." In this sense, the border is on the leading edge of massive social changes whose effects may reach the interior long after border residents have found solutions and made necessary adjustments.

Group Boundaries on the Border

In many respects, the Valley is a magnification of situations found elsewhere along the U.S.-Mexico border. Here rural meets urban, traditional confronts modern, enormous wealth grinds against abject poverty, and First World meets Third. It is a major entry point for both legal and undocumented immigrants from Mexico and other countries. Here, highly diverse groups mix, mesh, and mash into a kaleidoscope of cultural and social combinations.

Currently, some 30 million people live within two hundred miles of the two-thousand-mile border separating these two countries. Approximately 750,000 people live in the Lower Rio Grande Valley (Cameron, Willacy, Hidalgo, and Starr Counties). An almost identical population size (766,408) is found in the adjacent Mexican *municipios* (municipalities) of Matamoros, Río Bravo, Valle Hermoso, Reynosa, Miguel Alemán, and Camargo, all in the state of Tamaulipas.[1] These and other factors make the lower valley of the Rio Grande/Río Bravo one of the fastest growing areas in the United States and Mexico, and an area of tremendous cultural and socioeconomic diversity.

Groups emerge and culture changes at a rapid pace. Colonias, for example, are a relatively recent creation along the border. So are Winter Texans, maquiladoras, and *narcotraficantes* (drug dealers).

The lure of quick profits leads some Valley residents into drug smuggling, and this self-destructive turn to an underground economy is often repeated by those who smuggle aliens to the north or guns and electronic equipment to the south. Valley residents, however, largely reject such traps, as is evidenced by the low crime and addiction rates of Valley residents.

Traditions of collective self-help run deep in the Valley and are a source of many legal, religious, and charitable assistance agencies. When refugees fleeing violence in Central America began entering the Valley, for instance, people whose resources were already strained often gave them assistance.

The Research

The Valley is one of the world's prime sites for firsthand observation of social changes in such fields as sociology, political science, health care, multicultural education, and multinational development. Its uniqueness needs to be carefully described and analyzed through research.

Batos, Bolillos, Pochos, and Pelados is based on research from the Borderlife Project at the University of Texas–Pan American. I initiated the project in 1982 as a way to use student interviewers to investigate and describe elements of the South Texas–Northern Mexico border community. Today, the project has data from more than 5,000 exploratory interviews and 3,000 survey interviews with members of fifteen distinct sociocultural groups on both sides of the border. Most research topics include an exploratory (ethnographic) component and another based on survey research. (See "Borderlife Interview Projects," pages xxi–xxii, and Appendix B.)

For the exploratory interviews, students were given a wide selection of topics from which to choose. Subjects (whose names are fictitious throughout this book to protect their identity) were asked to describe their life conditions and to illustrate them with specific incidents.[2] The anecdotes were then examined to identify the most frequently recurring patterns. The patterns revealed by their stories suggested follow-up questions for the survey interviews, which we conducted to measure the prevalence of patterns that emerged from the exploratory interviews.

In most survey projects, using random samples was not possible because the populations under study were either hidden (e.g., undocumented immigrants) or inaccessible (e.g., maquila workers). Instead, student interviewers selected people they knew or someone introduced to them by a friend or family member.[3] Though this procedure produced a sample that may not be entirely representative of the larger group, the openness and trust in the interviews largely compensated, particularly with subjects involved in delicate or extralegal topics (illegal immigration, smuggling, etc.). The survey project did not sacrifice representativeness entirely, however. When these convenience samples are compared with the populations they represent, the correspondence to the known characteristics of these groups is strong.

Student interviewers were allowed to select the type of research—exploratory (open-ended) or survey—that they would conduct. At the end of each semester, students also chose whether to authorize the use of their material for the Borderlife Project. Those who authorized its use also had the option of having their names credited. All of the stories used in the text have been so authorized, and the students whose names appear in Appendix A have asked that their names be credited. We have not attached the names to specific stories, however, to further protect the anonymity of the interviewees.

In conveying the stories of the people quoted in the book, I found it necessary occasionally to select, edit, or transpose material. Always, however, I have tried to reproduce faithfully the meaning conveyed by the subjects. Because the students translated many of their interviews, and because they often provided abbreviated versions when they had been unable to make audio recordings, exact quotes were seldom possible.

Over 2,000 of the exploratory interviews conducted by our student interviewers focus on poverty-related issues. A slightly smaller number of interviews were conducted on topics related to the ongoing struggle between ethnic (or racial) groups in South Texas. The poverty and ethnic struggles they document are part of the very special character of the people in the South Texas borderlands today. This contemporary class and ethnic mosaic cannot be comprehended without knowing some history of the South Texas–Northern Mexico border region.

The Impact of History on Class and Ethnicity in South Texas

EARLY HISTORY

South Texas has a long history of ethnic, class, and racial conflict.[4] Less than thirty years from the day that Columbus waded ashore on San Salvador, Spaniards were exploring and mapping the Gulf Coast near the mouth of the Rio Grande. In 1520 Don Diego de Camargo sailed three ships up the Rio Grande (then called Río de las Palmas).[5] Like many Spaniards of his day, Camargo believed that a show of force would scare the Native Americans into submission, so he and his men descended from the ships on horseback and fired their guns. But rather than submitting, the Native Americans attacked the Spaniards, killing eighteen of them and all of their horses. In their hasty retreat, the Spaniards also lost a ship. Humiliated, they fled to the Gulf of Mexico with a fleet of canoes in hot pursuit.[6]

An opposite reception was accorded Alvar Núñez Cabeza de Vaca. In 1527 he and other Spaniards survived the loss of their ships in Florida, struggled across the Gulf of Mexico in makeshift rafts, and after many adventures made their way to the Rio Grande, probably not far from present-day Reynosa.[7] Here Cabeza de Vaca was treated well by the Coahuiltecan tribes along the river, most likely because he came as a healer, not as a conqueror.[8] Possibly as a result of the friendly treatment he received from the Coahuiltecans and other tribes, Cabeza de Vaca was one of the few Spanish conquistadors to advocate humane treatment of the Native Americans.

For nearly two hundred years, the Coahuiltecans managed to fight off most European settlement and slave raids in the Lower Rio Grande region. An important exception was the establishment of Cerralvo, Mexico, a mining and agricultural center founded in 1579. This site, within forty miles of present-day Roma, is at the base of mountains visible from Starr County. Then, in 1749, José de Escandón founded several towns along the Rio Grande, the first ones being present-day Camargo (across from Rio Grande City) and Reynosa Díaz (across from Mission). These first settlements on the Lower Rio Grande were planned, in part, to subdue the Coahuiltecans, who were resisting Spanish slave raids from Nuevo León. Roma, the first settlement on the north bank of the river, was founded in 1765 as a ranching outpost for Camargo.[9]

By 1850, war or disease had exterminated Native Americans along the Rio Grande. A few had mixed biologically and culturally with the Spaniards. Throughout Mexico, those of mixed blood, or mestizos, were emerging as the largest population group as Mexico gained its independence from Spain in 1821. The mestizos along the Rio Grande had finally begun to emerge from Spanish domination only to find a new threat from the north. Anglo settlers, originally invited into Texas to help colonize it for Mexico, soon fought for and gained independence from Mexico.[10]

After winning the Battle of San Jacinto, Texans forced Mexican general Santa Anna, a prisoner of war, to sign peace treaties. The treaties not only granted Texans their independence but moved the southern boundary of Texas from the Nueces River to the Rio Grande. Although the Mexican government was willing to grant Texans their independence, it repudiated the treaties and continued to regard the area from the Nueces River to the Rio Grande as part of Mexico. Thus this area became a source of intense conflict. Mexicans bitter from defeat raided northward into San Antonio. In 1842 Texans retaliated against Mexican raids by sacking Laredo. Then they launched an attack against Ciudad Mier, fifteen miles upriver from Roma. The Mexican Army captured the Texans and took two hundred of them to Salado, Mexico, where they were forced to draw from a jar of mixed-color beans. The army executed the seventeen who drew black beans, adding to the resentment against Mexicans, especially along the border.

When the United States annexed Texas in 1845, it sent troops into the disputed territory near Brownsville. Mexican troops attacked them to defend the territory, and politicians in Washington used the battle to justify a war with Mexico. Abraham Lincoln, then a young congressman from Illinois, introduced a resolution in Congress in an unsuccessful attempt to force President Polk to acknowledge that the battle had not

Juan Cortina, a few years after his raid on Brownsville (courtesy of Hidalgo County Historical Museum).

occurred on U.S. soil.[11] In the full-fledged war that followed, Mexico lost South Texas and most of the territory of the Southwest to the United States.

After this war, Mexican Americans living in South Texas lost much of their property to Anglo ranchers through theft, extortion, and trickery. Much of their land had been granted to their ancestors by the king of Spain centuries earlier. Juan Cortina, a veteran of the Mexican-American War, was one of these landowners, with property in Mexico and Cameron County, Texas. After witnessing a U.S. marshal harshly arrest a former employee, Cortina shot the marshal and escaped into Mexico. On 13 July 1859, he launched a raid against Brownsville, capturing Fort Brown and the local jail. He then freed the Tejano (Hispanic Texan) prisoners and killed several Americans suspected of brutalizing the Tejanos.[12] The governor of Texas sent two companies of Texas Rangers to put down the revolt. In their first battle, Cortina's men thoroughly defeated the Rangers. When the U.S. Army arrived, Cortina moved his forces to Rio Grande City. Eventually, his army of five hundred Tejanos and Mexicans was defeated by the larger force of soldiers and Rangers. Nevertheless, Cortina escaped unharmed amid a hail of bullets.

In 1870 Cortina returned to the border to launch raids against Texas ranches, some as far north as Corpus Christi. In 1875 Mexican troops arrested him and took him to Mexico City. He soon escaped and made his way back to the border. The U.S. government again pressured Mexico to capture him. He died under house arrest in Mexico City in 1894.

EARLY TWENTIETH CENTURY

Along the border, reaction to Cortina's raids turned into deep suspicion of anyone thought to be Mexican. U.S. troops and Texas Rangers began rounding up many local Mexican Americans and sometimes lynching them, in their effort to tame the area. Longtime residents still remember the raids and the hangings. During this period, Mexican Americans continued to lose large tracts of land by force or collusion between Anglo settlers and public officials.[13]

Artemio, a ninety-seven-year-old lifelong Valley resident, describes one incident that happened around 1917. "Some people from Mexico came over here and started trouble," he says. "They were telling us poor farmers that we could take back land that once was ours. They said we should get rid of the Anglos and be proud once again. That's when the Anglos called in the Texas Rangers. I remember seeing the boxcars ride into town and seeing those great big men on their horses with their hats and guns. Once the Rangers took charge, they didn't really know who started it or who was involved, so they would just go out and round up some men. If they saw you walking down the street, and one told you to come, you went. They would take a man to the outskirts of town and tell him to start running. They would shoot him in the back as he ran and report to the man in charge that they just shot another bandit. People were really afraid of them. They could do whatever they wanted, and no one ever questioned them. I still don't trust them."

Arturo, an older man from San Benito and a lifelong Valley resident, also remembers these times. His family lost thousands of acres originally granted to his ancestors by the king of Spain. "They slowly killed us," he says. "They would shoot our animals and force us off the land. My father lost much land this way, but they had other methods. They would also fail to send us tax forms, so we never knew when to pay our taxes. Then one of them would claim default on the land, pay the taxes, and become owner of our land. Since they had the sheriff and the lawyers, and since our people didn't understand the language or their system, they stole the land under our house. Many of us around here lost land to a wealthy man from Harlingen. People there still think he's a hero."

When the Valley shifted from ranching to farming early in the twentieth century, patterns of interethnic accommodation ended. Previously, many Anglo ranchers had married prominent Hispanic women. Anglo farmers and land developers, however, preferred to segregate Mexican Americans, though they continued to entice Mexican immigrants into the area as a source of cheap labor.[14]

María is seventy-five years old and has lived in South Texas all her life. She still remembers what it was like in those years. Her parents died when she was a young girl, so she moved in with her uncle Eduardo and his family. He was a skilled carpenter who worked for a prominent Anglo farmer. María remembers how her uncle would get up before sunrise and get home well after dark.

"He and his fellow workers always did what they were told," she recalls. "One day, his boss was angry about something and my uncle didn't exactly agree with him, so they exchanged a few words. At the end of the day, when the workers started for home, the boss told him to stay and redo something he hadn't done right. The others left. That night he didn't return home. We stayed up all night worrying. The next day we asked our neighbors about him, but no one had seen him. My cousin went to talk to his boss, but he said that Eduardo had left after redoing his job. Days passed and no one could tell us anything. Then, Saturday morning, they found my uncle in a nearby wooded area. His body was riddled with bullets and covered with cactus. The older people took him to the river to clean him and pluck the thorns from his body so they could bury him. But we had to wait until night because the neighbors were afraid of the KKK."

Trinidad Perález lived in South Texas during the same period. He found work with an Anglo family in Elsa. "In exchange for my labor," he recalls, "they gave me cornbread, beans, oatmeal, milk, and a small cot in the barn. They also paid me five dollars a week for chores like fixing the roof and shoveling cow manure. But the Anglos in town gave them a hard time for hiring a Mexican and for letting me live with them. They did not allow me in restaurants, stores, the church, or in the town theater. The only people that would speak to me were the couple and their two sons. As time went by, little by little, people began to nod their heads at me, but during the seven years I worked for them, I stayed pretty much in the barn or in the back of the house where my meals were served."

South Texas Today

With the passage of time and civil rights legislation, the situation of Mexican Americans in South Texas began to improve.[15] Indeed, had it not been for the continuous flow of poor Mexican immigrants across the border, the socioeconomic level of South Texas Hispanics might have risen as it has for other ethnic minorities. But today, economic crises in Mexico and a demand for cheap labor in the United States add thousands of impoverished Mexicans to the South Texas population each year. For this and other reasons, most Valley residents are still poor.

When the U.S. Department of Commerce measures per capita income among the three hundred or so urban centers in the United States, three on the South Texas border (McAllen-Pharr-Edinburg in Hidalgo County, Laredo in Webb County, and Brownsville–Harlingen–San Benito in Cameron County) generally rank at the bottom.[16] In addition, though rates of unemployment generally hover between 15 and 20 percent, the area suffers a chronic shortage of nurses, teachers, technicians, and doctors.

In spite of the poverty, South Texas also creates great affluence for some. Wealth is created as college students invade South Padre Island for spring break each year. Wealthy Mexicans come to shop and to protect their wealth against downturns in the Mexican economy by putting it in Texas banks and investments. The maquila industry on the south bank of the river brings highly paid managers to homes on the north bank. And retirees flock to the area each fall to enjoy the mild winters, the migratory birds, and the cheap prices just across the border.

This book examines the ways that class and ethnicity impact lives in South Texas. It also examines the ways the people of South Texas deal with each other and with the decided lack of control over forces that affect their lives. This lack of control is especially true of five distinct class groups on the South Texas–Northern Mexico border: migrant farmworkers, colonia residents, undocumented domestic servants, maquila workers, and street children in Mexican border towns.

Life at the Bottom

The Valley is home to the largest population of migrant farmworkers in the United States. They are among the hardest workers in this country. Their work is dangerous and tiring, yet they work for wages far below the poverty level. Most Valley farmworkers are U.S. residents or citizens, and many carry on a tradition of migrant farmwork that spans several generations. However, in spite of gains in legalizing their status and improving their level of education, many are no better off than their immigrant parents or grandparents, as we shall see in Chapter 1.

Rural housing settlements called colonias are home to many impoverished Valley residents, including migrant farmworkers. Colonia residents, whether migrants or permanent residents, frequently experience a class-based stigma over which they have little control, as is shown in Chapter 2.

Often, powerlessness accompanies the stigma of poverty. This is especially true for the many undocumented domestic workers, or maids, from Mexico who live in constant fear of deportation. Their lack of legal status makes them vulnerable to multiple forms of exploitation—low wages, long hours, and sexual harassment—as Chapter 3 delineates.

The struggle for survival, acceptance, and self-determination, though intense on the Texas side of the river, is often worse on the Mexican side, where many women work in large U.S.-owned maquiladoras (assembly plants). Their struggle near the bottom of the class hierarchy may involve sexual harassment, as well as grinding poverty. These maquila workers, however, are better off financially than the children who sell things on the street to help provide food for their families. Interviews with these children, as well as with maquila workers, are described in Chapter 4.

Ethnic Identity in South Texas

With the influx of newcomers from both south and north, problems of ethnic identity arise. Some local Hispanics are descendants of families that have lived here for hundreds of years, while others are recent immigrants. History and population shifts have combined to create a unique mix of race and cultures on the border. Here Mexican Americans outnumber Anglos four to one. Mexican immigrants even outnumber Anglos. Blacks make up only 0.2 percent of the Valley population. Some Mexican Americans who speak little English mix daily with Anglos who speak little Spanish. Both often cater to wealthy Mexicans who come to shop, although many of these Mexicans look down their noses at the *pochos* (assimilated Mexican Americans). While nearly 90 percent of the Valley is of Mexican origin, it is hard to find anyone here who likes to be called Chicano.[17]

Historically, conflict and ethnocentrism have characterized relations between Anglos and Mexican-origin residents of South Texas. In spite of

The Río Bravo/Rio Grande border at the Reynosa/Hidalgo bridge
(photo courtesy of George C. McLemore).

this, most scars of earlier years are largely gone. The groups discussed in the second half of the book—Mexican Americans, Anglos (newcomers, lifelong residents, and retired Winter Texans), Mexican immigrants, and Blacks—illustrate an ongoing process of interethnic adjustment. The stories collected in the exploratory interviews reveal how exploitation, racism, paternalism, accommodation, and assimilation may all occur simultaneously.

Though the Rio Grande Valley has endured more than four hundred years of intense conflict between racial and ethnic groups, few young people in the Valley know much about the battles, the lynchings, the land theft, or the segregation so common in earlier times. Some middle-aged individuals do recall a less violent form of discrimination in the schools, as we will see in Chapter 5.

Today, an important aspect of ethnic relations in South Texas is the presence of many Mexican immigrants, the topic of Chapter 6. One out of every four persons in the Valley is foreign born, with a large majority of them born in Mexico. Many immigrants miss the culture of Mexico and believe that Mexican Americans have "sold out" their culture and their language.

South Texas is one region of the United States where Anglos are a numerical minority, as Chapter 7 illustrates. Those who speak no Spanish often feel discriminated against or isolated. Knowing Spanish helps, although other barriers often exist.

Minority status depends on more than numbers. A minority group suffers considerable loss of power and is the butt of negative stereotypes. Anglos in South Texas still have considerable power. Often, this gives them options that Mexicans and Mexican Americans do not have. As one Valley Hispanic observed, "It's very hard even now to trust a White person, because they can always go back to being White."

The Anglos least likely ever to step out of "being White" are the ninety-thousand-plus retirees who migrate annually to the Valley, also featured in Chapter 7. While here, they live in special Winter Texan motor home parks, largely isolated from the local population. When they venture out to eat or to shop, they tend to go in groups. Thus, they seldom interact with local Hispanics as neighbors, coworkers, or fellow citizens. Rather, Hispanics wait on them in restaurants, stores, and service centers, so few relationships as equals ever occur. As a result, though Winter Texans regard Hispanics as very friendly, they seldom interact as friends. Rather, each group tends to overgeneralize and misunderstand the other.

In Chapter 8, we will examine the possibility that bias against Mexican Americans in South Texas has become less racist (and ethnocentric) and based more on social class. We will also see that it is often difficult to decide which factor is mainly responsible. Race, ethnicity, and class overlap to a great extent. Most South Texas farmworkers, for example, are poor Mexican Americans, many of whom are dark-complected. Virtually 100 percent of impoverished colonia residents are Mexican or Mexican American. Undocumented maids are usually Mexican, poor, and powerless. How does one separate out the factor that is the main basis for the abuse they often experience?

Class versus Race and Ethnicity

In South Texas, it is often hard to tell whether poverty and discrimination are the result of a group's class position, their race, or their cultural background (ethnicity). Tom, a Black mechanic who spoke no Spanish when he came to the Valley, searched for six months before he finally found a place to work. The rejection he experienced may have been the result of bias against his race, a reaction to his cultural background (including his inability to speak Spanish), or both factors working together. There may also have been prejudice based on his lower-class background.

María, a twenty-four-year-old Mexican American, offers an example of class-based bias. When she dated an Anglo named Jason, she was concerned because his mother seemed very prejudiced against Mexicans. However, Jason's mother explained that her prejudice toward Mexicans was only directed against the "lowlifes" on welfare, not against people like María who came from "good families."

Some sociologists have argued that class bias is replacing racial and ethnic prejudice as the main barrier to mobility for minorities in the United States.[18] Essentially, they argue that Americans today discriminate more on the basis of class differences than on considerations of race or ethnicity. Jason's mother seems to exemplify this bias against lower-class people. She seems to have stronger biases against lower classes than against someone's ethnicity or race. Otherwise, she would have rejected María simply because she was "Mexican."

Culture or Structure?

Perhaps the issue of abuse and discrimination is better framed by distinguishing between cultural and structural factors. The debate over which factor is most important is one of the oldest controversies in the social sciences.

First, we should clarify our use of the terms *culture* and *structure*. All social groups develop shared meanings, or understandings, of right and wrong, truth and error, good and bad. The way of life and the patterned ways they interpret or collectively understand things are their culture. Social groups also establish certain patterns, or forms, in the way they arrange social relationships. These patterns, or forms in the established relationships, constitute their social structure.

CULTURE

Culture potentially affects intergroup relations in South Texas in two major ways. First, culture makes each group ethnocentric. Cultural differences divide diverse groups and unite those who have the same culture. Anglos tend to feel affinity with Anglos, for example, because they share a common culture. Such cultural identification creates an in-group of those who are culturally alike and an out-group of those whose culture is significantly different.

Culture also gives advantages to groups whose culture "fits" the existing economic, educational, legal, or political systems (and gives disadvantages to groups whose culture is not "compatible"). Thus, though Mexican culture has an admirable emphasis on family solidarity, some argue that its emphasis on keeping young adults close to their parents may prevent some from moving around the country to find the best jobs available.

Some problems experienced by undocumented maids also stem indirectly from differences in culture. One student, for example, described her family's maid as excessively shy, always looking down when she talked to the family. The family apparently did not realize that in many parts of Mexico, looking down when addressing a person of higher rank is considered the correct way to show respect. People with this particular cultural orientation will often be misinterpreted, giving them an indirect disadvantage.

Some writers have taken the view of culture as a handicap to an extreme, alleging that minority groups are "culturally deprived" or that the poor in general have a "culture of poverty" that keeps them poor.[19] Both views promote the idea that the main obstacles to greater affluence are cultural. The implied solution to their poverty is to abolish key elements of their culture that are assumed to hold them back. We will return to this argument in the final chapter of the book.

STRUCTURE

One student who conducted interviews of colonia residents recognized how important structural position is as it affects life opportunities. "These colonia residents start with hardly any education," he said, "so they only qualify for field work. This type of work provides no benefits, such as sick leave or health insurance, and they earn the minimum wage or less. As a result, they have to buy property for a home in a colonia. Because of where they live, they send their children to schools that often are of low quality. The net effect is a continuous round of poverty; disadvantages lead only to more disadvantages." Thus, though we can discuss culture and structure, ethnicity and class, as separate concepts, in reality they are tightly interconnected.

Getting Along in South Texas Today

Many students who conducted interviews for the Borderlife Project were able to see the effects of culture and structure on life in South Texas. One student who interviewed several old-timers, for example, commented,

"Following my interviews, I left knowing something about how Mexican Americans had survived the gringo onslaught fifty years ago. Today, at least in the Valley, relations between these two groups have mellowed out. Gringos have learned they are outnumbered and must adjust if they are going to keep living in the Valley. Some Mexican Americans have an 'I wish they would leave' attitude, but it's very dispersed. Most Mexican Americans have become acculturated to the gringo culture. Today, most gringos and Mexicanos get along just fine here in the Valley, unlike fifty years ago when the gringos controlled everything."

Relations in South Texas have clearly changed over the past fifty years, perhaps in a way close to the pattern described by this student. Earlier in this century, Robert E. Park proposed that racial and ethnic minorities everywhere go through a cycle of race relations.[20] Park wrote that this cycle consists of four stages: contact, competition, accommodation, and eventual assimilation. He proposed that during the competition stage between two groups, one group eventually establishes dominance over the other. With time, the two groups eventually accommodate to one another or work out ways of getting along. Eventually, Park suggested, assimilation reduces major differences between the groups. They become so much alike that competition and dominance are no longer meaningful.

With some modifications, Park's stages might describe intergroup relations in South Texas today. Because of continuous immigration from Mexico, for example, contact for Mexican Americans in South Texas is not really a stage but an ongoing aspect of race relations. Therefore, we will concentrate more on the other stages, recognizing contact as the initiating process leading to subsequent adjustments. In the second half of the book, we will focus on the processes of accommodation and assimilation as hypothesized stages of intergroup adjustment.

Often, in the literature related to race and ethnic relations, these processes are treated as competing explanations.[21] Advocates of accommodation, for example, propose that highly diverse groups may never completely assimilate, even when they interact over many generations. Advocates of assimilation, on the other hand, believe that continued interaction among diverse groups will eventually lead to complete assimilation.

As we will see in the chapters that follow, life in South Texas today, as in the past, can be very different for those at the bottom than for those at the top. Similarly, quality of life in South Texas is closely related to one's ethnic or racial identity.

"Mamá, Nosotros *Somos Migrantes": South Texas Farmworkers, 1950–1990*

Chapter 1

WITH CRUZ C. TORRES
AND JUANITA VALDEZ COX

For years we had traveled to West Texas to work the cotton crop. I would hear people always talking about "esos migrantes" [those migrants]. "Look what they did," "Look how they left this place," "They're so dirty," "You can't leave anything out while they're around," etc. I had heard these remarks so often that I thought they were talking about gang members or people in trouble with the law. One day my husband was talking of some trouble, and I said, "Oh, it was probably 'esos migrantes.'" He looked at me and asked who I thought "those migrants" were. So I told him. When I had finished, he told me, "Mamá, nosotros somos migrantes [Mama, we are migrants]." I felt so ashamed and dirty that I cried. I said, "You mean all those times people were talking about me and my family as if we were no good?"

ROSA MORALES, 1988

Rosa became a farmworker when she married. Often she stayed in the migrant camp to care for her children. As a result, she was more sheltered than most. Still, she cannot understand why people think of farmworkers as lazy and shiftless.[1] She knows they work fourteen-hour days in brutal heat or freezing cold, bent over a hoe, for most of their life.

Most farmworkers know how people feel about them. Many learn the stigma at an early age. One middle-aged man, for example, recalled with some pain his experience in elementary school. Each year in April, as his family prepared to go north, his friends would ask where he was going. He was too ashamed to tell them that he worked in the fields, so he would say, "I'm going to visit my grandmother in California." In the fall, he made up stories about his summer with Grandma. "Years later," he says, "I realized that the other kids were also migrants and that they also lied about what they did during the summer."

Juanita Valdez Cox, an organizer with the United Farm Workers of America and a sociology major at the University of Texas–Pan American (UT–Pan American), read the stories from the interviews. She said, "When I worked as a migrant in the seventies, I felt like a burro in school because I just couldn't keep up with the other students. It was somehow our fault that we were so slow. They never allowed us to feel proud that we put food on the nation's table—that we did necessary and dangerous work that was worthy of respect."

Like Valdez Cox, many farmworkers are puzzled by the harsh stereotypes. They do backbreaking work, expose themselves to dangerous work conditions, and risk their children's safety every time they pack them into the back of a truck on those brutal twenty-four-hour trips.[2] In light of such conditions, it is hard for them to see how anyone can think they are worthless.

Not everyone, of course, shares the harsh view of migrant workers. Most of us rarely see them.[3] We forget that they provide the labor for most of our food and clothing. Those of us old enough to remember Edward R. Murrow's 1960 exposé of harsh treatment of migrant farmworkers (appropriately titled "Harvest of Shame") may think things have changed since then. We have civil rights laws now. Agriculture today is highly mechanized. So, many Americans express surprise when they learn that migrant farmworkers are still around and still suffer harsh conditions.[4]

Indeed, according to a recent study, the number of migrant jobs has tripled in the last twenty years.[5] Texas has the highest population of migrant farmworkers, though Florida and California also have large concentrations. The 1990 census classified 281,778 individuals in Texas as migrant farmworkers.[6] Not included in this figure are the 161,025 seasonal workers who do not migrate. The U.S. Census classifies migrant farmworkers as individuals "whose principal employment is in agriculture on a seasonal basis, who have been so employed within the past twenty-four months, and who establish for the purpose of such employment a temporary abode."[7]

Nearly 60 percent of Texas farmworkers reside in the four southernmost counties of the Rio Grande Valley.[8] Seventy percent of those live in Hidalgo County. Most Valley farmworkers live in rural colonias during the winter (see Chapter 2). They struggle to find work in local agriculture or in other temporary jobs. They are the United States' "stand-by" labor force—the hardest hit by NAFTA, agricultural mechanization, and the flow of undocumented workers from Mexico.

Nevertheless, some things have improved. Some adverse conditions portrayed in "Harvest of Shame" no longer exist. Programs have been created to help migrant children stay in school. Legal Aid attorneys have gained some concessions for workers. The United Farm Workers has won some important victories.

Still, the cost of living goes up while wages remain stagnant. Some housing and other benefits previously provided by farmers are no longer available.[9] Increasing numbers of undocumented Mexican migrants compete for available jobs. And farmwork is still the most dangerous occupation in the United States.[10]

In this chapter, we use data from the Borderlife Project to address two questions: What is it like to be a migrant farmworker? How have life conditions and treatment of farmworkers changed over the past fifty years? Using incidents related by migrant workers, we will follow them as they prepare to leave home, take to the road, find work and housing, work in the fields, interact in the towns and schools, and return to the Valley.

Preparing to Leave

Every year Monica's mom and dad would take her out of school. "I hated it," she says. "I knew I was going to spend the summer working long hours under the sun. Often I would ask, 'Why do we have to go? Why can't we stay?' They would only exchange looks, and I would get no answer." Not all migrant children leave school before the end of the spring semester. Some parents wait until school is out to head north. This works moderately well when a family knows a particular farmer who will save them a job. Otherwise, leaving late means getting the last pick of jobs and leftover housing. It also means a lot less money for a family struggling to survive. So the most needy parents take their children out of school early and return them late in the fall, making it even harder for them to ever break out of the poverty cycle.

In the Migrant Farmworkers Exploratory Interviews (1,398 respondents), many migrants said leaving school early was a problem. Though rich in insight, these personal accounts cannot reveal what proportion of migrants have had this problem, nor how it has changed over the years. Therefore, we initiated the follow-up Migrant Farmworkers Survey (Appendix B, no. 1). Each of the student interviewers found and interviewed 5 individuals who were teenagers in each of the past five decades (the 1950s through the 1990s). This produced 260 interviews (approximately 50 per decade) that provided answers to eighty-two standardized questions. These data show that 56 percent of those who attended school in the 1950s said migrants frequently had to miss school to migrate. Thirty-three percent of migrants who were teens in the 1990s said migrants today have to miss school frequently. Such factors as migrant school programs and somewhat improved economic conditions may have helped migrant children miss less school.

Falling behind is only one of the costs of missing school. Aurora remembers an incident when she was ten years old. "A huge truck pulled up in front of our house," she says, "with several other families already loaded in the back. As I walked out to get in the truck, all the neighbors were staring at us. It made me feel inferior to them. Worse, after I got into the truck, my best friend came up and peeked in. We both wanted to cry, so I just turned away."

Leaving school and friends also makes migrant children feel that they do not belong. Marisa's experience illustrates this. She remembers always being behind everybody else, even though her teachers put her in special classes and gave her extra help. "Not only that," she says, "I always felt different. After I graduated from high school, I got a job as a clerk in a grocery store. I was the first in my family to have a job working inside. Then I became a teacher's aide and things got even better. Now I help the teachers and the kids. I feel useful and important. I don't have to move anymore. I finally belong."

The feeling of not belonging contributes to high dropout rates. Hilario, now in his fifties, recalls how hard it was for his father to send him and his younger brother to school. They were the only ones of his six brothers and sisters to set foot in a school. "My brother and I had to go to school barefooted," he recalls, "and the children made fun of us. Once, a traveling shoe salesman sold my father some shoes for us. He had a very poor selection of shoes, so he sold us shoes two sizes too big. He said that would make the shoes last a long time. My father liked that. The first day we wore them, we had a hard time waddling the mile to school. The children, who always noticed everything, saw our big shoes and decided to call us 'ducks.' After that, we just stayed home and played marbles."

Antonio, another dropout, felt the same way. "Rather than suffer in school when the kids called me names," he says, "I decided to suffer in the fields where it could do me some good."

Many migrants never had a choice. Elena, for example, recalls when she was in the fourth grade. Her father said she had to drop out to earn money and take care of her younger brothers and sisters. "Papa explained that the whole family had to work together in the fields," she says, "because the wages were so low. I don't feel bad, though, because my brother and sisters graduated with honors. Two of them even finished college." Now that Elena has children of her own, she insists that they stay in school and do all that they can to get out of migrating. "I'm not saying that being a migrant worker is bad," she says. "Actually I have some fond memories of working in the fields. There's got to be a better life out there, though, than breaking your back to pick cucumbers."

Percent

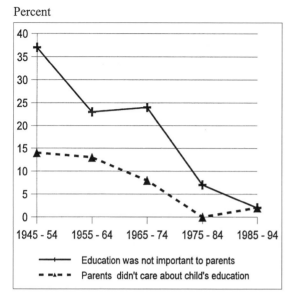

Fig. 1.1. Migrant farmworkers reporting their parents did not think school was important, or did not care about their schooling, when the workers were teenagers (Migrant Farmworkers Survey, 1993)

Migrant students still have high dropout rates. Today, more than half of them never finish high school. Some educators blame migrant parents for not keeping their children in school, claiming that migrant workers do not value education. To find out, we asked farmworkers in the Migrant Farmworkers Survey from each decade: "How important was it to your parents that you got a good education?" Figure 1.1 shows the percentage of respondents from each decade who answered either that their parents "didn't much care" about their education or that education was "not very important" to their parents.

These results clearly show that less than half of migrant parents, according to recollections of their children, ever placed a low value on education. More important, only a tiny fraction of the youngest group today believes that their parents do not value education. These findings support the claim that migrant parents should not be blamed for the dropout problem.

The socioeconomic costs of migration explain the high dropout rate better than the alleged "no value on education" hypothesis. Such costs include leaving school before the spring semester ends and returning after school starts in the fall. Also included is having to start over at so many different schools. One migrant student, for example, said, "I hate it because you study one thing here and start something else over there. I make many friends, but I can never plan any special school events. It's very painful always coming and going." Thus, structural factors interact with the feeling of not belonging to increase high dropout rates for migrant children.

Still, when it is time to begin the trip north, children and parents must put thoughts of school aside and prepare for the trip. Everyone has to pitch in to make it work. One migrant, now a grandmother, recalls, "I remember making dozens of tamales and cookies to eat on the way to Oregon. In the early days, we made our own food. We simply couldn't afford to eat in restaurants."

On the Road

Holding down trip expenses is only one reason that migrants prepared their own food. Another, revealed by the exploratory interviews, was outright discrimination by restaurants that refused to serve migrants. This pattern was especially pronounced during the years that the now-older migrants were children. María López, for example, remembers a trip in 1957 to Indiana. "We were packed like sardines in a big truck," she recalls, "thirty adults and twelve children. The journey was three days of pure hell because the driver wouldn't stop except for gas. On one of those stops, I needed to get some hot water for my baby's formula. The restaurant had a sign that read 'No Mexicans, No Negroes.' We just wanted water, but we had to wait till an Anglo lady came and got it for us. She made us pay fifty cents for a ten-ounce bottle of hot water."

Many older people have painful memories of being asked to leave a restaurant. The father of one interviewer described an occasion when he had decided to treat the family to a pleasant meal at a restaurant. "We walked in, and they stared at us like freaks," he recalls. "The owner told me that one of us could place the order but we'd have to wait for it out back because they didn't allow Mexicans in their restaurant." With anger in his voice, he added, "They were White trash, but somehow we weren't good enough to eat there."

Younger migrants report fewer direct forms of rejection. One man now in his twenties recalls an incident in Ohio. "We were hungry and tired from the long trip," he says, "so we went to a restaurant for hamburgers. The people just stared at us. We ordered eight cheeseburgers. They brought them but made the order 'to go' without even asking us. When we arrived at camp, we realized that each burger was just two buns with onion slices in the middle."

A similar pattern appears in the stories that describe how people treated migrants at gas stations. One woman recalls a trip to Bartlett, Oklahoma, in the 1950s to pick cotton. "We had to stop at a service station to use the rest room," she recalls. "The door to the ladies' room was locked and had a sign that read 'No Mexicans Allowed.' My mom asked what it said, so I told her. We were both mad and hurt. I decided to stand up to the owner of the gas station, so I asked him for the key. He was cold and mean and asked if I had read the sign. I said, 'Yes, but we're not Mexicans, we're Texans.' He didn't want to give us the key, but finally handed it to me. After we had finished, we dropped the key in the toilet and locked the door behind us as revenge for his unfair treatment."

Younger migrants report less blatant acts of discrimination. One young man, for example, describes an incident in the 1980s. He and his brother stopped for gas at the end of a long day on the road. "I walked inside," he says, "and immediately everyone was staring at me as if I had leprosy. I told the young man at the register, as politely as I could, that I wanted to fill my tank and pay for two cokes. When I got to the truck, I inserted the nozzle, but the pump would not turn on. I tried to get his attention, but he wouldn't look my way. After five minutes, I went inside and told him to please turn on the pump. He said he had, and if that wasn't good enough, I could pour my cokes into the tank and get the hell out of there. Everyone in the store was grinning. As I went to try again, the pump still wasn't on. My brother just wanted to get out of there. Humiliated and angry, we drove to a police station and filed a report. It did no good, but at least it gave us some peace of mind."

We asked 260 respondents in the Migrant Farmworkers Survey to describe how often people refused them food or gas service during their teen years. As Figure 1.2 shows, the frequency of both forms of discrimination has declined significantly over the years. While the passage of civil rights legislation in the 1960s may have produced some decline in discrimination, the pattern seems to have started at least a decade earlier.

Juanita Valdez Cox thinks the reason for the decline is that many migrants no longer just take the abuse. "We stand up for ourselves now," she says, "and that makes people angry. They want things like the old days when we just had to take it. They never stop to think that maybe we might just have a right to choose not to follow their orders or take their abuse."

John Howard Griffin, writing *Black like Me* in 1961, described the "hate stares" that made Blacks feel unwelcome in public places. Valdez Cox remembers a similar reaction to migrant workers in restaurants almost twenty years later. "The stares always hurt the most," she recalls. "My brother used to go in to order coffee or food. He would bring it out so that the rest of us didn't have to put up with it. Still, we got the looks

Percent Saying "Frequently"

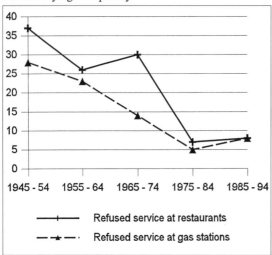

Fig. 1.2. Migrant farm-workers reporting they were refused food and gas service as teenagers (Migrant Farmworkers Survey, 1993)

that said, 'Who are these people?' 'Why don't they stay with their own kind?' We could never have a nice meal because they made us feel that we had no right to be in there with them."

Migrants experience other problems on the road. Virtually everyone, for example, has had a breakdown of their *mueble* (car) or *troca* (truck). Juan Cantú describes the time when their 1965 station wagon broke down and he walked to a farmhouse to get help. Dogs started chasing him. He got away, but an Anglo there started yelling at him. "I didn't go back," he says, "because I didn't think he'd help. We were stuck on the side of the road the whole day. Finally, a truck driver came along and helped fix the car. I gotta admit he treated us real good. He even gave the kids some crackers he had in his truck."

"When your car broke," recalls Valdez Cox, "you had to find someone to fix it. That could take several days, and you could only guess what the final bill would be. You had to find a place to park and hope the police wouldn't run you off. The people in those towns always let us know we were not welcome to stay in public places."

Sometimes, though, Good Samaritans appear in the stories. In 1987, the Gomez family was on their way to Lubbock, Texas, when their truck broke down. Mr. Gomez and his oldest son, Carlos, tried to fix the engine, but it needed new parts. After two hours on the highway, a state trooper stopped to help. He took Carlos into town for parts and then stayed to help fix the truck.

Even when their truck works well, migrants worry about the weather, especially when it is cold or rainy. A mother of eight remembers a cold day in Illinois when they and two other families were riding in the back of a vegetable-hauling truck. "Suddenly," she recalls, "the rain came down in sheets. The driver couldn't pull over, and only three people could fit in the cab, so everyone got soaked. My children were crying, so my husband and I held them close trying to protect them. I have never felt so helpless in my life. Finally, after we pounded a lot on the cab, the driver stopped and we got under the truck. It helped a little, but it just kept raining. Then God heard my prayers, and the rain stopped. We continued our trip with only the cold wind to dry us out."

Juanita Valdez Cox remembers what it was like on such occasions. "We would take it till we couldn't stand it anymore," she says. "Then we'd bang on the cab to let Dad know. Often nothing could be done. Babies and older adults simply couldn't trade places. One night, some of our friends suffered tragic consequences. They tried to let their parents know, but they had to go on. The youngest girl died that night, still on the way up north to work."

Sometimes children in the back of covered trucks are asphyxiated from carbon monoxide poisoning. Drivers do not discover the problem until they stop for gas. Often, it is too late. The children are either dead or close to it. The fumes give no warning. Sometimes they can save the children, but for some, it is too late.

"Even with all of this," Valdez Cox comments, "they brand us as lazy. Never mind that our desire to work might cost a family member. Then, even if we arrive safely, we're not sure we'll find work. Days of searching can turn into weeks. We may not even find a place to stay while we look. Thousands of miles of driving, just to go home with no money to show for it."

A Home Away from Home

Every year, Nelda's family would go to Caldwell, Idaho. "We'd head straight to the labor camp," she says. "My mother always hoped we'd get a clean house, but it hardly ever happened. Usually we'd find broken windows, rat droppings all over the floor, and faraway rest rooms that were always plugged up. The showers wouldn't have curtains, so we'd hold a towel across the door for family members. After work, everybody would race to the showers because a whole camp of twenty to thirty houses only had three or four showers. So we'd wait in line for an hour or more. At night one year, I could see the stars from my bed through a hole in the ceiling. I would make up stories to myself about the stars to help me get to sleep."

Migrant housing comes in two basic types. The first, described by Nelda, is the labor camp. Several small houses share showers and certain other facilities. Often a governmental agency runs the place, and it is only for farmworkers. Conditions in the camps vary from adequate and comfortable to dangerous and degrading.[11]

Housing provided by individual farmers is the other type. It can be anything from a converted shed or barn to a regular home. Most often it is barely livable. Juanita Valdez Cox comments, "Farmers often spend more money on fixing their equipment than on housing their workers. Often, we got worn-out mattresses and broken-down refrigerators or stoves. You never knew till you got there."

Some workers are lucky. When Nora's family went to Minnesota one year, she could hardly believe how nice the mobile home was. "We each had our own room," she says, "and they had carpeted all the floors. It even had an air conditioner. In fact, that house was better than the one we have down here. I would have been happy to stay there."

Due to a scarcity of housing,[12] such experiences are rare. Mrs. Martínez remembers a year when another family was assigned to share their house. "It had two kitchens, two bathrooms, and two bedrooms," she recalls, "so the owner said it was big enough for two families. But the other family's half didn't have a stove and their bathroom didn't work. We let them use our stove until the crew leader got one for them. I felt sorry because the other woman had to get up at three in the morning to use the stove to fix lunch for the fields. After eight weeks, the crew leader still had not brought them a stove. They finally bought one at a garage sale for forty-five dollars. Everything went better after that, except that we were still living together."

Sometimes, doubling up creates more serious problems. The Salinas family went to work for a farmer in Georgia who put them in a two-bedroom mobile home with a father and his three teenaged sons. "We soon found out," reports Mrs. Salinas, "that they were involved in drugs. My eight-year-old child was constantly in fear because of the yelling and screaming every night. We didn't know them and were scared of what they might do. One night, we woke up to loud screams and banging on the wall. All we could do was pray to God to protect us. We couldn't leave because it would mean finding a new job, and we needed the work just to survive."

Sometimes people ask why farmworkers put up with situations like

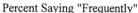

Percent Saying "Frequently"

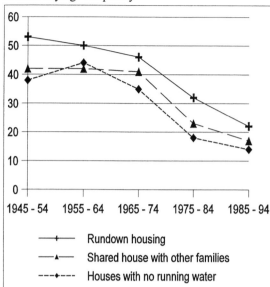

Fig. 1.3. Problems migrant farmworkers experienced with housing provided by farmers when the workers were teenagers (Migrant Farmworkers Survey, 1993)

this. Juanita Valdez Cox tells them, "You can't know what it means to have nothing to fall back on—what it means to tell your prospective employer that you don't like the housing he's offering. With no other housing, no money, and your car barely running, you simply can't shop around. You have to work. You have no choice. Sure, you can complain about the mattresses: you can complain—and he can tell you to leave. Then you won't have a job, and he might just call other farmers and tell them you're a troublemaker."

Some workers handle the difficulty by trying to see the lighter side of it. Imelda says, "The shacks where we lived in Michigan were battlegrounds for rats and roaches. At night you could see them commuting along the two-by-fours over our heads. At first we couldn't sleep, but soon exhaustion took its toll and we learned to ignore the nightlife. The bunk beds were two-by-fours with box springs, several with coils sticking out. Sometimes, you'd hear someone scream in the night when a coil attached itself to their rib cage. You learned to move carefully while shifting around in those beds."

In the Migrant Farmworkers Survey, we asked migrants how often, as teenagers, they had to live in rundown housing, had to share a house with another family, or had no running water in the house. Figure 1.3 shows that the frequency of all three problems has dropped over the years. Still, 20 percent of the youngest migrants believe farmworkers frequently have to live in rundown housing.

Despite the difficulties, life in a migrant camp can have its upside. Ana, a woman whose family has lived in many camps, says that she has established lifelong friendships in the camps. "While we were living in the *baracas* [barracks] in Uvalde," she says, "everybody helped everybody. Eight families became one big family. We women shared food and cooked together; the men drank beer and talked; and all of the children played together. That's where we met Tomasa, who is now our *comadre* [their child's godmother]."

Migrant camps can also be a place of young romance. Cindy Salinas, a student interviewer, described this aspect of the camps well. "At sixteen or seventeen," she writes, "a young boy or girl is desperate for change. You'll look up and find someone like yourself—working without choice and wanting something better. So you meet someone with common interests, the one you've been waiting for. At seventeen you decide you're getting married. Her parents think she's too young, but you don't agree. So you elope. One law of the camp is, if you spend one night out with her and don't bring her in by her curfew—she's yours."

In the Fields

Candelario Sandoval finds farmwork very difficult. "You could use a machine to pick your pickles," he says, "but Vlasic only wants small, firm, slightly green pickles. So you get on your knees and reach way down to pull up several cucumbers. You've got to fill each bucket to the top, carry it to the end of the row, and dump it in a big crate. Each bucket weighs thirty to forty pounds. Each crate holds approximately one ton. You fill about thirty of those crates, and you may have enough to pay rent on your house in camp. Each week it's the same thing, month after month, year after year. And it's seasonal because the fields can rest—but not farmworkers."

"THE WORK SEEMED ENDLESS"

Farmwork is hard, tedious labor. Shade is a luxury, breaks are few, injury is always a risk,[13] and chronic health problems later in life are a certainty.[14] Workers get deep-down dirty and earn just enough to bring them back next year, all the while hoping that their children can eventually break out of the cycle.

Farmwork is often hardest on beginners.[15] María, now forty years old, had never done farmwork before getting married. After a week in the fields with her husband, she told him, "My hands are cut. I have never been so tired before. My back is killing me." He listened patiently as she explained that the sun made her feel like she was burning up. "I don't see how I can work so many hours in the field and then come home to cook and clean house," she told him. "I could go on if I just worked fewer hours in the field." After a pause, he said, "There's no other way. We really need the money." She has stayed with it for more than twenty years but still remembers those first days as one of her most painful experiences.

Hard work is only part of the problem. In 1974 Benito's family started migrating. "Dad took us to Mayfield, Texas," he recalls, "because someone told him the work was good there. On the first day, we found work picking cucumbers. The next day, it started to rain. We expected the other workers to go home," he explains, "but they just kept working—so we did too. Soon the baskets were heavy with mud, and we were up to our knees in mud. The trucks kept getting stuck. We made almost no money that day. The next day, we packed up and went to Plainview, where we found work hoeing cotton. Since it had rained there too, the wet dirt made the hoes useless unless you scraped the mud off after each chop. Our shoes were so muddy, walking more than a few steps in the field was impossible. It's hard to work in those conditions," Benito explains, "but you can't make any money sitting at home."

Finding work is another problem. Therefore, many migrants work for a crew leader, often the owner of a truck. He transports them from place to place and contracts directly with the farmer. Some crew leaders take advantage of their workers, while others defend their interests with farmers.[16] Andrés may be one of the latter. He has been a crew leader for many years. "Once," he says, "I told my crew to take a short break because it was burning hot and we were still hours away from our lunch break. Many farmers don't like to see their workers take a break before lunch, so we were watching for the farmer. But then, we started kidding around and didn't see him drive up. He jumped out of his truck and yelled, 'Too little workee you.' We got up and headed back to work. I could tell the workers were upset, so I responded, almost loud enough for him to hear, 'We workee little *porque* [because] you pay too little.'"

Most farmworkers have stories of good farmers and bad—and of good crew leaders and those who were abusive. Many stories of abuse deal with farmers or crew leaders who cheat their workers in their pay.[17] Aparicio Gonzales, now a father of four, remembers when he first started as a migrant. He was young, unmarried, and trying to send money to his parents. He made an agreement with a farmer in Michigan to pick grapes for a set price. "When I asked the farmer for my money at the end of two weeks," he says, "he told me he could only pay me half of what he had promised. 'The price of grapes has fallen,' he told me, 'and I don't have enough to pay you.'" With a gesture of resignation, Aparicio says, "I was in a bind for the money, and there was nothing I could do. I took the money and looked elsewhere for work, hoping to find a more honest farmer."

Because of such experiences, many workers associate themselves with a crew leader. This arrangement is especially attractive to those who speak little English or who lack reliable transportation. Often, however, the result is no better. Tomás, a student at UT–Pan American, remembers a particular crew leader. "At first," Tomás recalls, "he told my father he would pay us twenty-five dollars per acre. Several days later, he said it would be only twenty dollars. I wanted to protest, but my father thought it was just a misunderstanding. The next week, the crew leader told us that the farmer would pay only eighteen dollars an acre. That's when I decided to do something. After work I found the farmer and asked him why he cut our pay. He was surprised and said he was still paying twenty-five dollars an acre. So together we went to the crew leader. We got him to admit that he was keeping the extra money for himself. The farmer made him pay us what he had stolen."

To learn how frequently such things happen, we asked respondents in the Migrant Farmworkers Survey how often farmers and crew leaders cheated their workers. Figure 1.4 shows some decline in abuse from the 1950s to the 1960s. Since then, little has changed. Approximately 15 percent of the youngest farmworkers said farmers and crew leaders still frequently cheat their workers.

Migrant workers recall other forms of abuse. One undocumented Mexican woman, for example, remembered a *contratista* (crew leader) who frequently abused his workers. "As we were cleaning a field," she says, "I became very upset at the way he was treating us. He told us to work faster or he would hit us. I told him we were not animals and that I would report him if he didn't treat us better. Later I heard that he was telling the other women that I was a prostitute from Reynosa who wanted their husbands. After that, they made me an outcast."

Juanita Valdez Cox remembers crew leaders and farmers as both good and bad. "My father never worked with a crew leader," she explains, "because they would charge a lot to take you up north. Once there, they were supposed to get you work and make sure you had mattresses. But it

Percent Saying "Frequently"

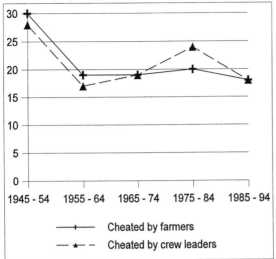

Fig. 1.4. Migrant farmworkers reporting they were cheated on wages by farmers or crew leaders when the workers were teenagers (Migrant Farmworkers Survey, 1993)

seldom happened. If you needed to go into town, they would take you, but it would cost you. Sometimes, if you went up north with a crew leader, you'd end the summer in debt instead of making money. So Dad always felt that we should work just with family members."

Some crew leaders and farmers risk the safety and well-being of their workers by allowing dangerous or harsh conditions. José is thirty-eight years old. In 1984 he worked in Minnesota for a farmer who didn't provide rest rooms in the fields. "It was not so bad for us men," he says, "but sometimes the women got sick from having to wait. Our boss kept putting us off till finally we went to his house and told him to put up rest rooms or we would stop working. He finally gave in. Boy, were we surprised. All we had to do was boycott."

Many bad working conditions are not so easy to resolve. Irma remembers once when she had to work in the dark. "I remember waking up at five one morning," she recalls. "Mom had been up since four to make meals for the family. That day we left early to top onions. It was still dark, and even the lights of a truck didn't help much. We couldn't see each other, and all you could hear was the sound of the shears topping onions. Suddenly, I heard a loud scream from the lady next to me. She had severely cut her finger because it was too dark to see where she was cutting."

Imelda remembers the summer of 1972 when her family was working in Colorado. "The previous day had been too cold and wet to work," she recalls, "so we were anxious to get started hoeing beets. As we worked,

Percent

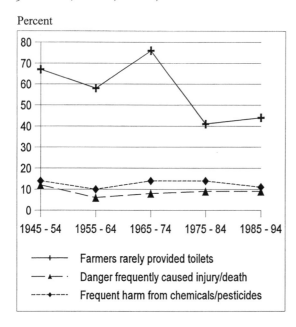

Fig. 1.5. Bad working conditions migrant farmworkers reported experiencing as teenagers (Migrant Farmworkers Survey, 1993)

we looked up and saw the farmer spraying pesticide close to where we were working. We tried to move away and not breathe the fumes, but some of it got on us. That day, my mother started vomiting and had severe headaches. For several days, I had nosebleeds."

Valdez Cox remembers once when a crop duster sprayed close to the workers. "The farmer said that we shouldn't worry. 'It's safe,' he told us, 'just medicine for the crops.' Even if someone went to the hospital, farmers would refuse to admit that their spraying contributed to it."[18]

How frequently do such things occur? And how have conditions changed over the years? Figure 1.5 shows how farmworkers who were teens in each decade remember three conditions: how frequently farmers provided portable toilets in the fields; how frequently farmworkers were exposed to dangerous chemicals, especially pesticides; and how frequently severe injuries or death resulted from dangerous working conditions.

Two things seem clear from this figure. First, not much change has taken place over the years. Portable toilets are somewhat more common in the 1990s than they were in earlier years. The risk from dangerous working conditions appears to remained virtually unchanged. Similarly, teens in the 1990s remember having about the same frequency of pesticide exposure as do those who were teens in the 1960s.

Figure 1.5 also suggests that farmwork remains a high-risk occupation. Pesticides also remain a problem. The Texas Office of Rural Health ranks agricultural work as the highest of all industries in work-related deaths, with a rate of 52 deaths per 100,000 workers.[19] This rate is roughly five times higher than the death rate in manufacturing industries.

Farmers and their workers cannot easily eliminate some unsafe conditions. They can do little about extreme weather conditions, for example. Snakes and insects are another problem. Ema, a young farmworker, remembers the time when her seven-year-old brother, Rudy, had just started working with the family. "We were hoeing a field of melons," she recalls. "Suddenly, I heard my brother scream. I knew immediately it was a snake. I ran over to him and started hitting the snake with my hoe. Rudy ran over to my mother and hugged her, trembling. The next day, we showed him how to move the weeds with his hoe to give the snake a chance to move away." Ema reports that it took Rudy a couple of years to lose his fear of snakes.

Despite the bad conditions often associated with farmwork, many migrants develop close ties to the land, other workers, and their family. Migrant children from an early age work alongside their parents to support the family. "Hell, I can't even get my kids to dump the garbage without charging me for their services," reports one former farmworker whose children have never worked in the fields. Though his children have more things than he did at their age, he misses the tight family closeness he felt as part of a migrant family.

Chances to enjoy life are an occasional part of migrant life. Lanete recalls one summer day in Virginia in 1969 when their farmer and his son rode up to their camp on two beautiful horses. "The horses amazed my children," she remembers. "Then, to our surprise, the farmer offered to let us ride. My kids had never ridden a horse before. We thanked him, and he just smiled and said, 'There's a time for work and a time for play. You folks have worked enough for today.' We'll never forget that man's kindness."

The Castañeda family also remembers an experience in Moorehead, Minnesota. One morning, the farmer came to tell them they did not need to work that day. "Since the children had worked hard," Griselda Castañeda says, "I wanted to take them for a ride. Their cousins had told them stories of traveling into Canada, so I wanted them to go too. I'll never forget their expressions when we crossed into Canada. They were amazed that the landscape never changed." Reflecting on it for a moment, she adds, "If we weren't farmworkers, they would never get to see any other country except Mexico."

Going to Town

After a hard week, migrant workers look forward to a trip into town. It provides a chance for relaxation and some shopping. Manuel ("Manny") liked it for a different reason. One summer in Ohio, it rained a lot. "When it rained," he says, "we couldn't work. We'd go to the barracks, change our clothes, get in our car, and head to town to go 'raiding.' 'Raiding' was finding Goodwill boxes. I'd jump inside and throw bags of clothes out to my sisters. Then we'd head back to camp. At the end of the summer, I had four or five pairs of good blue jeans for school."

Not all trips to town are good experiences. According to Juanita Valdez Cox, "Sundays were the only days we could go into town for a movie or a coke. We worked hard and just wanted to relax. Often, though, the store people made it impossible. It wasn't what they said. It was the stares and having them follow you around in the stores because they thought you wanted to steal something."

Carlos and his brothers seldom made it into town because they had to help fix up the house and work on the car. "We were lucky if we got one afternoon to ourselves," he says. "One Fourth of July, we only had to work half a day. With long lines at the shower, we couldn't clean up. We went to buy fireworks at a store called the Light House. I looked the cleanest, so I went in. As I was about to pay, an Anglo lady standing next to me said, 'Something smells awful in here!' I felt like putting her in her place, but my parents strictly opposed any sort of trouble with the residents."

Irene and her brothers had a similar experience. They got off work just before dark and had not had time to clean up. But they needed some groceries for dinner, so they made a quick stop at the store on the way back to camp. "In the store," Irene remembers, "some Anglos started staring at us. I heard one of them say, 'Look how dirty they are! How can they come in here like that?'" Irene replied, "We look dirty because we just got off work. We're sorry we don't look the way you want us to." The women were stunned. Apparently none of them thought Irene could speak English.

Juanita Valdez Cox says, "A lot of the time you just need milk or gas. You're just coming from the fields, so you can't clean up. They make you feel so uncomfortable that you only go to town in an emergency. Of course, they take your money, but only if they don't have to touch you."

Even when they can clean up, the reaction is often the same. Mario remembers when he and his uncle showered one night before going into town. "While I waited outside the store for my uncle," he says, "this man walked out with the stuff he had just bought. He was doing okay until he saw me. He freaked out! He actually jumped back a step. I felt like an alien from outer space or something."

Some reactions from townspeople are well intentioned but thoughtless. Ana remembers when a farmer in Uvalde, Texas, did not have a house for them, so they had to find one in town. "We just couldn't find anything we could afford," she says. "For several nights, the owners of a twenty-four-hour Mini-Mart let us sleep in our car in their lot. One day I was in the store to buy food. A lady started a polite conversation and then remarked, 'Oh, you're the family in the newspaper, right?' We were so embarrassed. We didn't wait to see our picture in the paper."

When trouble starts, townspeople see migrants as outsiders.[20] Abel and Javier are brothers who remember being thrown out of a town in Nebraska. One Sunday afternoon, they had gone to a local park for a picnic. "Two Anglo guys approached and began calling us 'beaners,' 'greasers,' and 'wetbacks,'" recalls Abel. "We wouldn't take it, so a fight started. The police came, but they arrested only the two of us. Then they called us every name in the book and told us to get out of town. Our whole family left Nebraska two days later. We've never been back."

Not everyone treats migrants as outsiders. Luis, a student at UT–Pan American, remembers living in Iowa when he was ten years old. Their farmer was unable to provide housing, so they had to live in town. "People there were quite friendly," he remembers. "We played with the neighbor children, and their mother would invite us over for cookies and milk. Once she even gave us a party. They would send over pies or cookies, and Mom would make tortillas to send back.

"One of our neighbors was a retired couple with no kids," Luis continues. "They loved having us over. Every Christmas until 1983, our families would exchange gifts through the mail. That year, they died in a car accident. My mother gets tears in her eyes every time we talk about them."

From stories like these, we designed survey questions to determine how people in the towns treated migrant workers. We asked migrants how often, when they were in their teen years, store clerks acted suspicious of migrants. We also asked how often townspeople treated migrants rudely.

Figure 1.6 shows the percentage of farmworkers reporting frequent rude treatment. Though the graph does not show it, a larger percentage reported occasional instances of rude treatment by clerks and townspeople.

While rude treatment has apparently declined some since the early

Percent Saying "Frequently"

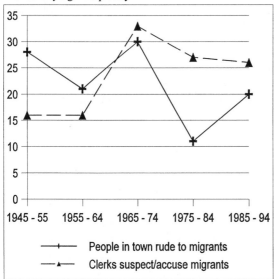

Fig. 1.6. Migrant farm-workers reporting towns-people were rude and store clerks suspicious of them when they were teenagers (Migrant Farmworkers Survey, 1993)

years, the reduction in both types of treatment is not statistically signifi-cant. Indeed, nearly 20 percent of the youngest category of farmworkers still reports frequent rudeness by townspeople, a figure not much differ-ent from that of the 1960s.

Heading Home

As the season ends, migrant workers begin returning home. For many, it is a time of happiness.[21] They're returning to family. If they managed to lay aside extra money, they can buy clothes and perhaps even a stereo. For some, farmers provide a special touch, as José discovered. Their farmer threw a party for all his workers. "There was plenty of food for all," he remembers, "but the biggest surprise came just as we were get-ting in our car to head back to Texas. He showed up at our place and gave us money for gas and twenty dollars extra to spend on the trip home."

Not all farmers are happy to see their workers leave. David, a student at UT–Pan American, recalls the summer of 1987. "We were in Michi-gan picking peppers," he says. "In August, I had to return early to regis-ter at the university. When the farmer heard I was leaving, he became an-gry. 'A good picker doesn't belong in college,' he said. 'You'll be wasting your time in school.' I paid no attention to him and went ahead with my plans to leave. All my family wanted to see me off at the bus station. When the farmer heard about it, he told my family that they had to work.

("We want fair wages")
Farmworkers must still
struggle for benefits other
workers take for granted
(photo courtesy of
George C. McLemore).

My father got mad and went to the union to look for another place to work. Luckily, he found one."

For some families, the trip home can turn into tragedy. María remembers one homecoming with great sadness. "While in Michigan," she recalls, "my sister became ill and died. My parents felt it necessary to bury her at home, but had no money to have the body sent home. So they put the casket in the back of our pickup truck. While the younger kids could ride up front, I and my older brother had to ride in the back with the casket. They did not allow us to speak while on the road, out of respect for our sister. That was the longest trip of my life."

Sometimes a tragedy at home causes migrants to return home early. Mary remembers the year her dad left the family at home to work in Idaho. One night a butane tank exploded in the family's home. Mary's brother Carlos managed to get the three smallest children out of the burning house. Then he saw his mother trapped inside and went back in

Percent Saying "Frequently"

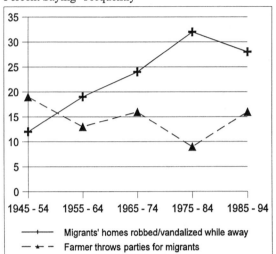

Fig. 1.7. End-of-season events migrant farmworkers reported experiencing when they were teenagers (Migrant Farmworkers Survey, 1993)

for her. Both were severely burned getting out. She was dead by the time firefighters arrived, and Carlos went to the hospital in critical condition. "When my dad heard about it," she recalls, "he got a loan from his friends and made it home in three days. He went straight to the hospital, just in time to see Carlos, who died a few hours later. To this day, my dad believes that if he had stayed home that year, it would never have happened."

For others, tragedy strikes at the end of the trip. Irma remembers coming home from Lubbock, Texas, in 1986. Like most migrant families, they had left behind their TV, VCR, stereo, beds, and everything else they were unable to take. "My dad and my brother had even put sheets of plywood on the windows," she recalls. "When we got back in October, the plywood was on the ground and the window was broken. We knew immediately what had happened, because some friends had been robbed the year before. We turned on the lights and, sure enough, no TV, no VCR, and no stereo. Damn! You can imagine how pissed we were. We didn't call the police because whoever broke in had had enough time to have come back for seconds."

We asked the 260 survey respondents how often farmworkers returned home to find their house robbed or vandalized. We also asked them how frequently, during their teen years, farmers gave them a party at the end of the season. Figure 1.7 shows that approximately 15 percent of farmworkers remember farmers giving parties to their workers. The figure also illustrates a pronounced increase in reports of vandalism and burglarized homes over the years.

Breaking Out

Not all migrants return home at the end of the season. Some find year-round work with farmers up north. Others find service jobs or positions in industry. Indeed, many Mexican Americans in the Midwest and elsewhere trace their ethnic roots to Mexico and the migrant streams from South Texas.[22]

This process of gradual dispersion is illustrated by the Gomez family. Ten years ago, they found a farmer they really liked. He paid them well and even let the older kids work in the packing sheds. "Later," says Martin, now a student at UT–Pan American, "we decided not to migrate anymore. We stayed year-round with the farmer. We grew up with his children, sharing all the holidays and going to church services in town with them. After a while, we moved to the city because we had started high school. Now I live with relatives here and only see my family during the summer."

The Castillo family left the migrant stream to work in a factory. Francisco, also a student at UT–Pan American, describes how it happened. "Three years ago, we were detasseling corn in Iowa. We got severely sunburned and dehydrated. Gatorade was the only thing that kept us going that summer. Then my father found work in the factory earning seven dollars an hour and working twelve-to-fourteen-hour days. Jerry, his manager, was pleased with his work and offered to hire my brother and me too. Now I don't have to worry about skin cancer and premature wrinkling."

Many farmworkers have mixed feelings about leaving a line of work that, for many, goes back several generations. Juan Perez, for example, met his wife when she was picking oranges with her parents. Now they have four kids and have been migrating for seventeen years.

"I do this work because it gives me freedom," he says. "I don't have to follow anybody's orders if I don't want to. If I don't like the crew chief I can quit and go somewhere else—just like my dad used to do.

"But it's not easy. People don't like to look at us. They don't want to see our clothes or get too close to us. The low pay is really tough. With no money, there's no doctor when the kids get sick.

"Some people say we don't take care of our kids. They don't know us. We love our kids and take care of them our way. It hurts when other kids make fun of their old clothes. They get into fights. So I want them to get away from this life. School can teach them how to do other things. Maybe they can get a job and settle down in one place. Ojalá [One hopes]."

Stories like this suggest that migrant workers feel trapped by their

Percent Saying "Frequently"

Fig. 1.8. Migrant farm-workers who felt trapped by cycle of migration as teenagers (Migrant Farmworkers Survey, 1993)

work and their lack of education. In the survey, we asked: "How often during your teen years did migrants feel trapped and unable to break out of poverty and the cycle of migration?" Figure 1.8 shows the percentage, in each of the age groups, that responded "frequently."

The perception of being trapped, according to these data, is both high and relatively stable. Only among the youngest workers is it less than 35 percent. Perhaps they do not feel trapped yet because the feeling has not had time to set in. Maybe in ten years, after experiencing setbacks and disappointments, 40 percent of those who are still migrating will also feel unable to break out, as is the case for each of the older groups.

These feelings of being trapped in the migrant cycle may be related to perceptions of whether life conditions have changed for migrant workers over the years. A quick review of the data presented in Figures 1.1 through 1.7 suggests that treatment on the road is not as bad as it once was and that housing conditions have improved somewhat. Nevertheless, much less improvement has taken place in working conditions. The same applies to being cheated by farmers or crew leaders, a situation that has shown very little improvement since 1960. Treatment by townspeople and clerks has improved only slightly. Worse, migrants now worry more about vandalism and burglary of their homes while they are gone than they did in earlier years.

We could guess that civil rights legislation has generally benefited

*Helping develop the land
of opportunity—for
everyone else*
(photo courtesy of
George C. McLemore).

migrants. Flagrant discrimination seems less common. But, as we shall see in more detail in Chapter 4, reducing bigotry does not end exploitation: it does not raise wages or keep children from missing important elements of a quality education. It also does not change cultural biases against people who migrate or get dirty because of their work.

For most migrants, education is the golden door out of the trap—if not for themselves, then at least for their children. While fewer migrants have to contend with parents who cannot see the value of a good education, they must still overcome major obstacles to get it. Marisa, for example, says, "I hated being called a migrant, but couldn't do much about it until I got older. That's when I decided to become a nurse. Each day after eight to ten hours in the sun, I'd rush home to see if my nursing and biology books had arrived. All of that hard work in the fields taught me to work hard, and now I'm a nurse. It's a shame that everyone can't be as fortunate as me."

It is not only the hard work that makes migrant life difficult. Many migrant children have to battle stereotypes and low expectations. Carla, who recently graduated at the top of her high school class, says, "I always feel weird when the Anglos up north speak to me. It's almost like being a two-year-old who doesn't understand. It doesn't even matter if you're valedictorian. They still talk to you real slow and in a loud voice so you'll understand their instructions."

Fortunately, though, some change has taken place. Antonio has seen the hardships and the change. He remembers the 1970s when the farmers never associated with the migrant workers. "They didn't want to be near us," he recalls. "The farmers made sure that they didn't go to town when we did. So on Sundays we had the town to ourselves. Nowadays, though, the migrants and the farmers mix more. In fact, the past few summers, we have a farmer who has provided good housing. He bought us a dishwasher. Last winter he even came to visit us here in the Valley."

Who knows? Maybe their farmer will be one of thousands of retirees who come to the Valley each year as Winter Texans. Then he will be the migrant.

"A Nice House":
The Colonias of South Texas

Chapter 2

We live in a nice house in a colonia. It isn't a perfect house. We don't have heating or air-conditioning, so the house is cold in winter and very hot in summer. There are lots of drafts, and the roof is falling apart. We have problems with mice and roaches. Still, it's our house, and we think it's nice.

MINERVA LARA, 1990

Minerva sees something "nice" about her colonia house that most outsiders fail to see.[1] She likes it because she and her family own it. Each year, they saved a few dollars for lumber, wiring, and concrete blocks. They built it with the help of family and friends. No contractor ever set foot on their property. So while it has certain defects, it is the fulfillment of the American dream of homeownership. Therefore, for Minerva and others like her, it is a "nice house."

In contrast, reporters and government officials almost never say anything good about colonias, the unincorporated rural settlements along the Texas-Mexico border. A June 1987 *Newsweek* article, for example, called them "rural slums," "prisons of poverty," "a grim new Appalachia," and "the worst America has to offer." Congressional reports have labeled them "The Third World within our borders."[2]

Colonia residents know that their homes are often in poor shape. They know their water supply may be contaminated, and they hate having to use an outhouse. It is hard getting into town, and they get tired of dust and pesticides from nearby fields blowing into their homes. They also know their homes will flood when it rains a lot.

The enormous growth of border colonias in the last twenty years should tell us something. Despite high interest rates, missing infrastructure, grinding poverty, and broken promises, colonia housing keeps expanding. From 1970 to 1990, the population of the Rio Grande

Valley doubled. A large portion of this growth was in colonias. In 1970 only 10 percent of the Valley population was housed in colonias.[3] By 1990, 26 percent were living in colonia housing. A recent report by the Texas Water Development Board counted 1,436 colonias in Texas, with a total of 339,041 residents.[4] Hidalgo County alone has 60 percent of these colonias. Presently, one-third of Hidalgo County's 400,000 residents live in colonias.

Before the 1950s, colonias were little more than worker camps on some larger ranches and farms. Then landowners found they could subdivide poor farmland (especially areas that flooded), grade some roads, put in occasional electric lines, and sell lots. Farmworkers and Mexican immigrants were willing buyers. By living outside city limits, they could get around loosely written and poorly enforced building codes. Here they could build whatever house they could afford.

Generally, they purchased lots with 14 to 16 percent interest on a "contract for deed." Such contracts gave them no equity in their property until they made the final payment. They were also unable to use their land as equity on a home loan. Worse, they could lose their investment if they missed a single payment.

Juan Garza is one of these colonia homeowners. In 1980 he saw a sign in Spanish along a country road advertising lots for one hundred dollars down. He felt he could afford that and the eighty-dollar monthly payments. Over time, he might even build a home. The lot was big enough for his two sons to build homes next to his when they get married. So he lived in an old mobile home while he and his sons built their house. A year later, however, heavy rains made a lake of the colonia. The developer had never told Juan or his neighbors this could happen. When they confronted him about it, he told them it was up to the county to provide drainage.

Mrs. Rodriguez was more wary when she bought her lot in a "rural subdivision." She checked to make sure that the area did not flood during heavy rains. In fact, her colonia had paved streets and even an occasional electric pole. She was thrilled because her children would not have to go to school all muddy on rainy days. The developer told her he would install water and sewer lines within six months at no extra cost. A year later, however, nothing had been done. She and her neighbors discovered that he had sold all the lots and moved away. County officials told her they did not have the personnel to control developers. "If you can find him," they said, "take him to court."

These descriptions of colonia life come from two research projects that inform this chapter. The first is the Colonia Residents Exploratory

Interviews, a series of exploratory interviews conducted as part of the Borderlife Project. The second is the Colonia Residents Survey of 545 randomly selected colonia residents, of which 89 percent were women, in twelve Hidalgo County colonias, which the Border Association for Refugees and Colonia Advocacy (BARCA) asked me to direct in 1994 (Appendix B, no. 2). We conducted the Colonia Residents Survey to evaluate BARCA's community development project in Hidalgo County colonias. Their project, funded by the Kellogg Foundation, seeks to develop a strong sense of community and to empower colonia women.

Foundation directors, academicians, and public officials have become increasingly concerned about colonias. Most reports, however, have focused on the "rural slum" aspect of colonias. Though this characterization does bring out such colonia problems as exploitation and the lack of a basic infrastructure, it distorts colonia life in at least two ways. First, it fails to convey the positive aspects of colonias and their potential strengths as a form of low-income housing. Second, it ignores the special character of colonias as a U.S.-Mexico border phenomenon. We will examine these two special aspects of colonias before describing their problems.

Potential Strengths of Colonia Housing

Colonias are essentially "owner-occupied" communities. In 1988 a Texas Department of Human Services study found that 87 percent of colonia residents in the Valley owned their homes.[5] In the Colonia Residents Survey of twelve colonias, 77 percent of respondents said they owned their homes, while an additional 14 percent said a family member owned it. Only 5 percent said someone outside the colonia owned their home, a remarkably low rate of absentee ownership. Homeownership in colonias even exceeds the national average of 63 percent reported by the U.S. Census Bureau.[6] This is particularly significant considering that high rates of homeownership are generally associated with community stability and high rates of civic participation.

In addition, many of these homeowners choose to live in colonias because they can build their own homes. Building codes or requirements for building permits can be largely avoided or ignored "out in the country." The Almendárez family, for example, first planned to build a home in a subdivision of Hidalgo, a town in Hidalgo County. When they found out they could not build there a little at a time, they decided to buy a lot in a nearby colonia. "It has taken us four years to finish our house," states Mrs. Almendárez. "Right after we bought the lot in 1987, we dug some

A colonia home of residents who have gone north to work in the fields
(photo courtesy of George C. McLemore).

holes for the foundation and then left to work up north. When we came
back, we found that someone had filled the holes and sold our lot to
someone else. We told the developer that we had gone up north to work
and that we wanted our land. He got the other family another lot and
gave us ours back, but we had to pay the three missed payments and an
extra thousand dollars."

Mr. Almendárez had learned carpentry working in a furniture store
in Linares, Mexico. "They made the furniture right there in the store,"
says Mrs. Almendárez. "My husband never went to school, but he
learned carpentry right there on the job." As she spoke, Mrs. Almendárez
showed her interviewer all the things her husband and sons had built.
She showed off beds, dressers, cabinets, closets, and tables, all beautifully
decorated with flowers carved into the wood. Her sons have even put
decorative burglar bars on the windows and doors to protect the house
while they are up north each year.

Many colonia residents who build their own homes do not possess
the same skills that the Almendárez family has. The Briones family, for
example, is about two-thirds finished with their house of block and cement. "The first day," says Mrs. Briones, "we only put up eleven blocks.
The second day we managed nineteen blocks, and on the third day we

did twenty-seven blocks." Their interviewer comments, "As I sat there talking to them, I caught a glimpse of sunlight through spaces between the blocks where the cement had not bonded. They plan to seal up the spaces later, though they have not figured out yet what kind of plaster to use to keep moisture out."

The Luna family put a small mobile home on their land while they built their home. "When my son got sick," says Mrs. Luna, "we couldn't make the payments, so they repossessed the trailer. Fortunately, we had four walls and the roof up, so we moved in." Her husband adds, "We didn't know much about building, so we just did what seemed natural and watched our friends work on their houses. In some places we messed up, but at least we have our own house. All our brothers come to help us on weekends, and one of them who knows about electricity put in the wiring."

Colonia residents continue the frontier tradition of building their own homes, using whatever materials and help they can muster. As a result, most feel a sense of investment and accomplishment. Mrs. Almendárez, for example, comments, "It was hard work, but we worked together and it was worth it."

Another potential strength of colonias is the high degree of cultural homogeneity that can enhance the sense of community among their residents. Ninety-nine percent of colonia residents in South Texas are Hispanics, many of whom have close ties to Mexico.[7] People with a common background, or those who speak the same language, often share a strong sense of community.

Maité González, for example, tells of a time in 1992 when her daughter turned fifteen. "She wanted a *quinceañera* [a special "coming out" celebration]," Maité reports, "but I didn't have the money. My neighbors collected about three hundred dollars. The one with the nicest home in the colonia decorated it for the party. My sister brought the cake, and my daughter's *madrina* [godmother] bought her a dress. Others brought a stereo. All the ladies helped make tamales, rice, and potato salad. Another neighbor took the pictures. It turned out really nice, and my daughter was very happy. Later that year, we did the same for another neighbor whose daughter was getting married."

A related strength of colonias is family solidarity. Colonia children learn early the importance of family, as one of our interviewers discovered inadvertently. As she talked to a young boy outside his family's small home, she could tell he was hungry. "I offered him an orange I had in my purse," she recalls, "and I'll never forget what he did with it. He shared it with his brothers, instead of eating it all himself. I asked him why he

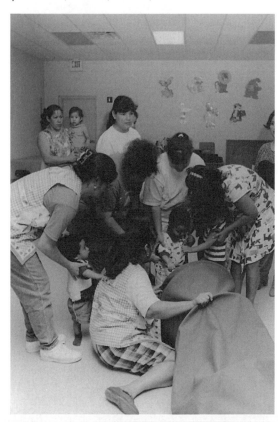

Colonia women often build a strong sense of community, especially in colonias where there is a place to meet
(photo courtesy of George C. McLemore).

did that and he replied, 'Son mis hermanos y lo que yo tengo es para ellos también [They are my brothers, and what I have is theirs also].'"

Family stability is also strong in colonias. In our Colonia Residents Survey, only 7 percent of adult women were separated or divorced; fully 81 percent were married at that time. A 1993 study by the Texas Attorney General's Office of colonia-dominant census tracts supports this finding. It found that only 9.6 percent of the Hispanic women in these areas were widowed or divorced. Further, only 13 percent of colonia homes had a female head of household.[8] These figures contrast with the high percentages of single-parent families in most "slum" areas and are even lower than the rate of 20 percent of single-female households in other parts of Texas.[9]

Colonia residents believe in family. Many move to a colonia to be close to family members. Mario García and his four married sons, for example, purchased five adjacent lots in their colonia so they could live near one another. All contributed to make the two-thousand-dollar down payment, and each alternately makes the monthly payments. This situation corresponds to findings of a Lyndon B. Johnson School of Public Affairs study. The study found that the main reason for moving to a colonia was to be near relatives. It also found that 80 percent of colonia residents have relatives living elsewhere in their colonia.[10] Mr. García, for example, has a nephew, two aunts, and an uncle living in his colonia.

While tight family solidarity is a definite plus for most colonia residents, it can also detract from a wider sense of community. When relatives live nearby, some colonia residents exclude nonfamily neighbors. One resident said, for example, in speaking of nonrelative neighbors, "We don't bother them, and they don't bother us."

In spite of such problems, colonias often have a strong sense of community solidarity. Those who see colonias only as "rural slums" often ignore this strength and the high levels of homeownership and family solidarity.

Colonias As a Border Phenomenon

Those who characterize colonias as "rural slums" also commonly ignore the special character of colonias as a border phenomenon. Colonias are not just another case of rural poverty—an Appalachia on the border. While rural poverty exists elsewhere in the nation, colonias do not. They are tied to the Texas-Mexico border in ways that make them unique.

The case of Erasmo Ramón, a resident of a colonia south of McAllen, is a good illustration. Four years ago, Erasmo came from his home in Monterrey, Mexico, 150 miles to the southwest. His aunt and cousins in McAllen invited him, helped him cross the border, and even found him a construction job that paid minimum wage. "My situation is not bad," he says. "I rely on my relatives for everything. Sometimes I go back to Mexico and cross through customs because I speak enough English to answer their questions. I like it here because there is more social order and I can be near my family. I plan to live here permanently and hope to legalize myself in the United States. The only thing that I don't like is the treatment from the [Mexican-American] coworkers who call me *mojado* ["wetback"] and tell me 'Ahí viene la Migra [Here comes the Border Patrol].'"

Erasmo does not have legal documents, so his employer risks being fined. He hired Erasmo as a favor to the aunt, though he only has to pay minimum wage. Erasmo argues that he does not hurt anyone because taxes are deducted from his paycheck. The Border Patrol has caught him several times. Nevertheless, with more than one million apprehensions along the border each year, little more is done than to take him to Reynosa, Mexico. He always returns to McAllen the same day.

Erasmo could get paid a lot more if he moved to Houston, but then he would be a long way from family. Getting picked up by the Border Patrol would also involve more than an inconvenience. He would also have to pass the "second border," the Border Patrol checkpoints on all highways heading north from the Valley, where officers are not easily fooled.

Erasmo's aunt became a legal resident of the United States with the amnesty provisions of the 1986 Immigration Reform and Control Act (IRCA). Many other colonia residents benefited from this legislation. Still, many are married to undocumented Mexicans who cannot become legal. Immigration officials claim they are "likely to become a public charge" because they are not earning more than $20,000 a year.[11] So, though many undocumented colonia residents qualify for legal status by having a spouse who is a citizen or resident alien, they cannot qualify on the income provisions. Approximately 90 percent of the households in our sample of twelve colonias (Colonia Residents Survey) had incomes less than $15,000, and 62 percent had incomes less than $9,000 a year.

With little hope for becoming legal residents, some colonia occupants get a "lawyer letter," an official-looking statement by an attorney or notary public saying they have initiated the long process of legalization. "Lawyer letters" provide no legal basis to prevent deportation, but officials may be more lenient toward those who have them. They provide a ray of hope for the undocumented and a steady income for lawyers and *notarios* (notary publics) who charge substantial monthly fees to keep them updated.

Other undocumented colonia residents borrow birth certificates. A few even purchase counterfeit documents. Many simply stay at home, unable to work because they are not legally in the United States, and unable to be here legally because they cannot earn enough to meet the income standards.

Though IRCA's fines for hiring undocumented Mexicans may have made it harder to get a job, it has not necessarily cut back on illegal immigration. Farmers and factory owners have found they can avoid fines by contracting labor from crew leaders. Some colonia residents work in local fields or packing sheds or get occasional jobs in construction. Others are self-employed, selling used articles at *las pulgas* (flea markets) or finding odd jobs in the area.

Some take articles to Mexico for resale. Others even have jobs or small businesses in Mexico, commuting daily or weekly using a *mica*, a border-crossing card issued by the INS at ports of entry from Mexico.[12] The pass allows Mexican border residents to spend up to seventy-two

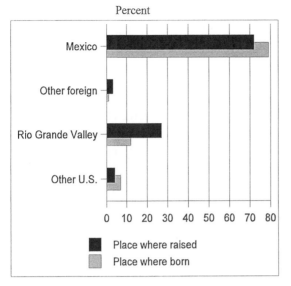

Percent

Fig. 2.1. Places where born and where raised of adult female residents of twelve Hidalgo County colonias (Colonia Residents Survey, 1994)

hours in the United States for shopping, visiting, and other errands. Though it carries no work authorization, officials rarely check to see whether *mica* holders actually leave within the time limit. Colonia residents holding *micas* thus have a quasi-legal status, having entered legally but lacking authorization for long-term stays or employment.

Some colonia residents pass for U.S. citizens. Roberto came illegally to the United States, but in school he learned to speak English so well that no one knows he is in Texas illegally. His mother's friend used false documents to get him across when he was twelve years old. "This friend passed me off as her grandson," he relates. "She brought two of her own grandchildren and passed me off as a third by using someone else's birth certificate. She even brought a set of clothes for me to put on. As we drove up to the agent at the border, I was scared. The agent didn't even question her, however, so we made it safely. I was very happy to be reunited with my mom."

If children of illegal parents are born in the United States, by law they are full U.S. citizens. As a result, many colonia homes have a mixture of citizens, legal residents, quasi-legal "guests," and illegal residents. Discretion dictates against questioning the legal status of colonia residents, so we did not address the issue in the Colonia Residents Survey. Nonetheless, we did ask the adult respondents where they were born and where they were raised. The results of the responses are summarized in Figure 2.1.

These figures show a very heavy concentration of adult colonia women who were both born and raised in Mexico. The Texas Department of Human Services survey finding that 71 percent of household heads in Valley colonias could not speak English is indirect support for these conclusions.[13]

Though colonias are quite homogeneous in terms of national origin and social class, they are highly diverse in the orientation of their residents to the international border environment. In terms proposed by Oscar Martínez, we can find many Mexican nationalists (those who passionately assert Mexican interests), American nationalists (those with similar feeling for the United States), and many others who are binational and bicultural.[14] In addition, colonias have become home for many settler migrants (those who live in the borderlands for prolonged periods), as well as a stopping-off place for transient migrants (those who pause only briefly before moving farther north).

For most low-income colonia residents, owning a home close to the border has certain advantages. They have a wide choice of Mexican radio and TV programs and movies, as well as other entertainment. In addition, rural land close to border cities is cheaper in Texas than it is in Mexico. Homeownership also allows most colonia residents who have relatives in Mexico to receive visitors for weeks, months, or years. Landlords seldom allow such visits in rental housing.

The flexibility of a border location is often a matter of survival for many colonia residents. Many cannot afford medical treatment in the United States, so they go to Mexico for lower-cost treatment. They can also purchase prescription drugs in Mexico without a prescription. Though self-prescription can be dangerous, people on low incomes often rely on it to save the cost of visiting a doctor just to get a prescription.

Finally, the border environment provides needed flexibility for those whose employment status is highly unstable. Many residents need to be able to work or sell things on both sides of the border. Likewise, having family on both sides of the border provides a safety net during periods of unemployment. As Martínez points out, being able to have many options is a matter of survival for those at the bottom of the social order.[15]

Problems of Colonia Housing

Nevertheless, major drawbacks offset these advantages of colonia housing. The same lax subdivision codes that have enabled many families to buy and build homes have also created enormous infrastructure problems. Many colonias lack potable water. Most are not connected to sewer lines. Poor drainage is a problem for many, as is the lack of paved streets. In addition, colonia residents have many social problems associated with poverty and marginal social status.

PROBLEMS OF POOR INFRASTRUCTURE

Of the 868 colonias counted by the Texas Water Development Board in 1995, 204 still lacked treated water. More than 750 lacked wastewater connections.[16] Mayela lives in one of these colonias. Every day she must visit her aunt in a nearby colonia to shower and fill a huge ice chest with water. She takes it home for cooking, drinking, washing, and even for a recently added "luxury"—an indoor toilet.

Joaquín's family went without potable water for thirteen years. During the 1960s, some residents of their colonia obtained water from a nearby canal. Others used barrels or tubs to store water. Then most of them obtained cement or metal cisterns in their backyards that could hold a one- or two-week supply. Colonia residents who owned flatbed trucks brought water from the city water pump for their neighbors. Finally, with government funding, a water supply corporation brought water lines to the colonias.

Colonia residents like Joaquín have discovered that some things are improving. In 1990 the Texas Legislature created the Economically Distressed Areas Program. This legislation made it more difficult for developers to start new colonias without providing water, paving, drainage, and adequate sewage disposal systems. In addition, federal and state agencies have allocated funds to bring some infrastructure to existing colonias, though red tape keeps many colonias in the "planning" stage. The Texas Water Development Board estimates that 123 colonias have been connected, another 481 are in the planning stage, and 264 are not yet included.[17]

Even when water and wastewater lines do arrive, however, some residents cannot afford the connections. Others run into problems getting lines onto their property. The Támez family lives in a colonia recently connected to the North Alamo Water Supply Corporation. Nonetheless, they still have to haul their drinking water from her father's house down the street. The water company told them that their neighbor has to give permission to put the line through her property. So far, she has not. "I keep telling myself," says Mrs. Támez, "that someday she'll be nice enough to let the water line through. But it's been six years, and we're still waiting."

Most people have a hard time imagining what it would be like to live without running water. Susana vividly remembers the times when they did not. "One week in 1989," she recalls, "it rained for days. The roads were muddy and covered with water. My grandmother and I both knew that my uncle's car would get stuck if he hauled the water for us like he usually did. We were getting desperate for clean water. I knew I had to go, but my grandmother was afraid that snakes or rats forced out by the rain might bite me, so she went with me. That night, while we were gone, my grandfather got very sick. By the time we got home, his fever was so bad that we had to take him to the hospital."

Flooding is a serious problem in many colonias. The 1988 Texas Department of Human Services study discussed above found that 45 percent of Valley colonia residents reported flooding. In our Colonia Residents Survey, 20 percent of the respondents reported that the area around their colonia homes frequently floods during heavy rains. Another 22 percent said they occasionally experience flooding. Even when no water comes into the home or yard, flooding makes colonia life very difficult. María, a UT–Pan American student, remembers a year ago when a friend from the university gave her a ride home after class. "It rained a lot that day," she says. "Because our colonia has no drainage, our street flooded. On the way to my house, I warned my friend to stop and let me walk, but she wouldn't let me out in the water. It came up past the car floor, but she made it without stalling. Later, I found out her ignition system shorted out after she took me home. I was so embarrassed."

Antonio Garza hates the flooding for another reason. "After a few hours of rain," he says, "the yards become covered with water. The worst part, though, is that it stays there for days because there is no drainage or sewer system in our colonia. It not only turns brown but smells awful." And with the smell come mosquitoes. Alejandro Cabrera remembers a few years ago when it rained for an entire week. After the rain stopped, he went out to drain the water. "I finally had to quit," he says, "because I was covered with mosquito bites. A few days later, I got a fever that kept me in bed for a week with fatigue and aching muscles."

Residents of colonias with no paved roads suffer in other ways. Lydia remembered what rainy weather was like when she was in junior high. "They did not allow the bus drivers to drive into the colonia on rainy days," she recalls. "They would drop us off on the paved road. We had to walk four blocks in the rain and mud. Our shoes would stick in the mud. I remember my mother waiting for me at the door with a clean pair of shoes."

When residents cannot get in or out of flooded colonias, the situation is worse. Mrs. Cavazos remembers once when it rained for two weeks. "The bus stopped over a mile away," she says, "because of the mud. We didn't have a car, so the kids just missed school. They hated that because they're smart and love school. They held my daughter Melisa back a grade because she fell behind. I talked to her teacher, but she couldn't do anything. Since then, we started a committee to do something about our terrible living conditions. By working together, we got paved streets."

Paved streets also help alleviate the dust. Martín Morales says, "We moved out here because this is all we could afford. People here are good neighbors and help each other when they can. But with no paved streets, everything we touch is covered with dust. It's on the furniture, the clothes put out to dry, and even the food we eat. Neighbors across the street have it even worse. The wind usually blows out of the southeast, so every passing car dusts people on the west side of the street. It's impossible to keep our cars or houses clean."

Sewage disposal is another major headache. The Texas Department of Human Services study found that less than 10 percent of colonia homes in the Valley were connected to sewer systems; 70 percent used septic tanks, 12 percent used outhouses, and 8 percent had cesspools. The González family has tried all of these systems except the municipal sewer. "We've had many problems from not being connected to a sewer," Mrs. González comments. "The smell gets really bad in our neighborhood, and we always have flies. At first we had an outhouse, but I hated it. Keeping it clean was impossible, and it always smelled bad. I was always afraid one of the kids would fall in or would get bitten by spiders or snakes. My kids were afraid to go at night, and I never let them go alone. My husband dug a cesspool, but that was almost as bad. Finally, we were able to afford a septic tank."

José Rodríguez says that septic tanks also create problems. "The pipes to the septic tank are constantly getting clogged," he says. "The water sometimes comes out under the house. It's green, stagnant, and smells like dead animals. One day I called a professional to clean my septic tank, which usually costs about fifty dollars. When he saw a big puddle, he said I'd have to get new plumbing. He told me colonia people should petition to get connected to a sewer system. We've tried that, but nothing ever happens. It's not right. The city incorporated our colonia so now we pay city taxes. They still won't connect us to the sewer system."

Most colonias are too far away for cities to incorporate them, connect them to their sewer systems, or allow them to benefit from other municipal services, such as trash collection. Since many cannot afford expensive trash collection services (when such services are available), they burn garbage. Marilu Saenz says that around five in the evening, everyone closes their doors and windows, even when it's hot, because of the smoke from burning trash. Even when pick-up services are affordable and available, dogs often run loose in colonias and tear up the bags. Then, the wind blows trash all over the neighborhood.

Another problem of colonias in agricultural areas is the danger of pesticide contamination. María lives in a colonia south of Pharr. One July morning in 1985, a strong, bitter odor awakened her. As she got up, she got a headache, nausea, chest pains, and a general muscle weakness. She remembered these symptoms from working in sprayed fields as a farmworker, but she had never felt them so strongly. When she went outside, she saw a plane spraying a cotton field southeast of her home. The prevailing southeast wind was carrying it directly toward her house. She checked with her neighbors and found that many of them were also complaining of headaches and nausea. She went to the migrant clinic where a doctor told her to rest and take aspirin. She returned home, and that night her symptoms became even stronger. Finally, she went to the emergency room at the local hospital. The doctors told her she had "severe high blood pressure," a condition she still has. Until that day in 1985, she had never had blood pressure problems. Her doctor says she will remain on medication to control this condition for the rest of her life.

Health Problems in Colonias

In the Colonia Residents Survey, we asked respondents how often, in their colonia, they had to breathe air contaminated by pesticides. Twenty-three percent said "frequently"; another 28 percent said "occasionally"; and 50 percent said "rarely or never." Colonia residents who are exposed are often unable to do much about it. Carmen remembers waking up to the sound of an airplane. She went to the window and could see one spraying a field near her house. "This frightened me a great deal," she says, "because within seconds, a cloud of spray surrounded our house. My children began to cry because it was hard to breathe and it stung their eyes. My neighbors and I tried to get them to stop spraying, but they wouldn't leave until the field was done. We were all sick for days, and our clothes all smelled bad. I am tired of complaining, but nobody will listen."

Colonia residents do not need another cause for poor health. Many poor infrastructure conditions discussed earlier cause health problems.

Contaminated water contributes its share, as does flooding and poor sewage disposal. Martín Montoya, a longtime colonia resident, sees this connection. In 1969 his colonia did not have a good source of treated water. "There was a cotton gin close to us," he says, "where we could get water. The people there were very helpful and never denied us water. A few years later, we saved enough money to install a *noria* [water well]. That made it easier to get water, but we still had problems. Often we could see dirt at the bottom of the containers, and the water wasn't clear. Once my four-year-old got sick and started throwing up. We took him to the doctor, who told us he had an infection due to contaminated water."

Because of conditions like these, colonia residents have rates of illness much higher than the general population. Even diseases that have been "eradicated" elsewhere are common in Valley colonias. Six percent of Valley colonia residents surveyed by the Texas Department of Human Services study, for example, have had tuberculosis. Another 10 percent have had hepatitis.[18] Water-borne fecal contamination, often the result of sewage improperly draining into the water table, spreads most of these diseases.[19]

To make matters worse, most colonia residents have no health insurance. In Texas as a whole, 42 percent of people below the poverty line have no health insurance. More than 71 percent of colonia residents are uninsured.[20]

With high medical costs and no insurance, colonia residents often rely on home remedies. Mr. Guajardo says that his wife uses household remedies to cure their children's illnesses because there simply is not enough money left for medical treatment after paying the bills. For many, the cost of conventional medicine is exorbitant. "All they want is our money," said one resident, "and they don't care if we get better or not. They'll tell us to go back for another checkup, and another and another, so that they get every cent we've got. The only thing that gets better is their wallets—not our health." Her sister agreed. "We don't have money to be going to the doctor every ten days, especially if there are no results. That's why I'd rather go to a *curandero* [folk healer]. He doesn't try to take our money, and besides, he has faith in God. Through his faith and mine, he can heal me, if its God's will."

Another colonia resident trusts doctors but explains the way other costs are involved. "We have only one car," she says, "which my husband takes to work. I have to walk four blocks to phone him if a child needs to go to the doctor. Then, he'll miss work because you have to sit all day at the clinic to see a doctor. To take a bus, I'd have to walk two miles to the bus stop, carrying a sick child all the way. Usually, we just wait to see if the illness goes away. Sometimes we go across to Reynosa, but transportation is still a problem. Most of the time I just pray to get better because going to a doctor is expensive and a lot of trouble."

The Valley lacks a general purpose public hospital. Even in emergencies, local proprietary hospitals sometimes turn away colonia residents because of their perceived inability to pay. Until recently, one hospital in McAllen had security guards whose uniforms closely resembled those of Border Patrol agents, presumably to scare away those afraid of the Border Patrol. In this situation, even children whose birth in the United States makes them citizens may be kept from medical attention when neither they nor their parents have proper documents.

Economic and Social Uncertainty in Colonias

Problems of poor health are, of course, related to poverty in colonias. Illness or injury can deplete resources needed for food or other living expenses. Alicia, for example, remembers one night when her little brother became very sick. The family had to choose whether to use their grocery money to take him to the emergency room or just wait to see whether he got better. Knowing that they would have very little food, they chose to seek medical attention. With great emotion, she says, "Teníamos que sacrificar para nuestro hermanito; la comida no tiene el valor de su vida" [We had to sacrifice for our little brother; food isn't as valuable as his life].

For people who live on the economic edge, almost any emergency can bring disaster. Sicknesses, the breakdown of the family car, losing a job, and the septic tank overflowing are not only more serious for colonia residents but are also more likely. When funds are low, repairs to homes and vehicles, as well as health needs of family members, are put off until they become full-blown emergencies. Often, they have no "safety net" of insurance, a second vehicle, or savings.

As a result, colonia residents learn to live with a great deal of uncertainty. As we have seen, public services that most of us take for granted, such as clean water, sewage disposal, drainage, and well-maintained roads, are available only with great effort. Without savings or insurance, the health care system is undependable. In addition, employment is often seasonal and temporary. Attitudes of residents of nearby cities are also unpredictable, as is police and fire protection. A brief examination of each will illustrate these points.

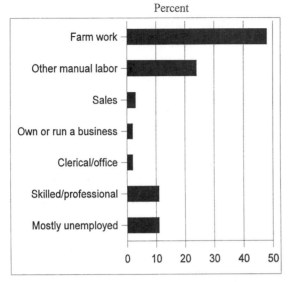

Percent

Fig. 2.2. Employment categories of residents in twelve Hidalgo County colonias (Colonia Residents Survey, 1994)

UNEMPLOYMENT

By conventional definitions, about half of colonia residents are unemployed.[21] Such figures, however, are deceiving. Farmwork, for example, is seasonal, leaving those who do it "unemployed" during winter months. Construction work is also temporary for many workers.

In the Colonia Residents Survey, we asked respondents in the twelve colonias, "What kind of employment do members of your household mainly have?" The results are presented in Figure 2.2, which shows that only 11 percent of respondents said people in their household were "mostly unemployed." Almost half claimed farmwork as their main source of employment.[22]

Farmwork affects colonia life in many ways, including the way residents talk about their occupation. Anglo society usually asks, "What kind of work do you do?" In colonias, it is often, "¿En qué trabajas?" [What do you work in?]. The common response is something like, "Trabajo en el tomate [pepino, etc.] [I work on tomatoes (peppers, etc.)]" to describe not only field labor but the specific type of crop they follow.

As we pointed out in Chapter 1, most migrant families do not have a regular year-round income. Often while they are in the Valley, they find temporary work in local fields, packing sheds, construction jobs, janitorial positions, or warehouse labor. They need these jobs to help pay for the trip up north. For others, farmwork is what they do when other occupations fail to provide sufficient or steady income. One young woman, for example, has been unemployed for about six months. "I was working for a supermarket in McAllen," she says. "I only worked for two weeks before they laid me off. The employment commission had nothing for me, and I have not found anything on my own. My father says I need to help him pay the bills, so I guess I'm going to have to go back to the fields."

Even with several members of a household working, disruptions in employment are a serious matter. One young mother says, "We were all working when, all at once, I lost my job and couldn't find another. We couldn't do many things we were planning, like getting a TV or eating out occasionally. We did grocery shopping only when we had to. Luckily, no one had to go to the doctor. We wouldn't have had money for that."

Still, colonia residents are very resourceful. A young couple with three young children live in a two-room house in Las Milpas. He does odd jobs, but she is presently unemployed. She wants to work but cannot find a job. Besides, she cannot find day care in the area, and she has no way to get to and from a job. So she sells food items that he brings from Mexico. The only time they go out together is to shop and to make their weekly visit to his family in Reynosa, Mexico.

POVERTY IN COLONIAS

Colonia families want to work. Many avoid welfare, even when they are eligible. Most families, including the older children, work when they can. Still, it may never be enough. Anabela and her husband, for example, are farmworkers. They have never had a steady income. They managed to avoid any welfare assistance until 1979. That year she could not go up north with her husband because she was pregnant. On his way back, the car broke down. "That took just about all the money we had made," she says. "We needed new tires, and we owed my sister a hundred dollars she had lent us for the trip. That left only enough money for a couple of months, so I had to ask for food stamps. It's always the same. We work very hard but never have enough."

It does not help that many jobs for colonia residents provide no benefits, such as sick leave or health insurance. Some jobs do not even pay the minimum wage. Often, work is temporary, so they are not eligible for unemployment compensation. In addition, certain federal benefits may have regulations that exclude some colonia residents.

Still, many people in colonias do not think of themselves as poor. Though they cannot buy their children toys or snacks, other families are

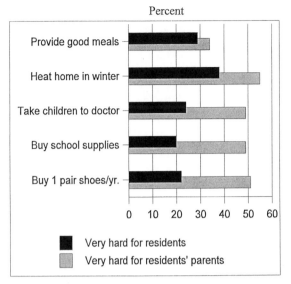

Percent

Fig. 2.3. Expenses colonia residents in twelve Hidalgo County colonias reported were "very hard" for their parents and themselves (Colonia Residents Survey, 1994)

in worse shape. Many preschool colonia children think of themselves as middle class because some families in the colonia are better off and some are worse off.

In addition, because many colonia adults grew up in Mexico, life in a Texas colonia may be much better by comparison. One Mexican immigrant, for example, said, "In Mexico when kids in your neighborhood get hungry, you have nothing to give them. They'll eat whatever they can find. I've seen children eat an onion as if it were an apple, or an uncooked jalapeño. Because they are so hungry, anything tastes good. Things are really bad in Mexico. People are too poor, hungry, and sick. Here I have it much better."

Hortencia also feels her life is much better than it was for her parents in Mexico. "Raising us was hard for my parents," she says. "Both of them had to work in the fields. One day my dad was sick. He had to put food on the table, though, so he went to work feeling pain and tightness in his chest. There in the fields, he collapsed and died. I'll never take food for granted. My father died for us, his children, to survive. Fortunately, it's been a lot easier for my husband and me to feed our children."

In the Colonia Residents Survey, we asked respondents how hard it was, when they were children, for their parents to afford to do the following things for them: buy them shoes once a year; pay for school supplies; take them to the doctor occasionally; heat their home in winter; and provide good meals. Then we asked them how hard these same things were for them as parents. Figure 2.3 shows the results.

It is clear, from this figure, that most colonia residents struggle to provide even the most basic needs of their children. Almost 30 percent, for example, say that providing good meals for their children is very hard for them. It is also clear, however, that most of these colonia residents feel better off than their parents. As for income, colonia residents are the poorest of the poor. In attitude, though, many (especially first-generation immigrants) believe that they are better off than their parents. Stoddard calls this condition relative poverty, or personal feelings of one's own state of economic well-being based upon comparisons with others.[23]

STEREOTYPES OF COLONIA RESIDENTS

The belief that colonia residents are upwardly mobile is not widely shared in Valley cities. One colonia resident attending UT–Pan American, for example, relates a common experience. "I was talking to some of my friends," he says, "when they introduced me to a female friend. We were having a nice talk until I mentioned the colonia where I lived. Suddenly, she backed off and said she had to go. I knew why she left. She got scared of me. It's happened before. It's hard to make friends when people get scared just because you're from a colonia."

Another student describes her experience in high school. "To get to and from school, we had to take the bus. That was one of my worst nightmares. Every time we got on the bus near our colonia, the other kids would start calling us names. I remember them saying, 'Ya se subieron la bola de rateros [The gang of thieves just got on].' We knew this wasn't true, but we couldn't do much about it, since they outnumbered us and the teachers thought they were the 'good kids' in school."

Since Mexican Americans are often the perpetrators of such incidents, much of the prejudice against colonia residents may be more a matter of class than either ethnicity or race. One colonia resident, for example, said that Anglo and Mexican American students in the McAllen schools think that anyone from a colonia belongs to a gang or is a *cholo* (delinquent).

Women from the twelve colonias we sampled report much less discrimination once they leave the public schools. Perhaps this is because they do not spend much time outside the colonias. One woman said she commonly experiences stereotyping by Mexican Americans who believe that colonia residents are illegal Mexicans who come to take away jobs or to get on welfare. When we asked them how often people in Valley cities discriminate against colonia residents, only 8 percent said "frequently," while another 20 percent said "occasionally."

Often, the stereotypes have economic consequences. One young man from a colonia north of Edinburg recalled a job interview in McAllen. "I dressed up very professionally," he says, "because I knew you have to look good for those jobs. I was on time, and they took me in right away. The young man interviewing me asked where I lived before asking about my experience or education. When I told him, he wanted to know: Did I ever use drugs? Did I have an alcohol problem? Had I ever been in a gang? Did I have gang members as friends? Was I a convicted felon? These questions insulted me, but I thought they were part of the interview. But then he said he needed a person with class and good manners and that people from colonias don't usually have these qualities. I just got up and excused myself. I couldn't believe what I had heard."

CRIME IN COLONIAS

As this account and the ones preceding it illustrate, colonia residents are often stereotyped as gang members, criminals, or people in trouble with the law. As with many stereotypes, there is a bit of truth to this image. Colonias do have problems with crime and gangs. Nevertheless, colonia residents are more often the victims of crime than the perpetrators of it. In the Colonia Residents Survey, 42 percent of respondents said their colonia frequently has problems with gangs; 38 percent said homes in their colonia were frequently vandalized or burglarized. Much of this is related to the fact that many colonia residents leave their homes for extended trips to Mexico or to do migrant farmwork. Mrs. Morales gives an example. "Not so long ago," she says, "they burned down the home of some people who are up north working hard. We can't reach them, so they're going to be real shocked when they get back."

Colonias are vulnerable in another important way. They have only minimal police protection. Carmen discovered this when she saw some kids breaking into her neighbor's house last year. She called the police, but they would not come because she lived outside the city limits. They told her to call the sheriff. She did, but it took more than an hour for the deputy to come. "Now I'm always afraid to leave my home," she says. "How are we going to go up north if gangs are going to vandalize our house?"

It is hard to blame the sheriff. Almost half of Hidalgo County's 400,000 residents live outside incorporated city limits. His office has only fifteen officers per shift to cover fifteen hundred square miles. Besides, the sheriff holds elective office and few colonia residents vote, so they do not have high priority.

Perhaps these factors explain the reaction Mrs. Sosa got last year when she called for help after finding her home burglarized. She called the sheriff's office and told them it was an emergency. They did not come until two hours later. "I asked them why they took so long," she says, "but it looked like they weren't listening to me. Here I was, devastated, calling for help, having to wait two hours, just so they can ignore my question."

For some, the threat of personal assault is a more immediate danger. One September afternoon in 1991, Yolanda was walking near her home. Two drunk men accosted her. "They tried to hurt me," she says. "They were drunk, so I was able to get in my house where I called the police. It took them forty-five minutes to get to my house, which is easy to find in this colonia."

Some colonia homes are not so easy to find. Addresses in rural areas are often nothing more than a mail route and box number. Many colonias have no mail delivery to their homes, so their address is one mailbox among hundreds near the colonia entrance.

Because of the difficulty in getting reliable police protection, many colonia residents find their own solutions. According to one student interviewer, "Every house has at least one dog not because it's 'man's best friend' but because it is the poor man's best security. Every Sunday, one neighbor goes to his backyard and fires thirty-two rounds with his .22 rifle. He doesn't do it for practice, but to warn his neighbors that he has a gun and is ready to use it."

Others, like the Garzas, rely on family. "Now when it's time for us to go up north," she says, "my husband and the boys go, and I stay here with the girls." Thus, colonia residents not only lose their possessions from burglary or vandalism; they also lose income when wage earners have to stay home to guard the house.

In one colonia, residents got together to put up a few security lights. "With the lights," says one resident, "we don't have many gang members walking around, looking to see what they can get their hands on. We also help each other out in other ways. If my neighbor is going out of town, for example, he'll tell me, and I'll watch his house to make sure nothing unusual is going on. Our colonia is very united and peaceful. That's what I like about it."

A SENSE OF COMMUNITY IN COLONIAS

With a strong sense of community, colonia residents can more easily endure the lack of basic services. One woman remembers, for example, when her neighbor needed surgery. "Tenchita's family is very poor," she says. "They didn't have insurance, so we had some meetings and did bingo and raffles to help her out. After that, we kept working together on other things. We got the county to give us better drainage systems and even got them to pave our roads. The feeling of unity is what I really like about this colonia."

Unfortunately, not all colonias have this sense of unity and neighborliness. Maribel Salinas, for example, wishes her neighbors cared more about each other. "One afternoon," she recalls, "I was making lunch for my family. Suddenly I heard a scream. A mother had just discovered her two-year-old drowning in a *tina* [water tank]. I screamed for help but none of the neighbors wanted to get involved. Finally, my sister called the paramedics who were barely able to save him. As we talked about it later, the neighbors blamed the child's mother for leaving him alone. I thought to myself, 'Why can't people be more helpful, especially when a child is concerned?'"

In spite of all their problems, colonias have certain cultural and structural properties that could produce a strong sense of community. Their small size makes it easier for neighbors to know each other. The high level of homeownership provides stability and an economic stake in the colonia. Cultural, economic, and language similarity also provide the basis for a shared sense of identity. The need to find solutions to common problems has the potential for bringing neighbors together. Even the fact that almost half the colonia residents have the same occupation (farmwork) provides the potential for a strong bond.[24]

Other cultural and structural factors, however, pull in the opposite direction. Many colonias are new, so residents often do not know their neighbors. It is also hard to get to know migrant neighbors who are gone for several months a year. The strong emphasis on family in Mexican culture can also produce clannishness among extended family members to the exclusion of neighbors. In addition, most colonias are just groups of houses. Potential gathering places, such as schools, churches, or markets, are usually outside the colonia.

In the Colonia Residents Survey, we asked three questions designed to determine how strongly residents feel a sense of community. First, we asked how frequently people in their colonia watched out for each other and protected one another's property. Next, we asked how frequently residents of their colonia help each other when someone is sick, has an accident, or is in danger. Finally, we asked how often people in their colonia felt a sense of belonging with each other. The results are presented in Figure 2.4.

Percent

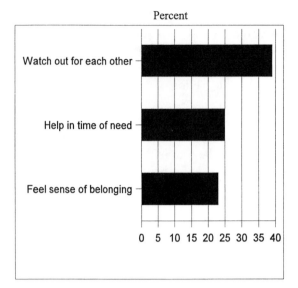

Fig. 2.4. Respondents' sense of community in twelve Hidalgo County colonias (Colonia Residents Survey, 1994)

The data in Figure 2.4 show that colonia residents are more likely to watch out for each other than they are to feel a strong sense of belonging, or to help each other in time of need. The willingness to watch out for each other may be because of the lack of adequate police protection—colonia residents have only each other to rely on. The sense of belonging may be low because colonia residents feel such a strong sense of family identity that neighbors are kept more at a distance. Such people would also likely see family, rather than neighbors, as those to whom one first turns in time of need.

Having extended family members living in the colonia is important. Nonetheless, entire colonia communities will need to work together to get water lines installed, roads paved, drainage improved, and sewage systems that do not contaminate drinking water. Some organizations have been successful in organizing entire colonia communities. Valley Interfaith, for example, is modeled after Saul Alinsky's Industrial Areas Foundation. They pressure public officials to meet the needs of some larger colonias and have been effective in training colonia leaders, especially those close to cities. Another organization, BARCA, conducts community-wide programs in some smaller outlying colonias, working mainly with women to help them develop networks within the colonia through which they can pressure public officials to make needed changes.

Often, such organizations must overcome formidable obstacles when they begin their work in colonias. Residents are often unfamiliar with the bureaucratic channels of U.S. systems of government. Most are not registered voters, and few have any real skills in working with politicians. Coming from backgrounds of poverty and having little English, many feel intimidated when approaching government agencies. They also know that public officials and people in nearby cities do not really want to deal with colonia residents.

As Ramona, one resident, says, "Those rich folks in the city don't like us. When they see the conditions we live in, they don't even want to pave the roads out here. They pave Trenton Road, for example, all the way from McAllen right up to our colonia. Then the pavement stops, and a dirt road is all that comes into our colonia. Doesn't that tell you something?"

"Only a Maid": Undocumented Domestic Workers in South Texas

WITH CRUZ C. TORRES

Chapter 3

In 1986 I came from Mexico so my kids could eat and stay in school. I found a job as a maid that paid fifty dollars a week. They provided free meals, and I even had my own room. But they wouldn't give me time off to see my family. They wouldn't even let me call home. There wasn't much I could do about it because I was only a maid.

ANA CAMACHO, 1991

Sometimes, Ana has a fatalistic way of looking at things. She feels that she cannot do much about what happens to her. Nonetheless, as we listened to hundreds of women like her, we became convinced that their "fatalistic attitude" is an accurate perception of life, not an orientation acquired from Mexican culture. Powerlessness, more than culture or upbringing, seems to produce such fatalistic attitudes.

Occasionally, "fate" can be kind. Some employers treat undocumented Mexican women much better. Lourdes, for example, found work with an older Anglo couple. They introduced her to friends as their adopted daughter. "At first," she says, "I had trouble talking with them, but after a few months we got used to each other's way of speaking English and Spanish. I worked for them for five years. I was lucky to find them. Those were the best years of my life. Then my boyfriend and I got married. They were happy for me, but sad I had to leave. They offered us a room at their house to keep me working for them. But we wanted a place of our own, and my husband didn't want me to work. I've never forgotten them. They were a father and mother to me. I still go to their graves once a month to leave flowers."

Lourdes, like Ana, believes that she found these employers by fate or luck. Though both women rightly perceive that they cannot control the way they are treated, something besides fate or luck is responsible. Factors in the social situation of undocumented maids, more than luck or destiny, produce these results. We will use data from hundreds of exploratory interviews and two survey research projects to illustrate.

The Research

In the initial research, we conducted exploratory interviews to get mini–"case histories" to see how undocumented maids are treated by family, immigration officials, smugglers, and employers. The patterns suggested by these Undocumented Maid Exploratory Interviews helped us to develop our Undocumented Maids Survey, in which we administered a fixed-response questionnaire (Appendix B, no. 3). This study consisted of 162 face-to-face interviews with undocumented maids. We then repeated this process with maids' employers: first we conducted the Employers of Undocumented Maids Exploratory Interviews with 214 respondents, then the Employers of Undocumented Maids Survey with 136 respondents (Appendix B, no. 4). To invite open expression, we avoided interviews with either a maid or her employer if we had already interviewed the other. Finally, if maids were afraid to talk about their current employer, we gave them the option of discussing a previous employer.

Hiring an undocumented maid or being one is illegal, as Nannygate exposés of politicians who hired undocumented maids have shown. As a result, both employers and their undocumented maids tend to shun interviews. These factors rule out random sampling techniques, so our interviewers used "snowball sampling." Sixty-five percent of the students who interviewed maids, for example, approached friends, relatives, or neighbors to arrange an introduction. These interviewers then asked those they interviewed to recommend others to whom they could speak with confidence.

For most student interviewers, this was an eye-opening experience. One student, for example, interviewed her own mother, formerly a maid of many years. "My mother described some really hard experiences," she says, "but said her first job was much better. An Anglo couple had gone to Mexico and chose her when she was only thirteen years old. They brought her to live with them in Houston. They made her part of the family[1] and even gave her a big surprise party when she turned fifteen. When we finished the interview, I had a lump in my throat. I had to go outside, so my mom wouldn't see me cry."

Another interviewer, the son of a doctor, remembers his father saying that maids could never be trusted. "I learned," he says, "to suspect the maid anytime I lost something. One morning, for example, I lost my wallet. I decided she must have taken it, so I went to her room and searched. I found nothing. Later that day I found it in the laundry. As I look back, I can see how I must have made her feel. I had learned to think of her as nothing more than a servant."

The Life Situation of Undocumented Maids

Many employers forget that their maid has a family, a right to privacy, and a life beyond the job.[2] Undocumented maids speak little or no English. They are "illegal," come from a foreign country, and do not understand local ways of doing things. As single women, cut off from family, afraid to seek police protection, they are frequent victims of exploitation.[3]

Carmen's case illustrates this point. "When I came to the United States in 1985," she says, "I didn't know anyone. So when a woman offered me twenty-five dollars a week until I proved myself, I took the job. She had three children and a big house. I had to get up at five-thirty every morning to make lunch for her husband and breakfast for the kids. After five or six months she hadn't increased my pay, though she liked my work. Then she gave me yard work on weekends, saying her husband was too tired. One month she said I couldn't take my monthly weekend home because she and her husband wanted to leave town. I was very upset because I needed to see my family. I told her, 'Well, at least pay me so I can send money home.' She said 'No, because we need the money for our trip.' I had no choice because I really needed the job. When I got ready to leave for home the next month, she wouldn't pay me the hundred dollars she had missed. She said, 'That way I know you'll come back.' Well, I never did. Gracias a Dios [Thanks to God], I have a better job now."

Some factors in the situation of undocumented maids promote treating them as one of the family.[4] Frequent interaction, especially in highly personal settings, for example, has been shown to produce friendship even among dissimilar people.[5] Live-in maids interact with their employers in the most personal family setting, the home. They are there twenty-four hours a day, seven days a week.[6] Their interaction is personal, intense, and covers an extended duration. Theoretically, such conditions should produce positive relations, unless the family takes measures to prevent them.

What is it about the situation of undocumented maids that might produce such extremes in their treatment? In this chapter, we will examine some specific aspects of the unique experience of undocumented maids in South Texas, including why they leave home, how they cross the border, how they find a job, how they are treated on the job, and what relations they maintain with family in Mexico. From this, we can identify several factors that might explain both good and bad treatment.[7]

WHY THEY COME

What motivates a young girl to leave family, friends, and the only home she has known, travel to an unknown country, live with strangers, and hide from authorities? Though "economics" is the correct answer, it fails to convey the complexity of the "push" situation. Antonia's case illustrates. One day eight years ago, she came home from school, a happy thirteen-year-old. "When I walked through the front door," she says, "my mother was crying. I asked her what was the matter, but she said to ask my father. At first, he didn't look at me in the eyes. He just asked if I wanted to work in the United States. I said no, that I couldn't leave my family. He said, 'Well, get your clothes ready because you're leaving tonight.' I felt like someone close to me had died. Tears came to my eyes, but I bit my lip. I begged him to find me some work nearby, not to send me so far away. I'll never forget what happened next. He looked me straight in the eyes and said, 'We have no choice. We need the money and that's that.' I was crying real hard. Then, for the first time in my life, I saw my father cry."

In our Undocumented Maids Survey, 29 percent of the women said they came to help their parents financially. Another 25 percent said they came to help their husbands support the family. One maid, for example, said, "The only reason I work in America is the dollar. I get paid more than my husband, who works as an attendant in a Mexican hotel." Another agreed. "If I could get the same pay in Mexico, I would never leave," she says.

An additional 23 percent said the lack of work in Mexico was their main reason for coming. Inocencia, for example, is an eighteen-year-old former maquila (assembly plant) worker from Ciudad Camargo who works in Rio Grande City. She quit her job at a maquiladora owned by a U.S. company because she was only earning thirty-four dollars a week. "Then I'd have to pay bills," she says, "buy food, and pay rent. Here, I earn forty dollars, and I don't have to pay any other bills. Now I can save money for school in August."

Five percent said they came to escape a bad personal experience in Mexico. That is what brought Martina to the United States four years ago. "One day," she says, "my stepfather raped me. My mother wasn't there because she had gone for tortillas. When I told her what happened, she called me a liar. The next day I packed my clothes, broke my bank, and left. I crossed the river at Roma and found work with the Garza family. They treated me like a daughter. Mr. Garza told me I needed to be in school. In the summers, we would migrate up north and work in the fields. But I was happy because I had four 'brothers and sisters.' They were the family I always dreamed of."

CROSSING THE BORDER

For some undocumented maids, getting into the United States is routine, while for others, it is very painful.[8] Flora remembers five years ago when she and her sister came to Reynosa. A friend led them to a coyote who charged them three hundred dollars to get them across the river. "He swam while pushing a tire tube," she remembers, "with us piled on top of each other. I have never been so scared in my life." Flora has gone back and forth often during the five years since then. She laughs while saying, "The coyote now gives me a discount because I am a regular customer. The last trip only cost me fifty dollars."

Most coyotes are not so generous.[9] One maid from San Luis Potosí and some friends hired a coyote in Reynosa to take them across. "We didn't really know him," she says. "After paying him five hundred dollars, we thought, 'This is it, U.S.A., here we come.' That night, he took us down to the water, took us across on tubes, took our money, and disappeared. We were sneaking around until some people told us we had just crossed the Anzaldúas Canal in Reynosa and were still in Mexico."

Some coyotes do more than steal money. In 1990 Paula came with an older lady. "When we arrived at the border," she says, "they told us we could cross the bridge with false papers for $175 each or pay $50 to cross on tubes. Since we had borrowed money for the trip, we decided to cross through the water. When we got down to the river, the men told us to take off our clothes to keep from drowning. The humiliation was so unbearable that I cry every time I remember. It was a cheaper way to cross, but it gave us a lesson we'll never forget."

The student who interviewed Paula adds, "She gave me the impression that something worse had happened that night. It made her very distressed to talk about it, however, so I decided to ask nothing further about the incident."

In the survey, we asked the 162 undocumented maids, "Have you ever hired a coyote to help you enter the United States?" Only 30 percent of the respondents said yes, so apparently most maids do not use a coyote. Rebeca's father takes her across on a tube whenever she enters the

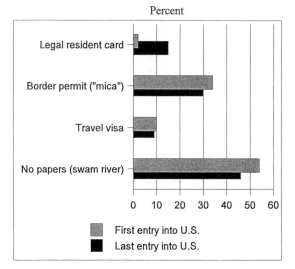

Percent

Fig. 3.1. How undocu-
mented maids reported
entering the United States
on first and most recent
entries (Undocumented
Maids Survey, 1993)

United States. Her friend Juanita does not have anyone like that to help her. She crosses on her own. "Many of us have a *mica* [border-crossing permit]," she says, "but I don't have one, so I have to swim. One night I was almost across when the Migra [Border Patrol] saw me. I tried to turn back, but they caught me. They took me to Mexico and said I'd never get a *mica* to enter legally. Somehow, I got the courage to try again that same night. This time, I wore dark clothing and traveled farther down the river. I made it and called a friend who took me to my job the next morning. I haven't returned to Mexico in three years because I'm afraid I won't be able to get back. I can't take the chance because my family needs the money too much."

We asked the maids we surveyed how they crossed the border the first time and how they made their last entry. The results, summarized in Figure 3.1, show that more than 10 percent of the women have become legal since following their first entry. It also shows that fewer women used the river on their last entry than on their first.

Though women with a *mica* can cross at the bridge, they too experience occasional problems. When Chela first crossed with a *mica*, she was frightened. "It must have been obvious," she says. "When the officer asked to see my border-crossing permit, I was trembling. He snatched my purse away from me and dumped everything on the table to look for American addresses. He wanted to make sure I was planning to return to Mexico."

Aída had a more serious problem. "I crossed in a taxi one day," she

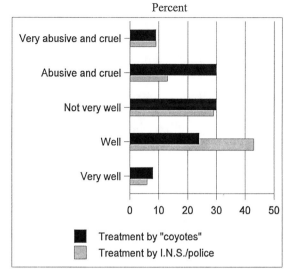

Fig. 3.2. Treatment of undocumented maids by coyotes and immigration officers/police, as reported by undocumented maids (Undocumented Maids Survey, 1993)

says. "The officer looked at my *mica* and told the driver to pull over. They asked me if I had any drugs, and I said no. Two female officers took me to a room and ordered me to take my clothes off. I was scared because they had guns. They checked my body for drugs. It was the worst experience of my life. I cried the whole time they searched. When they didn't find anything, they said they had received a tip that a woman was bringing drugs in a taxi. Now, I'm really nervous every time I cross to work here."

In the Undocumented Maids Survey, we asked, "From your experience, and that of others you may know, how do you feel police and immigration officers generally treat maids?" Figure 3.2 shows the responses to this question and to a similar one about how coyotes treat them.

Relatively small percentages of respondents said maids are treated either very well or very poorly by smugglers and law enforcement personnel. Most believe smugglers treat women badly, while slightly less than half believe that immigration officers do so. We also asked, "Have you had any problem with police or immigration officers in the United States?" Eighty percent of the women said no. Apparently, many women with negative impressions of immigration officers get such ideas from talking to others, rather than from personal experience.

Some women are more afraid of police in Mexico than of the Border Patrol. Rosa recently came from Guatemala and found a low-paying job. "One winter day," she says, "I went to buy some warm clothing. Unfortunately, when I saw the Migra, I got nervous and gave myself away. They took me in, but I convinced them that I was from Chiapas and had relatives in Reynosa. I didn't want them to send me back to Guatemala. They made me promise never to return and released me at the bridge. I wandered around in Reynosa looking lost and hungry. The Mexican police stopped me. They knew I was not Mexican and took me in to search for drugs. They undressed me and found my money. They took it and finally let me go. A kind person in Reynosa found me. Because I was sick, she took me to the doctor. Later, I crossed again and found a job with my current employer."

FINDING A JOB

Often, finding a job is also a nightmare. Ramona, for example, had a *mica* and took a bus to McAllen during her first attempt to find work as a maid. At the bus station, a man stopped his car in front of her. "He called me to his car," she says. "I got in, thinking it was the McAllen doctor who said he might hire me. As we drove down the street, he locked the doors and headed away from McAllen. Then he started touching me. I was terrified. Finally, he stopped at a red light, and I unlocked the door and jumped out. I yelled at some men working on some electric poles to please help. He saw them and drove off."

In light of recent news reports, Ramona was very fortunate. In at least five cases in 1995, a man lured Mexican women at bus stops into his car, drove them to isolated places, and brutally raped them. Unlike Ramona, however, these women could not jump out because he had fixed the car door so it would not unlock.

Most undocumented women rely on friends and family to find a job.[10] Sixty-two percent of maids in our Undocumented Maids Survey said they used a friend or relative; 15 percent found out about the job through another maid; 6 percent said an employer offered them the job; and only 4 percent said they got the job from an ad. Clearly, most undocumented maids use informal channels and networks of friends or relatives to find work.[11]

AS ROSA'S EXPERIENCE SHOWS, BEING DETAINED BY MEXICAN POLICE MAY BE FAR WORSE THAN DEPORTATION.

That is how Socorro got her current job. As a child, she helped her mother in the home of a very well-to-do family. She learned a few English expressions from them, including the term *hand-me-downs*, as the woman occasionally gave them used clothing. Her mother said that one day this job would be a hand-me-down. Sure enough, Socorro got the job when her mother moved on to something better.

Women who have no informal networks often experience great difficulty finding a job. In 1985, for example, Elena went door to door looking for work. Almost no one invited her in. Many would ask, "Where are your papers?" or "Do you have recommendations?" After many hours with nothing to drink, she asked one woman for a glass of water. "She went in the kitchen and got a glass," Socorro remembers, "but she told me to go outside to get the water from the tap. I kept going house to house until I found one with children playing outside. They hired me, but they put me in a shed with no toilet, lights, or water. I quietly left a few days later."

Another woman, Delmita, had searched for three weeks. She was discouraged and thinking of returning to Toluca. "I came to a house having a garage sale," she says, "so I stopped to see if they needed a maid. To my surprise, the lady took me inside, fed me, and gave me some clothes. Then she gave me my own room with a color TV and, if you can believe it, my own bathroom. They even gave me weekends off and let me eat with them at the table. They were a blessing from God."

Treatment of Undocumented Maids

These accounts illustrate the extreme variations in the way employers treat undocumented maids. Some find warm acceptance as virtual members of the family. Other experience abuse, exploitation, and outright cruelty. We will examine each form of treatment before we consider why such differences occur.

ONE OF THE FAMILY

Like Delmita, some undocumented women are surprised when the family includes them in meals, leisure activities, and family celebrations. Many come from a class-conscious society where many "high-class people" do not mix with servants.

As a result, some U.S. employers find their maid reluctant to join their family activities. One Anglo employer, for example, says, "We think the world of Janie, but she keeps her distance. She insists on calling us Mr. and Mrs. Smith, and only recently have we been able to get her to eat dinner with us. I can tell she isn't real comfortable with it, but I just want her to feel like she belongs. I hear so many people say that their

Percent Saying "Frequently"

Fig. 3.3. Good treatment of undocumented maids, as reported by undocumented maids and employers of undocumented maids (Undocumented Maids Survey, 1993 and Employers of Undocumented Maids Survey, 1993)

maid is 'just like a member of the family.' I don't know. It's hard to have someone from a completely different culture fit in as if they had lived with you forever. We do appreciate the importance of a dependable, trustworthy employee, though."

Some employers want to be friendly, but not friends with their maids. They want her to feel included, but only as an employee.[12] A few go beyond such boundaries. Martina, for example, had worked as a live-in maid for a family of five for thirteen years when interviewed. "The first day I walked into their house," she says "I felt at home. Not once did they treat me as an outsider. They eventually included me as part of the family, and I became close to each of them. Two years ago, one of the children was killed in a car accident. I felt almost as if he were my own child. On the day of the funeral, they included me in the funeral arrangements. I'll never forget that feeling of belonging."

Both the Undocumented Maids Survey and the Employers of Undocumented Maids Survey included items that measured how much maids are included in key family activities. We also asked maids and employers how often the maid was treated like a friend or a member of the family. The responses are shown in Figure 3.3.

About half the maids and the employers said the maid is included in key family activities. Maids were more likely than employers to report inclusion in the four family activities mentioned, with the greatest difference in reports of how often the maid eats with the family. Perhaps the discrepancy can be explained by how each category interprets "frequently."

Letting your maid sit down with you for dinner or TV might or

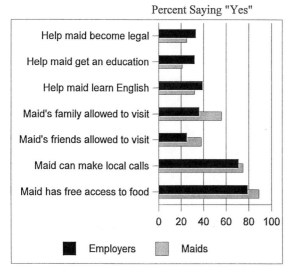

Percent Saying "Yes"

Fig. 3.4. Various ways employers help their undocumented maids, as reported by undocumented maids and employers of undocumented maids (Undocumented Maids Survey, 1993 and Employers of Undocumented Maids Survey, 1993)

might not show that you feel she should be treated as one of the family.[13] A few employers went beyond including her in family activities to truly helping their maids in times of need. Camila, for example, describes an elderly Mexican immigrant couple that took her in when she was alone, fourteen years old, and pregnant. "I was very lucky to find Mr. and Mrs. Valenzuela," she says. "They found a *partera* [midwife] for me. I even had my baby in their house because I was afraid to go to the hospital. After I had my baby, they helped me become legal. They completed every application form for me and even got me some documents from Mexico. Eighteen months later, I was legal and my little boy was a United States citizen."

Irma also got help to legalize her status. In 1987 her employers took her to the immigration office in Harlingen to file for legal status. "I was really afraid to go," she says, "because I thought they would arrest me. But instead, they treated me really well. After that, Mrs. Valenzuela enrolled me in night classes. They even let me borrow their car to go to school."

Three questions included in both surveys compared how frequently employers help their maid: (1) become legal, (2) improve her education, and (3) learn English. Four additional questions asked how accommodating the family was of their maid's personal needs, specifically, whether they let her (4) have visits from family, (5) see friends in their home, (6) use the phone for local calls, and (7) have free access to food (for snacks, etc.). The frequencies of responses to these items by maids and by employers are compared in Figure 3.4.

This figure shows a high correspondence between maids and employers on most items. It also shows that more employers than maids said they help their maid become legal, get an education, or learn English. Nevertheless, employers appear less likely than maids to say they permit her to receive visits in their home, let her have free access to food, or use the phone for local calls. Finally, Figure 3.4 shows that few maids or employers say the employer helps the maid do things that would make her become independent, like legalizing her status or getting an education. These findings lead us to believe that most employers do not regard the self-improvement of undocumented maids as part of their responsibility, though a substantial proportion do.

An Outsider in the Home

Employers who fail to recognize the integrity of a maid's personal life, or to give her a space to call her own, frequently mistreat their maid. Luisa, for example, worked for a single mother in a rent-subsidized apartment. One day last February, her boss told her that apartment inspectors would come some time between eight-thirty and five the next day, so the apartment had to be clean. "The next morning," she says, "she woke me up at five to straighten everything up. Then she told me I had to be out of her apartment by eight and not to return until five that afternoon because she wasn't supposed to have anyone else living there. I had no money to buy food. She just threw me out on the streets. My employer didn't care where I spent the day, whether I ate, or how bad the weather was. I felt like a dog and not a human being."

Alma had a similar experience. "One night I was sound asleep," she recalls. "Around two o'clock in the morning, my boss came in and shook me awake. 'You'll have to go outside and find a place to sleep for the night,' she said. 'I have some business to take care of.' When I got up, I saw three couples kissing and carrying on in her living room. I knew it was her home and she could do as she pleased, but it was really cold outside. I spent the night sitting on a concrete block in the alley."

Behind such treatment is the clear message that an undocumented live-in maid is an outsider.[14] Even her room is not really hers. Nearly 30 percent of respondents in the Employers of Undocumented Maids Survey, for example, said that, at least occasionally, they go into the maid's room to see if they can find something they suspect she has taken; 39 percent said they do not trust the maid around jewelry or personal items.[15]

"The hardest part of this job," reports one maid, "is when your employer accuses you of taking something. If something is missing, blame the maid—go to her room and rummage through her things. Once I

When the maid's duties are not clearly defined, any job can be hers
(photo courtesy of George C. McLemore).

worked for a woman whose son was addicted to drugs. He would steal her money. Automatically, she blamed me. My parents taught me right from wrong, and I have never stolen anything in my life. I decided if she couldn't trust me, I'd look for work elsewhere."

Not all maids, of course, are innocent. One employer told of a time at the end of one weekend when she gave her maid a ride home. "As we were getting ready to leave," she says, "I couldn't find some papers I needed. I looked everywhere. I checked her bag. To my surprise, it was full of food and other things that she had taken without my permission. I decided to say nothing until we were in the car. Then I confronted her and asked why she stole those things. She said nothing. She just dropped her head and kept quiet. So I told her I wouldn't be needing her any more."

Living in her employer's home creates many opportunities for a maid to take valuables and even more opportunities for them to suspect her of doing so.[16] It also creates other problems. There is no clock to punch, and most homes have no fixed working hours. Because the maid is present in the home, she is often expected to be available around the clock.[17] Lupita, for example, says her present employers are very insensitive about her right to have some time of her own. She recalls an incident a week prior to her interview when *la señora* (female employer) summoned

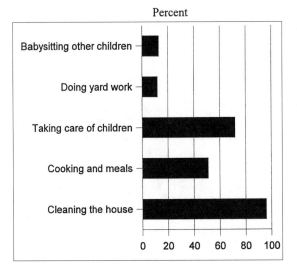

Percent

Fig. 3.5. Work duties undocumented maids reported assigned primarily to them (Undocumented Maids Survey, 1993)

her at two o'clock in the morning to come into their bedroom. "Her husband had too much to drink," she says, "and had vomited all over their bedroom. His wife refused to clean it up, so they called me. It makes me feel like I'm their slave. They have no respect for my feelings at all. But I can't leave until I get another job because I'm sending money home to my family."

Pati found herself in a similar situation. When a family of seven hired her, she only had to do basic housekeeping chores. Gradually, new duties were added. "One day," she says, "Mr. Cardenas ordered me to clean the large toolshed in the backyard. I refused to do it. I told him, 'For fifty-five dollars a week and every other weekend off, I will not do a man's job.' I was told to leave immediately. I asked Mr. Cardenas to take me to a friend's house. That was a big mistake. Two days later the Migra showed up there and took me back to Reynosa."

Just what are a maid's regular duties? In the Undocumented Maid Survey, we asked respondents to specify the duties for which they had primary responsibility. Their responses are summarized in Figure 3.5 and show that maids are expected to do most of the housecleaning and child care. About half are primarily responsible for cooking, and small percentages are expected to do yard work and babysit someone else's children.[18]

Some employers pay more when they add work to the maid's duties. Often, however, they forget that she has a life outside their home.[19] Tencha is an undocumented maid who lives with her family in a colonia. She commutes every day. "Last year," she says, "Mr. Jiménez pressured me into cleaning his office after working all day at his house. I didn't want to work late because I need to spend time with my children. He gave me extra pay, but it was just too much work. I did it for a while, then told him I couldn't continue. He just kept pressuring, telling me how lucky I was to have the extra work. I didn't want to lose the job, so I finally gave in. Besides, I thought he might call the police if I refused."

Most undocumented maids cannot get home to family as easily as Tencha. Many go weeks or months without a visit home. This situation tempts some employers to keep the maid on her weekend off. Seventy-five percent of employers surveyed said they had asked their maids to stay during a scheduled day off. One employer, for example, was indignant when she described one occasion when her maid refused to stay the one weekend a month she was allowed to go home. "I became ill with the flu," she states, "so I was expecting her to offer to stay that weekend to take care of the house and the kids. She knew I couldn't do it myself because I was ill. But she refused to stay, saying that she had arranged to see her kids. I told her she could take the next weekend off instead. I pay her to work, and I expect her loyalty. I told her if she left she would have no job to come back to."

Unclear duties and the inability to control their own time make the situation of undocumented maids highly insecure.[20] So does the issue of pay. Some employers expect a lot of their maids but give almost nothing in return.[21] Rosa, for example, works for a lady who just had a baby. "Now I have to look after a crying baby," she says, "and the three-year-old who always misbehaves. I still have to clean the house, do the laundry, and run errands. She gives me thirty-five dollars a week. With all the added work, I deserve more than that."

Almost no employers pay their undocumented maid the legal minimum wage.[22] Despite a wide variance in weekly pay, we found that the average (median) weekly salary is approximately sixty-five dollars. But according to the Employers of Undocumented Maids Survey, 59 percent of maids work ten or more hours a day. Half of them also work six or seven days a week, so most are putting in sixty-five-hour weeks. That makes the average pay only about one dollar an hour. If they're expected to be available during the night, it is even less than that.[23]

Some maids would not complain about the size of their paycheck if they knew they would get it on time. Seven percent said they frequently were not paid on time, while another 17 percent said it sometimes happens. Isela Lopez frequently experiences delays. She described how the Castillo family expected her to clean the house, do the laundry, iron, cook, and take care of the children. "When any guests spend the night," she says, "I have to take care of them. But they never pay me anything extra. Even worse, they never pay me on time. At first, I was supposed to get paid weekly. Then they said it would be every two weeks. Sometimes I even had to wait a month. They always have excuses, like 'I have to pay car insurance,' 'The car broke down,' 'The light bill was too high,' or 'The kids need new clothes for school.' I have a family to raise too. I'm always on time with my work. But if I ever complain, they make threats."

The most disturbing threat, however, is the possibility of sexual assault or harassment.[24] Twenty percent of the maids surveyed said they had experienced sexual threats or harassment in at least one of the homes where they had worked. When the Cantú family hired Angelica, for example, the *señora* told her that she did not trust her husband with another woman living there. "I told her," she says, "that if he ever showed any disrespect, she'd be the first to know. One of my chores was to serve them breakfast in bed. One morning, when I took it in, I was surprised to find him alone. His wife had gone to the doctor. As I brought him his breakfast, he grabbed my arm, and tried to kiss me. I kept telling him to stop, but he wouldn't. Finally, I broke free and ran out of the room. A few minutes later, he came out and told me not to tell his wife or he'd kill me. The way he said those words, I knew he meant it. After a week, I decided to quit. I told both of them that my family in Mexico needed me. She was understanding, but he knew the real reason. He paid me that week's work and told me to pack and get out. Not far from their house, some immigration officers picked me up and took me to Reynosa. I was happy, though, because I'd never have to see him again."

Husbands in these homes are not the only perpetrators of sexual assault. Fourteen percent of the maids surveyed did not feel safe alone in the home with older sons of the family. One night, for example, a nine-teen-year-old son came home intoxicated and woke up Rocio. "He ordered me to make him something to eat," she says. "Then he started making sexual advances toward me. That really scared me. I went back to my room, but he followed me and began forcing himself on me. He became violent, and I started screaming. His parents came in and saw us struggling on my bed. They accused me of trying to seduce him and of taking advantage of him while he was intoxicated. *La señora* demanded that I leave at once, or she was going to call immigration. They didn't even pay me for the days they owed."

Other problems arise when a maid, as a

THE THREAT OF BEING PICKED UP BY IMMIGRATION OFFICERS IS OFTEN USED BY EMPLOYERS TO TAKE ADVANTAGE OF THEIR MAID.

single female, comes to live with a family in their home (53 percent of the maids in our survey were single). Thirteen percent said that the *señora* in at least one house where they worked acted suspicious that something was going on between the maid and her husband. Isela experienced this when she began working for a young couple. One day, the husband asked her a question that she cannot even recall. "I answered him," she says, "and his wife got upset with me. Later, she told me to go to the store with her. But instead of the store, she took me to Reynosa and dropped me off saying, 'The next time you feel like flirting, do it with someone who's not married.' She was jealous, but what could I do but answer his question?"

Frequently, the abuse is more verbal than physical. Lupita's boss started asking her to serve drinks to his friends. "They had no respect for me at all," she says. "They would get drunk and say all kinds of things to me. My boss just sat there and let it happen. One day I decided to confront him about it. All he said was, 'Don't take things too personally, and I'll talk to them the next time they come over.' I didn't wait for that to happen. I just packed my bags and left when they weren't around."

Not all verbal abuse takes sexual forms. Constant increases in the workload and treatment of a maid as less than a full person often cause undocumented maids to suffer great emotional strain.[25] Rosie, for example, got a job with the García family. "I had to wake up at six each morning," she says, "and I never got to bed before midnight. They never called me by my name. They always called me the *criada* [maid]. Nothing I ever did in that house was good enough. I was either too slow or I didn't do it right. Once I spilled a gallon of milk on the floor. The *señora* told me, 'You can't do anything right. Eres una burra [You're dumb; You're unteachable].' Several times they said they would call immigration and have me sent back to Mexico. I lived in fear because my family needed the money I sent home."

The use of rude or discourteous forms of address are often cited by undocumented maids as forms of abuse.[26] So is the use of threats.[27] In the Undocumented Maids Survey, we asked, "Have you ever been verbally abused or insulted by an employer?" One-fourth of the maids answered affirmatively. In addition, 13 percent said their employer had, at some time, threatened to report them to immigration officials.

Understanding the Range of Treatment

As we have seen, some undocumented maids are horribly abused and exploited. Most, apparently, are not. A few are even treated with consideration and kindness, or taken in as members of their employer's family. Why the differences?

Most people explain abuse or good treatment in terms of personality or character.[28] According to this point of view, harsh or uncaring individuals abuse their maids, while kind people treat them kindly. Though there is some truth to this "intrapsychic" point of view, it fails to consider the "sociological" context within which maids and their employers work. The nature of this social situation, as much as personality, produces the results we have outlined.

Let me illustrate. Marta has worked as a maid in the Valley since 1987. Unlike the other maids that have been described, she is legal: a "resident alien." She is also not a live-in maid. She works eight hours a day for several employers and then goes home. When one employer tried to pay her less than the amount they had agreed upon, she went to Legal Aid and made the employer pay the full amount. Now she writes out contracts detailing what work she will do and how much they will pay. She hardly sees some of them and that is fine with her. None of them treat her like family (though some are friendly), but then, none of them abuse her. As far as she is concerned, she is an employee, but that ends each evening when she walks out the door.

Though Marta's personality and that of her employers certainly affect how she is treated, the main difference is her situation. Unlike undocumented live-in maids, she is in Texas legally, has clearer schedules, lives in her own home, and has friends and family in the United States. Undocumented maids, on the other hand, are relatively powerless, have unclear schedules and work assignments, live in their employer's home, and as foreigners live cut off from family and friends. These situational factors explain much of the abuse of undocumented maids. Let us examine each factor to see how.

Powerlessness

As pointed out earlier, undocumented live-in maids have little control over their work, their pay, or their time. They have virtually no recourse to law when they are cheated or abused. In addition, their status as women, as "aliens," and as poor, unskilled laborers contributes to their powerlessness. Even their place of residence is not their own, as employers can enter to search for lost items.

Two additional forms of powerlessness compound this situation: paternalistic treatment and limited authority with children. Paternalistic treatment involves treating the maid like a child. Limited authority with children means giving her the responsibility, but not the authority, to take care of them.

PATERNALISM

Paternalistic treatment is often a harsh version of treating the maid like a member of the family—but as one of the children. Several employers said their maid was incapable of handling her own financial affairs. Unfortunately, none of the survey questions directly addressed the issue of paternalism, so we have only anecdotal evidence of it. One employer, for example, said, "I make sure she sends a certain amount of her pay to her kids and that she does the right things with her money. It's part of my duty to her. If I don't, she might spend her money on things like makeup and trinkets."

Another woman said her maid often asks for advances on her pay. "I won't do it unless she says what the money's for," she says. "I can't lend money for something frivolous." Another employer said she feels an obligation to "protect" her maid from relatives. "She's not used to having money and is an easy target for relatives," she says.

Lucía described how her employers are paternalistic in other ways. "I was invited to a party," she says, "but they wouldn't let me go. I overheard Mr. Garza tell his wife that I was too young, that I might fall for some guy and run away. I felt so humiliated I wanted to leave. I couldn't because my family needs the money."

LIMITED AUTHORITY FOR CHILD CARE

Approximately 75 percent of the maids surveyed said that they are primarily responsible for their employer's children. The measure of a maid's powerlessness is how much authority parents give her to discipline them. Another is how much they trust her if the children accuse her of something. Adriana's case illustrates. "I had just cleaned the kitchen," she says, "when one of the kids came in and made a mess. I told him politely to clean it up because I had to clean the bedrooms. He did, but when his mom came, he told her that I made him clean the whole kitchen. Before I could explain, she was yelling at me."

Even older children present similar problems for the maid. Hilda describes how the parents in one family would leave town frequently. "During those times," she says, "the kids were monsters. They did many things their parents wouldn't allow, like get drunk and stay out all night. Then when their parents returned, they would say I gave them permission. The kids got away with it, and I got in trouble because the parents wouldn't believe me."

Several questions in our two surveys allowed us to compare the responses of employers with those of maids on this issue. First we asked respondents in both surveys whether the maid was authorized to discipline the children. We then asked who the parents were likely to believe if the children blamed her for something she denied. Figure 3.6 shows the comparison.

Roughly half of both employers and maids said the maid is authorized to discipline children. Nevertheless, if the children complain about the maid, only 16 percent of employers said they would believe the maid over their children. The fact that 48 percent of the maids thought parents would believe them shows they seriously overestimated how much parents trust them.

Such data show the powerless situation of maids. A classic problem of powerlessness, one dating back to slavery, is that powerful groups often interpret the powerlessness of oppressed groups as inability. They judge "inferiors" as incapable of handling their own affairs (paternalism). In addition, abuse is not seen as such because they "are only a [slave, servant, maid, etc.]." Powerlessness, then, as much as abusive personalities, produce abuse and paternalistic treatment of undocumented maids.

An Unclear Division of Labor

Often, employers want the maid to "help" with the kids, but fail to clearly establish what their role is, vis-à-vis that of the parents. Zoila remembers a family that wanted it both ways. "I took care of the kids day and night," she says. "The parents were never home, so I treated the children like my own. They were very nice. I taught them Spanish, and they taught me English. When they got home from school, we'd eat together, they'd do their homework, and then we'd all sit and watch TV. At night, I would sing to them and put them to bed. One evening their parents returned from Hawaii, and the kids didn't pay much attention to them. The next morning, my employers called me into their office. They accused me of trying to take over. I said I was just doing my job. Still, they fired me. First they tell me to take good care of the children, and then they fire me for doing a good job."

Some employers also fail to clearly define the maid's household duties.[29] Araceli found a job, and for three months everything went well. Her duties included housecleaning, child care, and light cooking—about the same things her friends did for their *señoras*. "A short time later," she says, the *señora* asked me to give her a body massage every evening. I guess she thought I was good at it, because she began to lend me out on weekends and evenings to her friends. I thought she'd

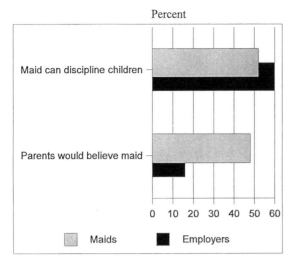

Percent

Maid can discipline children

Parents would believe maid

0 10 20 30 40 50 60

Maids   Employers

Fig. 3.6. Trust in undocumented maids as adult caregivers, as reported by undocumented maids and employers of undocumented maids (Undocumented Maids Survey, 1993 and Employers of Undocumented Maids Survey, 1993)

pay me extra, but when I asked, she became upset and told me that I was lucky to get thirty-five dollars a week plus free room and board. She said that if I didn't like it, she could call Immigration. I continued giving the massages for two more months until I was able to get another job."

When work duties are not clearly defined, it is difficult for employers to avoid adding new tasks to "the maid's job."[30] Thirty-seven percent of the maids surveyed said that their employer had asked them to do tasks that were not originally part of their job; 81 percent said that their employer expects them to be willing to do anything they want done (39 percent said "frequently" and 42 percent said "sometimes"). Such figures show that a clear division of labor is lacking in the work situation of many undocumented maids. As Araceli discovered, when tasks are not clearly delineated, employers will not see the addition of extra duties as an abuse. Thus, the lack of clarity in the division of labor, as much as personality, produces much of the work-related abuse that undocumented maids suffer.

Living in the Employer's Home

Seventy-six percent of the respondents included in the Undocumented Maids Survey worked as live-in maids. This very closely matched the Employers of Undocumented Maids Survey, in which 77 percent reported having a live-in maid. Employers often fail to realize that the workplace for their live-in maid is also her home. By living with them, she gives up much of her privacy and has no place where family or friends can visit.[31]

This peculiar situation of living twenty-four hours a day in an employer's home strains the relationship. When the maid is only a room or two away, many employers are tempted to give her something to do during her "off hours." Twenty-eight percent of the maids said they were unable, at least sometimes, to use their free time as they wished. In addition, being present in her place of employment twenty-four hours a day means that unpleasant tasks that arise after regular work hours will be requested of the maid. This was confirmed in the two surveys by 31 percent of maids and 41 percent of employers, who said that the maid was expected, at least occasionally, to care for sick, hungry, or intoxicated family members during the night.

In addition, the live-in situation creates problems of sexual abuse, jealousy, and suspicions that the maid might steal something. She is from another country, resides in this country illegally, speaks a foreign language, and comes from a lower social class. She is an outsider.

Nevertheless, in other ways she is very much an insider. She is in the employer's home twenty-four hours a day, seven days a week. She eats with them, sits down in the evening to watch TV with them, and helps raise their kids. Such activities can produce highly personal relationships unless steps are taken to prevent it.[32]

That is what Nora's first employer did. "At first," she says, "I thought they were going to treat me equally. Then, they said I couldn't eat in the dining room with them, but had to go to the kitchen after they had finished eating. Then, they told me not to watch TV with them. They provided an old set for my room. I was not supposed to come out when they had company. Next, they told me not to use their bathroom or shower, but to use the one provided for me. The *señora* also gave me my own spoon, glass, plate, and fork, so I wouldn't have to use any of theirs. I felt real bad and cried every night. I had no choice because my father was out of work and my mom was sick."

Nora's employers kept her at a distance by erecting social and physical boundaries. In essence, they were saying, "Those are your things, and these are ours. You have your place, and we have ours. You are an outsider, and not one of us." The maid is kept at a distance and feelings of attachment do not develop. She is kept "in her place" as an outsider inside the home.

Such exclusion may hurt more than outright abuse. Margarita remembers one day when the family she worked for got her up at five in the morning to help prepare for a big family gathering they were planning. "Once I had everything done," she says, "they sent me to my room for the rest of the evening. They said I would feel better there because I didn't have the proper clothes and wouldn't fit in. I felt so hurt I cried all night."

Some boundaries are more subtle. Calling the maid by her first name but requiring that she address her employers as "Mr." and "Mrs.," for example, puts distance in the relationship. So does addressing the maid as "tú" (the form of *you* that Spanish speakers use with their maids, children, and close friends), while expecting her to use "usted" (the form of *you* used by adults in formal circumstances and by children to address adults). Fifty percent of the employers said that they do not allow their maid to call them by their first name, or allow it only occasionally. Sixty-three percent of the maids said their *señora* does not usually like them to use the familiar "tú" form when addressing her.

Employers who set up boundaries in the relation with their maid seldom feel close to her, which makes it easier to exploit her powerlessness. They will likely take advantage of an unclear division of labor to ask her to do things that were not supposed to be part of her job. That is, the close personal nature of working and living in someone's home twenty-four hours a day produces a familylike situation in which a maid's relative powerlessness and unclear duties will not necessarily produce abuse. Unless boundaries are established, the employers will likely come to see her and treat her much like a family member. Boundaries that clearly proclaim "You are an outsider"—that polarize the maid as distinctly apart from family—are likely needed if exploitation is to take place.

SOCIAL AND CULTURAL ISOLATION

Some boundaries, however, are involuntary.[33] Families that do not speak Spanish unintentionally isolate their maid. Josefina has been the Camp's maid for a year and a half. She says they treat her well. Still, both she and they are frustrated. "When they want something done," she says, "they have to use sign language or call a Hispanic neighbor who can translate for them by phone."

Language differences can cause serious problems for both parties. Veronica described a time when her employer told her not to let the kids play outside. "I misunderstood," she says. "The kids went outside and the three-year-old nearly got run over by a car. The neighbor told my employer about the incident, so she fired me."

Even when language is not a problem, however, cultural differences can prove divisive.[34] Marisa, for example, worked for a Hispanic couple. She remembers the time she tried to celebrate El Día de los Muertos (Day of the Dead) according to her Mexican customs. "In Mexico," she says, "we make little skulls of sugar and eat them on the Day of the Dead. Well, these people saw me making sugar skulls and said I was a *bruja* [witch]. They insulted me and told me to leave, so I went to my cousin's place. Several days later, they called to apologize and said someone had explained the custom to them. They asked me to come back, but suggested I observe my customs only in my own land. I declined because my customs are part of me."

Different customs divide in other ways. Cindy worked for a family with a fifteen-year-old daughter. The mother's work took her out of town every other week. One night while the mother was gone, Cindy discovered the daughter and her boyfriend in bed together. "She started yelling at me," Cindy recalls, "and refused to have him leave. When my boss came home, I was afraid to tell her, thinking she'd fire me for letting him in. Finally, I decided I had to tell her. She was hardly even surprised and said she'd talk to her about birth control pills. I didn't know what to say so I told her that in my country we wait to have sex until marriage. She said she would raise her daughter the way she wanted and for me to pack my things and leave. I was glad to get out of a house where they live like that."

Nonetheless, the most serious difficulty of living illegally in the United States is the strain it puts on relations with the maid's own family. Twenty-six percent of maids said they can go home only once a year or less. Sixty-one percent said they visit once a month or less. Vicky is a twenty-two-year-old maid who left her children with her mother in Mexico. She was gone for two years before being able to return. "I was so happy to see my children," she says, "that I just cried and hugged them. What really hurt was that they hardly knew me. They were even calling their grandmother 'Mamá.' I'm really scared I'm going to lose my children."

LANGUAGE, CLASS, AND CULTURE ARE IMPORTANT BOUNDARIES THAT KEEP MANY MAIDS FROM GETTING CLOSE TO "LA SEÑORA."

Most of the maids surveyed (93 percent) said they were sending money home each month to family members. Years ago, Amalia was happy in Mexico with her family. Then her husband was killed. She had to support her two girls and could not do so there. "Since I came here," she says, "I have been able to send my girls through school. That makes me very proud of myself, but it hurts that I can't be there to see them grow up. I hope they understand."

Always a Maid?

Almost all the women we interviewed said that when they first came to Texas, they had no intention of staying.[35] Those who are abused often leave, preferring a life of poverty in Mexico to suffering in the United States. Eloísa, a woman interviewed in Mexico, for example, came when she was eighteen years old and worked a short time for an Anglo family. "One day," she recalls, "Mr. Starnes chased me around the house as nude as the day he was born. I left for my hometown and never even tried to collect my money." With bitterness, she adds, "I will never return to that country. ¡Gringos estúpidos! [Stupid gringos!]"

Many, however, manage to endure the hardships and hang on. We asked respondents in the Undocumented Maids Survey, "Do you plan to return to your own country some day?" Thirty-nine percent said yes, for sure; 38 percent were undecided; and 23 percent said no. Gabriela is one of the undecided. After six years here, she has a chance to become a legal resident. "The question that now plagues my mind," she says, "is do I want it? Perhaps all the hurt, pain, and humiliation I have endured could help others back home learn to work and live in the United States."

Those who plan to stay in the United States are often young unmarried women who have learned to adjust to life here.[36] When we asked the women whether they prefer life in the United States or in Mexico, 43 percent preferred the United States. Silvia is one of them. "My parents have a hard time accepting my independence," she says. "Being responsible for a home and children has made me mature. When I go home, however, my parents still expect me to ask for permission to go out with my friends. I love the freedom girls have here in the U.S., though some of them don't respect that freedom." She has tried explaining this to her family, but they just do not seem to understand it.

Flora has also decided she wants to stay. "Each time I return to Tula," she says, "I just can't get used to being in Mexico. The longest I can ever stay is a month. Then I become restless and anxious to return to the U.S. Now I feel out of place in Mexico."

Mónica, one of the interviewers and the daughter of a former maid, says she can relate to these stories. "My mother worked for a family in an

Anglo middle-class neighborhood for several years," she says. "She did her job with pride and always had a positive attitude toward our future. Maids will always have a special place in my heart and will be treated with respect in my home. As a child, I used to go with her to a 'nice' neighborhood. While she worked, I would sit there and dream. Because of her, I now live in that same 'nice' neighborhood."

Social Class on the South Texas–Mexico Border

Chapter 4

My mother used to work for a very wealthy family in Mexico. I lived with her in their home. They treated me all right, but they made sure I knew my place. Every summer, as their children came home from Europe, they'd have lots of parties. Once I met a friend of their son. At the time, I was wearing some American clothes my mother had bought at a flea market. I thought he might be interested in me until later when he saw me helping my mother prepare for the party. I cried that whole summer when I realized that, because of my mother, I was poor—just like the people in the streets.

Martha Alonso, 1989

Valley residents have two stereotypes of Mexicans. One portrays light-skinned wealthy Mexicans, like the family Martha lived with. Valley residents commonly see them in expensive restaurants, hotels, and malls. In good times, they provide almost half the retail trade of cities like McAllen. Some store clerks and waiters say wealthy Mexicans treat them like servants, have spoiled children, and seldom tip. Realtors like them because they buy investment homes in well-to-do sections of town. Bankers cater to them because they bring huge deposits to local banks whenever rumors spread that the Mexican peso will be devalued.

Then there is the stereotype of Mexican peasants—undocumented, uneducated, dark-skinned, and eager to work. This is the image U.S. tourists get when they cross the bridges into Mexico. Poor Mexican street children try to sell them gum or trinkets. *Limosneros* (beggars) surround them in the market, and young men swarm over their cars to wash the windows. Some tourists will even see the shanty towns, not very far from the industrialized maquila (assembly plant) parks. Unlike the United States, poverty is not hidden in Mexico.

Still, as Martha's story illustrates, the rich and the poor of Mexico live in two different worlds. Social class affects life there as profoundly as race does here. Carlos, a Mexican student studying at the University of Texas–Pan American, recalled life in Mexico City. "When I lived there," he says, "I never went

Percent of Household Income

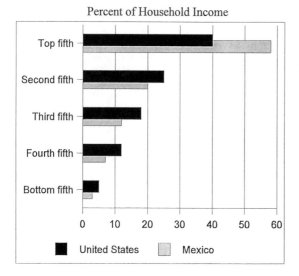

Fig. 4.1. Total household income received by each fifth of the population in Mexico and in the United States (World Bank, World Development Report, *Table 26)*

into McDonald's. Only the 'preps' went there. When my friends and I would pass by, we'd always want to go in, but we didn't dare. We didn't have the right sweaters. You know, all of the schools in Mexico have a uniform or a sweater, so it's easy to tell who's rich and who's not. The rich kids would stare and make us feel very uncomfortable, so we stayed away. When I came here, I saw that it didn't matter who went into a McDonald's. Still, the first time I went to one, I was afraid to go in. I still don't think I could go to one in Mexico City."

The extent of social inequality in Mexico is partially illustrated in Figure 4.1, which compares the distribution of income in Mexico with that of the United States. As shown in the figure, the best-paid fifth of Mexico's population receives a percentage of income considerably greater than the top fifth in the United States. Although the difference at the bottom is not as great, the poorest fifth there gets a smaller portion of income than the poorest fifth here.

Still, social class depends on more factors than the amount of money earned. In Mexico and elsewhere, class position depends on how much wealth you control, how important people think you are, and how much power you wield. These marks of class in Mexico are even more unevenly distributed than income. Mexico is a land of extreme differences between the top and the bottom.

In Mexico, as in most societies of the world, people can change their class position only with great difficulty. Mexico's wealthy have their restaurants, their schools, their parks, and even their churches. They speak and dress differently from poorer people. All of these differences serve to maintain class lines. Mexicans teach their children to maintain their "place" in a highly stratified social world. As a result, people like Carlos have deeply ingrained fears of crossing class lines to enter a McDonald's.[1]

In Mexico and along the border, these class lines profoundly affect individual lives. Marisa remembers attending a private *colegio* (high school) in Mexico. "One day," she says, "my friends started making fun of a low-income classmate attending on a scholarship. I felt bad because she was crying. I told them to stop. They accused me of not being loyal and called me a *naca* [lowlife] just like her. For several days, they completely isolated and ignored me. I couldn't stand it, so I went along with them, though I felt bad doing it."

Most of the well-to-do Mexicans interviewed believed they could easily determine a person's class from clothes, grooming, and speech patterns. "People of the lower class have bad taste in clothing," said one. "In addition, their hairstyles distinguish them from us." Another said, "Lower-class people use slang terms and bad grammar that set them apart from us. They also lack culture, education, and social skills. It would be very difficult for them to be accepted in the upper class even if they had the money to move up. They will always retain their background."

Nevertheless, many poor Mexicans do not allow their self-image to be dictated by the stereotypes that wealthy Mexicans have of them. One former campesino, for example, says, "When I wasn't working in my field, I would sell corn on the cob on the streets. I wasn't lazy. I was always doing something. One day, I passed two well-dressed men drinking *refrescos* [soft drinks]. When they saw me with my corn cart, one of them said, 'Mira al pobre diablo vendiendo elotes [Look at the poor devil selling corn].' I pretended I didn't hear and kept walking. I knew I was better than them because at least I was working."

As we have seen in previous chapters, however, negative stereotypes are hard to resist. Some migrant children attempt to hide that they work in the fields. Colonia residents sometimes feel ashamed to admit they live in a colonia. Undocumented maids can be made to feel undeserving of respect and fair treatment. Some people in these situations break out of poverty. A few overcome the harsh treatment. Occasionally, the cycle of powerlessness, stereotyping, and internalized feelings of inadequacy is broken. For most, however, it is not. Social class becomes "fixed" by means of internalized self-definitions *and* through external powerlessness and stereotyping. Class position is perpetuated from one generation to the next almost as surely as if it were genetic. In this chapter, I will propose some reasons for this.

The personal accounts in this chapter come primarily from the Maquila Workers Exploratory Interviews (75 respondents) and the Mexican Street Children Exploratory Interviews (90 respondents). In addition, they come from 39 exploratory interviews related to class distinctions in Northern Mexico and South Texas that have not yet been developed into a formal project.

Poverty and Deprivation on the Mexican Border

On the Mexican side of the border, poverty is more the rule than the exception. Campesinos have been pushed off their *ejidos* (communal farms) by a combination of government edicts, overpopulation, and drought. Massive migrations bring them to the cities and to the border. For example, Reynosa and Matamoros, the border cities facing McAllen and Brownsville, have grown by 600 percent since 1950. Such rapid growth is a boon to developers but often hurts those at the bottom.

MAQUILA WORKERS

Rosa and her husband came from San Fernando a few years ago. Both of them work in a U.S.-owned maquiladora in an industrial park outside Reynosa. They live in a tiny two-bedroom apartment with their two children and his mother. "We would move to a bigger place if we could," she says, "but there's no housing available. Our rent constantly goes up because the landlord knows the apartments will not stay vacant for more than a couple of days. He raises the rent because he knows someone is always willing to pay more. It's hard to get by, but we've learned to manage."

Maquila plants generally prefer women workers, though less so now than a decade ago. Often, they hire young women from the interior of Mexico who take the job to help families back home. Florencia fits this description. She has rent payments in an extremely expensive housing market. She lives with several other workers in makeshift housing not far from her place of work. Since the peso devaluation in 1995, her take-home pay is less than one dollar an hour. She sends whatever money she can to her parents. "I work," she says, "to help my mother send my younger brothers and sisters to school. I don't want them to end up a *burra* like me."

Teresa, who works for a U.S. toy manufacturer in Matamoros, struggles to support her ill mother as well as her two children. With low wages, she finds it very difficult to buy her mother's medication. "Some days," she says, "I barely have enough money for food. I'd rather starve, though, than not support my mother and children. I find myself asking friends and neighbors for money until I get paid. But by the time I get the check, I owe it all. Le pido a Dios que me de la paciencia para sobresalir estos días difíciles [I ask God for the patience to overcome these difficult times]."

Often, survival requires the effort of many family members. Yolanda Rincón and her husband both work at maquila plants. "I have to get up at four in the morning," she says, "to get my kids dressed and take them to my parents' house. Often, I don't get back to pick them up until around eleven-thirty at night. My husband also works long hours and rarely has time to see them. It's sad to see my children coming to think of my parents as their mom and dad. I have to remind myself that I'm working for their well-being and that they're safe."

In spite of the low wages, some maquila workers consider themselves fortunate. Andrés is twenty-eight years old and has worked in maquiladoras for the last twelve years. "It took me that long to become a supervisor," he says. "I see maquiladoras as a blessing for our economy. Here you have a secure job, good income, and some benefits. I know many people who want to work in the maquiladoras because their only other choices are to work in the fields, sell tacos on the street, or work in town where the hours are longer and the pay is worse. At least the maquiladoras provide cafeterias with microwave ovens and a choice of foods. I have managed to save enough money for a car. It's not new, but it is a decent one. My three brothers and two sisters also work in the maquiladoras. Together, we have been able to build a concrete block house for our parents."

Maricela, who is twenty years old, likes the teamwork she finds in her plant. "Once," she says, "we had to get a certain number of products made by a certain date, so we had to work really hard. We even stayed late several days. We couldn't talk to each other like we usually did, but it wasn't bad. Our bosses had pressure on them to get the work done on time, so we had to be patient with them, and them with us. When we finally finished, they gave us a big party with cake and punch and let us take half the day off on Friday. That was really nice."

Roberto also likes the camaraderie. "I felt sick one day," he says, "and my head hurt really bad. But I couldn't afford to miss work. Some people that work next to me let me take their breaks so that I could go rest in the nurse's office, and I didn't have to go home."

Still, many workers believe that the low wages are unfair. Enrique is an engineer for a large corporation. "I don't make enough money for what I do and for my level of education," he says, "but there is really nothing I can do. The pay is the same everywhere unless you cross the river to Texas, and I don't want to go there." Roberto agrees. "I work just as hard as any of the American engineers who work here," he says, "but I don't get even half of what they make."

Estela Castañeda says that the worst problems of maquiladora workers are not in the workplace but on the outside. "The city is not responding to our needs," she says. "The maquila plants are in industrial parks miles away from the city. The city needs to develop ways to help us get to work much faster, safer, and easier. Transportation is our main problem. We have to depend on the *peseras* [minivan taxis] for transportation. I have to walk three miles just to get to the road where one can pick me up because they will not drive where the roads are not paved. Sometimes when I work overtime, I don't get home until about midnight."

Being out when it is dark puts many women workers at risk. "When I'm ready for work," reports Cecilia, "it's only five in the morning and it's still dark. There are always many men standing around who have been drinking. They seem to be looking for a victim to rob or rape. Luckily, they have never raped me, but I have been robbed. Once, after my husband had given me a watch for my birthday, I was going to work early. As usual those men were staring at me. One of them wouldn't take his eyes off me. As I waited to get on the *pesera*, he grabbed my arm, pulled the watch off, and ran the other way."

For some women, working conditions are the most serious problem. Doña Josefina was employed as a maquiladora worker for many years. Two of her five children still work at maquiladoras in Reynosa. "When I started working there," she says, "I heard that working for an American company would mean better wages and good health conditions. But it wasn't true at that plant. The wages we received didn't meet even basic needs. In that plant, I had a job that required me to use many chemicals. From my first day there, I felt sick. Those chemicals hurt my skin and I had to quit. Now my two older daughters have to sustain our family."

Though poor working conditions do exist in some plants, many U.S. companies voluntarily maintain worker protections similar to those in their U.S. plants. Stoddard proposes that multinational maquiladoras provide a much better workplace and better worker relationships than do many Mexican-owned plants.[2] Belén González agrees. She used to work for a Mexican clothing plant in Reynosa. "The place was ugly," she says. "There was only one bathroom, and it was very unsanitary. The work areas were also filthy, and the machines were all old and unsafe. The building was also poorly ventilated. A few days before I quit, I was coming down some stairs that had no railing on either side. I fell and broke my leg and had many cuts and bruises. They paid some of my medical costs, but they didn't cover even half of what I had to pay for my injuries."

If workers feel powerless against poor working conditions and wages, they get little help from Mexican labor unions. Powerful labor organizations in Mexico City have prevented maquila workers from electing their own union leaders. Labor unions exist, for all intents and purposes, for the benefit of almost everyone except workers. Stoddard claims they are an extension of the political system, used mainly to maintain loyalty to the government and party leaders.[3] One worker said, "We might be able to get some things we desperately need if union officials weren't so greedy. They do almost nothing to get us higher wages, a five-day work week, and safe working conditions."

With virtually no support from unions, workers can do little more than depend on the goodwill of their U.S. employers. Sometimes they are fortunate and sometimes they are not. Some, like Martina, get pressured into sexual relations with their U.S. supervisors. Martina started working at a large electronics assembly plant in Reynosa five years ago. A U.S. supervisor there pressured her to have sex with him. Though she initially refused, he continued to insist. "I know that this is not an excuse," she says, "but I had family in Zacatecas, and I had to send them money. This man hinted that I could lose my job if I didn't agree. He also said that if I went out with him, I could get a better job and a higher wage. Finally, I agreed. I was with him until two months ago. He's the father of my two children. When my family realized what I did, they told me never to return home. A few months ago, he was transferred. I don't know how I'm going to maintain my children."

Women cut off from family face very scary prospects in Mexican border cities. Diana Guerrero has to work to provide for her four children. "My husband was never reliable," she says, "so we soon separated. My sister also has to work, so I had no one to leave them with. Some days, I just had to leave them to take care of each

THOUGH THE PAY AT AMERICAN MAQUILADORAS IS VERY LOW, BENEFITS LIKE BASIC MEDICAL ATTENTION MAY BE BETTER THAN THOSE PROVIDED BY MEXICAN COMPANIES.

other. Then I found that they began to sell candy in the streets to help me out. I didn't like it, but what else could I do?"

Street Children

Many children do end up in the streets. Though it is hard to get an accurate count, recent estimates place the figure at around 1.3 million in all of Mexico.[4] Our Mexican Street Children Exploratory Interviews include 90 children who were selling gum or other items in the streets of Mexican cities bordering South Texas. Some were helping their struggling family survive, while others were homeless and could depend only on other street children in their daily struggle for survival.

Though it is hard to find any studies of street children in Mexican border cities, UNICEF and other agencies have studied street children in Mexico City. They report that in 1995, 47 percent of Mexican street children were under age twelve, up from only 25 percent in 1992.[5] Two-thirds of the children who were selling items on Mexico City streets were doing so to help their families.

Children in Mexican border cities also find themselves forced onto the streets by poverty and bad economic situations. Antonio and his family lost their home when his father lost his job. "I remember," says Antonio, "when we had a house. We were poor but not homeless. Now we all have to work if we don't want to starve. When I ask my dad why things are the way they are, he just looks at me but doesn't say anything. He's always looking for a job, but he can't find one. I'm getting used to selling gum, but I wish things would get better."

It is hard for many Americans to understand the poverty that brings people like Antonio's family to the border. Mrs. Martínez and her children sell items on Reynosa streets. She remembers a time in her home community in Central Mexico when it did not rain for a long time. "We had no money and nothing to eat," she says. "No maíz, no frijoles, ¡nada! [No corn, no beans—nothing!] For a week, we lived on cactus that we gathered from the desert. We cut them up in little pieces and put them in a tortilla. When there were no beans, we suffered a lot. Once when I was young, four others and I in my family had to share one hard-boiled egg for breakfast."

Carlos and his two brothers sell gum near the Reynosa bridge. "Three months ago," he says, "my mom got pneumonia. I am the oldest of five, and my dad left us a year back. Until she got sick, my mom worked so we could go to school. When she got sick, I had to earn money to eat and pay for her medicine. I feel very lucky because the first day I started selling gum, I sold ten boxes. That was one hundred pesos for my family. Since then I feel God is always helping me. My mom always gives us a blessing before we go out to sell."

Surprisingly, most of the street children can read and write.[6] Jorge, for example, quit school in the third grade. "One day," he recalls, "the teacher told the class that we were going to have a *bailable* [dance] for Mother's Day. To participate, we had to buy a *traje de charro* [Mexican cowboy outfit] to dance a polka. I wanted to participate, but I knew we couldn't afford such an expensive suit. When the teacher asked me if I would participate, I answered no. Another boy started saying I was poor and my parents wouldn't even come to the dance. I got angry, even though I knew it was true. I got up from my desk and hit him in the face. The teacher went out to call the principal. While she was gone, I ran out of the school. They never found me because nobody even knew where I lived."

Some children try to stay in school while they work. Apolonio, for example, goes out to sell immediately after school. Often, he works until midnight. "One day," he says, "I had not done my homework, and my teacher asked me why. I told her I had been working all day and I didn't have time to do it. She didn't believe me and made me stay after school. When my parents found out, they were mad because I didn't start selling right after school. I didn't know who to please. When I'm in school, I have a hard time paying attention because my mind is always somewhere else. There are times when I even fall asleep during class. Sometimes I just want to stop going to school."

Some children use the money they earn on the streets to stay in school. Maria is twelve years old and sells fruit cocktail in plastic cups. "I attend a secondary school," she says, "and tuition costs increase every year. My mother cleans houses and irons for other people. She earns only enough money to pay rent, food, and utilities. When I finished primary school, I knew I would have to pay my own tuition if I wanted to stay in school. So what I get from selling, I save up for tuition."

For many children, school and stable families are only dreams. Juan, for example, is eight years old and plays a guitar for money. "My mother is a very hard worker," he says. "She sells *nopales* [cacti] and carries my eight-month-old sister around with her while she works. This work is very hard, and we have to wake up very early in the morning and walk several miles to get here. My father always stays home and does nothing. When I tell my mother that I don't think that's fair, she gets angry and tells me to be quiet. I will never understand. Why do we have to work while he gets to say home?"

Many children selling or working on the streets have suffered abuse.[7] Lupito, for example, is seven years old. "I will be eight in just a few days," he says. "When I was about five or six years old, two of our uncles came to stay a few weeks. When my parents went to work, my uncles watched us, but they were very mean to my brothers and sisters and me. They would hit us for no reason, especially one uncle. He made us sit on the sofa the entire day without getting up. If we left the sofa for any reason, we would get a beating. He would bring us water if we asked for something to drink, but we went most of the day without eating. One day, as my parents were leaving for work, my little sister refused to stay another day with them. When she told them why, my parents asked all of us if what she said was true. When we all said it was, my parents made them leave and never return. They are still not welcome in our home. But now we have to go with our parents to help sell things."

Some children leave abusive homes and attempt to survive on their own. Marcos, for example, lives on the streets with other children. "When I was younger," he recalls, "my dad used to come home drunk and hit me a lot. My mom couldn't do much to stop him. Because of his drinking, he could never hold a job so I had to work to help my family out. The work was tiring, but what I hated the most was coming home to find my dad drunk and violent again. Since I am the oldest, he always blamed me for his ruined life. One day I just couldn't take it any more. I never went home. I met some other kids, and I've been with them ever since. It's been two years. I miss my mom and brothers. Sometimes I wonder what they're doing."

Guillermo also has no family. "About a year ago," he says, "my mom abandoned me. One day I didn't find her at the corner where she always sold things. She just left me. For several days, I walked around alone. One day I met three other kids like me. I began to hang around with them. When they felt they could trust me, they gave me gum to sell. Since then, we help each other. You need others to make it here. I don't have my family, but I have them."

Some abandoned children stay with relatives. María Cisneros is eleven years old. "I work every day selling the flowers my grandmother makes," she says. "I can't go to school because my mother has the documents they require for school, and she left us five years ago. She ran off with a man from the Dominican Republic, so now we live with my grandmother. I hate living with her because she makes me do chores after I get in from selling. Also she hits me if I don't sell all the flowers. I wish I could go to school to become a teacher."

Eight-year-old Pedro lives on the streets of Reynosa with his older sister. "Once," he says, "I was crying on the streets because I hadn't eaten in two days. I didn't have any money to buy gum to sell. An older man came by and asked what was wrong. I told him I was very hungry and couldn't work because I didn't have anything to sell. This old man bought me some food and gave me some money. I now call him *abuelo* [grandpa]. Since then I go to his house when I'm hungry. He always gives me food."

When the children can find no one to help, they may be reduced to begging.[8] Manuel, aged seven, and his five-year-old brother Marcos started begging in the streets when their father died. "My father was a good man," says Manuel. "He worked hard, and we always had something to eat. When he died, my mother had to take care of the baby, and we just about starved. So we had to go out begging in the streets. When we have something to sell, we like the American tourists because they often give money to my little brother, Marcos."

Though there are exceptions, many children like selling to U.S. tourists. José Luis, aged thirteen, says, "Sometimes, people from *el otro lado* [the other side] bring bags of clothes and shoes to give to the kids on the street here. One morning, I was on the sidewalk trying to sell when two ladies drove up in a nice car. They got out and opened the trunk and took out two large garbage bags full of clothes and shoes. Thanks to them, I now have shoes and don't have to burn my feet on the street when it gets hot."

One reason some children prefer the U.S. tourists is because they often volunteer much more money than is requested for a sale. "Mexicans," says Antonio, "want to get what they pay for. The gringo tourists, though, often take fewer packages of gum, but they give us more money. Sometimes, when we try to give them more gum or change, they shake their hand, to let us know they don't want it."

Guadalupe feels uneasy about some of these transactions. "Some people are very nice and will buy something because they know we need the money," he says. "Others just give us the money. We're thankful for it, but I don't want them to think I'm a beggar. I work for my money. Sometimes, people treat us like we have some kind of disease. If we get near their car, they close the windows and yell from inside for us to leave."

Selling to people in cars can cause problems. Carla remembers one day when she had sold a lot of gum. "I went up to some people in a car from Monterrey," she says, "and asked them to buy some gum. I had six packs and expected to get my money in return. Instead, they just rolled up the window and laughed, making fun of my stupidity. I kept asking myself, 'How can they do that and just laugh about it?'"

Tacho dislikes higher-income Mexicans, in general. "I was selling gum at the plaza," he remembers, "when a nicely dressed man said he didn't want any of my gum. He said I should be in school and do something useful with my life. I was angry and just turned around and left. What makes him think I like selling gum on the streets? I really want to go to school and improve my life, but we can't afford to buy the uniform, the shoes, and the school supplies. The school won't accept me with these rags I call clothes. Can't he see that at least I'm working and not begging or stealing?"

Sometimes, the children risk more than humiliation by selling on the streets. Arturo said that though most of the people who buy from him are very nice, he has had a few bad experiences. "One night," he says, "I thought I was going to die. It was seven o'clock on Saturday night, and I only had one box left to sell. I was very tired but decided to keep trying a bit longer. Then I heard someone say, 'How much for your box of gum?' It was very dark and I couldn't see his face very well. I answered that I would sell it for two American dollars. The words weren't even out of my mouth when he gave me a kick in the stomach and took my gum. I told the police, but they never caught the man. I still have nightmares about that incident."

Many children avoid the police.[9] Eleven-year-old Manuel sells gum near his father, who sells corn on the cob. One day, two years before the interview, he says, a police officer came up to him and told him that he and his father could not sell because they did not have a permit. "My father," he says, "had tried many times to get a permit from the municipal office, but they never want to give us one. When the policeman saw me trying to sell a while later, he came up to me and knocked the gum out of my hands and threw me against the wall. I hit my head and started bleeding. All he did was yell at me that he just wanted to scare me."

Juanita is ten years old and sells garlic, cheese, or gum in Nuevo Progreso. "I have always worked very hard," she says. "I don't mind that because my family lets me keep some money. The only thing that really bothers me is

POLICE OFFICERS ARE OFTEN MORE OF A THREAT THAN A PROTECTION TO MEXICAN STREET CHILDREN.

that I always have to be on the lookout for *la liebre* [the jackrabbit]. That's what we children call the police officer who chases us off the streets because he runs very fast. We all hate him because we always have to be on the lookout for him. He has only caught me once, but when he did, he took my box of gum away. I went home that day with no money and no gum. I hear that he even hits some of the kids. I wish he could understand that we have to make a living too."

A favorite spot for many children is the international bridge. Arturo remembers a time when he and his friends went to the bridge and tried to sell gum to the long lines of cars waiting to enter the United States. "A policeman came over," he says, "and told us we couldn't sell there because we were disturbing the people. I didn't listen and kept selling. Suddenly, he came and grabbed me by my neck and told me to leave or he was going to put me in jail. We all got scared and left. Now we don't get near the bridge."

Some children are not so easily scared. A few even cross the river to sell or work on the U.S. side. "I was in a parking lot in Roma," reports Miguel, "when I spotted La Migra [the Border Patrol]. They saw me too, so I took off running and went inside a clothing store. I knew they would come in after me, so I waited until they came in one door, and I ran out the other. I escaped that day, but I'm not always so lucky."

Miguel says he must swim the Rio Grande each time he crosses because he does not have a crossing card. Sometimes he brings tools for cleaning windshields and hides them in the woods near the river. "I'm used to crossing the river," he says, "but I'm constantly being chased by the Border Patrol. When they catch me, I get sent back to Mexico. I keep coming back because my family is poor, and I need to help my parents with the extra money."

Though police and Border Patrol agents can be a problem, many children have a greater worry. "If we find a good place to sell," one says, "some older boys will appear and claim we're selling in their territory. Sometimes they don't warn us but beat us up and take our gum and money. We can't do anything if we're alone. The four of us just go farther away and stick together. Even then, sometimes they'll beat up on us. I hate it because they leave me without any money to give to my mother."

Some street kids in Reynosa become very hardened by life on the streets. A Border Patrol agent, for example, caught some children inhaling paint thinner on the U.S. side of the river. "When I took them in," he says, "I told them that stuff would fry their brains. I asked them why they used it. They said that when they got high, they didn't feel hungry."

The same agent recalled another occasion when he chased one of them into the brush by the river. "Without realizing it," he explains, "this kid got himself into an area with no way out except past me. As I came upon him, I could see he was only about eleven or twelve years old. When he saw he was trapped, he reached down and grabbed a broken bottle. He held it up, threatening me with it. I drew my gun to scare him into dropping it. He didn't even flinch. It was a standoff. I had to either shoot him or let him go. He wasn't about to back down, so I holstered my gun and stepped back. When he saw I wouldn't shoot, he ran past me to the river."

Though many children use their earnings for food, clothing, and help for their parents, some use the money for drugs or alcohol. Pancho, for example, spends half his earnings on Resistol, an intoxicating shoe glue abused by children throughout Latin America. He gives the other half to his mother. When asked whether his mother knew about his addiction, he replied, "Yes, she knows. At first, she would cry and hit me if she saw me drunk or high. But after a while she lost hope in me, and now she doesn't say anything. Sometimes I wish she would, but the only time she pays attention to me is when I give her money."

Many children that we talked with lived with relatives. Veronica, for example, is thirteen years old and lives with her aunt and uncle and their five children. "I just moved here from Oaxaca," she says. "My parents sent me here so that I could make money, since there just isn't any work in Oaxaca. I really miss my family very much. I haven't spoken to them since I left Oaxaca about a month ago. Nobody can tell me when I will be seeing them again. I get very sad and I wish I were back home with *mamá y papá.*

Homeless children often must rely on other children. "I have some friends that I work with," says Felipe. "We sell gum and put our money together. With it we can afford more food than each of us alone. The nights are also very scary when you're alone."

Class Differences and Abusive Treatment

Being alone is a key aspect of powerlessness. In this and preceding chapters, we have described several groups whose class position leaves them without many allies and vulnerable to abuse and exploitation. On the Texas side of the border, farmworkers continue to labor under "harvest of shame" conditions eerily similar to those described in the 1960s by Edward R. Murrow. Colonia residents live in squalor that rivals Third World housing. Some undocumented maids are not much better off than plantation house slaves in the early 1800s. Even with NAFTA, conditions in Mexico remain deplorable for many maquila workers and street children. Why?

The most defining characteristic of the South Texas–Northern Mexico border is not its poverty. Rather, it is the enormous range of inequality between those at the top and those at the bottom. Some farmers and townspeople, for example, have such low regard for farmworkers that they see no absurdity in calling them "lazy." Colonia residents, with so much less public and private wealth than city dwellers, are virtually invisible. Undocumented maids have so little power, in relation to their employers, that outright rape and theft are not even reported. Similarly, maquila workers assemble some of the most complex electronic devices of the twentieth century—at nineteenth-century wages. Finally, near the bottom are Mexican street children. With no wealth, no power, and low prestige, their economic activity is seen essentially as begging.

Poverty and inequality exist elsewhere in the United States, but not with such wide gaps between rich and poor, served and servants, elites and the "underclass." Though South Texas is home to many impoverished groups and individuals, it is also an area of considerable prosperity. In 1996 *Money Magazine*, for example, ranked metropolitan McAllen as the twenty-sixth best place to live among the three hundred largest metropolitan areas in the United States. Factors considered included job creation, affordability of housing, available medical services, clean water and air, and a low crime rate. According to the *Wall Street Journal*, the McAllen-Edinburg-Mission area topped all U.S. metropolitan areas for job growth in 1993, with a rate three times the national average. Bank deposits for the Valley in 1994 totaled 5 billion dollars.[10]

Much of the abusive treatment of the poor is related to the huge gap that exists between them and those who most enjoy the area's prosperity. In 1952 John Kenneth Galbraith proposed that in industrialized nations, massive abuse of one economic or political entity by another would be avoided by the emergence of "countervailing power."[11] Unions, for example, would gain enough power to counter the domination of workers by management. Government power would counter the economic power of banks and multinationals. Well-informed consumers and voters would counter the power of political and economic elites.

To some extent, this has happened in the major industrialized nations of North America, Western Europe, and Japan. Though workers and consumers have not achieved full equality with industry, blatant abuses like those seen in the early stages of industrialization have been largely curbed. Servants cannot be beaten with impunity. Workers have rights. Buyers have some protection by law and in the courts from unscrupulous vendors.

But there is much less protection along the South Texas–Mexico border. Here the economy of Mexico meets that of the United States, resulting in an enormous inequality between citizens of the two countries. Though Mexico's population is now about one-third that of the United States, its gross domestic product is only one-twenty-fifth the size of the GDP of the United States. This means that on a per capita basis, each U.S. worker produces at least ten times as much wealth as each Mexican worker, resulting in the largest income gap between any two contiguous countries in the world.[12]

So much inequality creates a powerful magnet for Mexican workers. With severe restrictions on legal immigration, "undocumented entry" becomes the only real possibility for finding work in the United States. Though the consequences for being caught are generally minor, undocumented workers are isolated from those with similar class interests and effectively stripped of protection by police or judicial agencies. Law enforcement officers become the unwitting allies of employers who themselves violate immigration laws by illegally hiring undocumented workers. As a result, employers who should pay a minimum wage and honor a work schedule seldom give their undocumented workers those "luxuries."

On the border, laws that protect workers in all other segments of the U.S. economy strangely exclude migrant farmworkers. Their union is often ignored or "busted" by corporate growers. Here also, state laws that require developers to pave streets and install water lines in colonias are not enforced because public officials lack the power or resources to do so. On the Mexican border, the maquila industry is vastly more powerful than the workers. The government of Mexico needs the influx of dollars, so they do little to protect workers. Mexican labor leaders often side with management against the workers. As a result, when U.S. companies cross the border to Mexican cities, the power of unions and governmental controls is largely missing.

In addition, trade between the United States and Mexico is stacked against Mexico. NAFTA and other agreements opened markets in both Mexico and the United States, but the size of the U.S. economy means that U.S. investors have much more capital to invest in Mexico than Mexicans can invest in the United States. What Mexico needed from a free trade agreement was the freedom of workers to "sell" their labor where they could get the best price. Unlike the European Economic Community, where workers can freely cross boundaries, NAFTA permits no such freedom of movement for Mexican workers. This produces a situation like two neighbors wanting to trade with each other, one having apples to sell and the other pears. The one with apples wants free movement of apples between them, but not pears. The fact that the apple seller is willing to let apples go both ways does not make it a fair agreement.

This same lopsided relationship exists in other ways. Though Americans can freely cross into Mexican border cities without permits or even identification, Mexicans cannot legally enter the United States without first obtaining a visa or visitor's permit. Getting a permit usually requires long waits at Immigration and Naturalization Service ports of entry or U.S. consulates in Mexico. Mexicans have much less freedom of movement across the border than do citizens of the United States.

In this situation, allowing the "market" to set pay and working conditions creates conditions ripe for abuse. Rosa discovered this. She works for a maquila plant in Reynosa. In 1990 her take-home pay was the equivalent of about fifty-five dollars a week. That year, a study published in *Twin Plant News*, a trade publication of the maquila industry, reported that the average maquila worker was only earning about half the money needed to buy a "basket of goods and services."[13] In other words, her pay was only half what she needed for her most basic needs. By going without some of these needs, and by pooling her resources with some friends, she has managed to hang on.

In early 1995, Mexico had another peso crisis. Overnight, the peso dropped to less than half its previous value. It was a bonanza for U.S. corporations: labor costs were cut because dollars could now buy twice as many pesos. The Mexican government allowed workers' salaries to rise only very slowly. Rosa hoped the maquiladores would pass some of the "savings" on to the workers, especially since the cost of rent and imported goods had doubled or tripled. She was disappointed though. With only thirty-two dollars a week in take-home pay, she had to drop out of night school and move to a shanty town near work to save on rent and bus fees.

Rosa and her coworkers got no help from the union, in part because the Mexican government was pressuring unions to hold down wage demands to fight inflation. Even some sympathetic U.S. managers were of no help. They answered to the home office that had moved operations into Mexico to reduce labor costs. In addition, some reported that local maquila associations were pressuring them to hold the line on labor costs. If one plant raised wages, they were told, then others would have to follow suit or lose workers. So they kept each other in line and reported even larger profits for their home offices. This, of course, did not hurt the record of managers hoping to be promoted up and away from the border.

Maquila managers argue, however, that they do not exploit Mexican workers. Most of those we talked to are decent individuals who respect their Mexican workers. They point out that their industry is second only to petroleum in Mexico's economy and provides direct employment for nearly a million workers. Competition for these jobs is intense, and maquila jobs often pay more than most workers made in previous jobs. They also point out that the plants provide many noncash benefits to their workers, such as paid vacations, health care, and Christmas bonuses.

Guillermo Sáenz, a Mexican worker who has become a supervisor after twelve years as a worker, agrees. He recognizes that salaries are low, but blames it on the government and the recent peso devaluation. "The maquiladoras provide many benefits," he says. "I know many people who want to work here because the only other choices pay much less and make them work longer hours under very poor conditions."

Still, it is interesting to ask the U.S. managers how low the pay could go before they would consider it a form of exploitation. Most do not have an answer. They have not had to think about it. They are used to wages being determined by the countervailing forces of the market, union negotiators, or government regulations. The term "exploitation" introduces moral considerations with which they have not had to deal. The more balanced power situation in the United States makes considerations of what is morally right largely unnecessary or irrelevant. On the border, however, letting the market, rather than moral considerations, determine pay rates invites abuse and potential exploitation of workers.

Abuses on the Texas Border

Employers of undocumented maids in Texas cities run into a similar quandary in deciding how much to pay their maids. Farther north, families who employ a maid do not have to worry much about it. Such matters are well established by minimum-wage laws, a tight market for household help, or even tradition. The phrase "I don't do windows" reflects a degree of countervailing power of domestic workers in the United States.

If undocumented workers had some form of countervailing power on their side, abuse would be far less common and people would be inclined to behave "morally." Tomasa's case illustrates. She came from Guadalajara with her mother at the age of fourteen. Her mother found work with a judge in Edinburg. When a local school teacher was looking for help, the judge recommended Tomasa. At first, she was only supposed to clean the home. "The first day I cleaned the house," she says, "my boss was surprised at how fast I worked. The next day she bought some paint and asked me to paint all three bedrooms. I finished them in one week. She said I could do this type of work because I was young and full of energy. The next week she asked me to paint the fence. On payday she said she was going to give me used clothes instead of money. My mother told the judge. He called the teacher and told her to pay me what a painter would have charged. That was about triple what she had agreed to pay. I got my money, but I had to find another job."

This account is unusual, not because of the abuse but because the maid was able to summon power to counteract it. Most undocumented maids do not have powerful allies who can make people behave honorably. Likewise, farmworkers, especially in the early years, were unable to summon power when farmers or crew leaders cheated them on wages. Today colonia residents are generally unable to force developers to install legally required infrastructure. Some maquila workers find it difficult to resist intimidation by managers. Even though their job pays little more than thirty-five dollars a week, it is all they have, and the threat of losing it pushes some into very disagreeable situations.

Nevertheless, poverty is not all that keeps workers locked in a low-class position. The presence of an international boundary has much to do with it. Barriers to legal immigration, for example, such as limiting Mexico to a quota of only twenty thousand legal immigrants a year, leave almost no avenue for legal entry. With jobs north of the border going begging, many workers cross, only to be stripped of allies and legal protections in the process. While the border allows industrial capital to flow one way, Mexican labor is stripped of power as it flows the other way.

North of the border, the situation is not much better. Migrant farmworkers lose bargaining power when the job market is constantly glutted with undocumented workers. An increased demand for cheap housing, often from migrants from across the border, plays into the hands of unscrupulous colonia developers. Maids and other undocumented workers are subject to exploitation when the dominant culture views their illegal search for jobs as more criminal than employers who illegally hire them and pay them wages far below the poverty line.

Cultural and Structural Factors

Often the situation does not improve much for Mexican immigrants who manage to become legal residents. This is illustrated when colonia residents who become legal still have notoriously low rates of political participation. The reasons are much deeper than apathy or a lack of interest, however. Many colonia residents who are migrant farmworkers are often gone during elections. Officials almost never locate polling places in colonias, and many residents would have no way to get to the polls, even if they knew where they were. Such structural factors produce a high degree of powerlessness for many South Texas residents. With the powerlessness comes a great deal of discrimination, though much of it may be indirect or unintentional. As we will see, the inequality of power, more than prejudice and racism, keeps Mexican immigrants and Mexican Americans at the bottom of the South Texas class system.

Forms of Domination or Discrimination

As I indicated in the Introduction, Robert E. Park proposed that some form of domination generally follows contact between the dominant society and immigrant groups. Domination, which we roughly equate here with intergroup discrimination, has several forms or manifestations. One is bigotry, or intentionally harsh treatment of a group based on prejudice or racist attitudes. This was the form most common in South Texas during the first half of the twentieth century. Luisa remembers the bigotry of Anglo students when she attended school forty years ago. "We were very poor," she remembers, "and almost never had sandwich bread, except for Daddy's lunch. The rest of us ate tacos made with Mom's handmade tortillas. But I wouldn't dare take my tacos to school because I would have died of embarrassment. The Anglo kids would have called me a 'beaner,' like they did with other Mexican kids. School food wasn't free back then. If you wanted to eat in the cafeteria, you had to work for it. I washed dishes in the cafeteria during recess just so I could have lunch at school. The Anglo kids still laughed and called me names. I never could understand why. I was working for my food."

Bigots seldom tried to hide their racism or class bias, since the prevailing ideas of the time held that racial and class inequality were a fact of life. As a result, even public facilities were segregated. One student's uncle, for example, remembers trying to go swimming with his friends at the only swimming pool in McAllen. "I begged my father to let me go," he says. "Finally, he said we could. When we got there, an Anglo said

Mexicans were only allowed to swim on Thursdays. When we asked why, he said they always cleaned the pool on Friday, so that left Thursdays for the Mexicans."

Cultural bias is another form of domination (or discrimination) based on beliefs and attitudes. Unlike bigotry, where harm is deliberate and motivated by prejudice, cultural bias has indirect causes. Some problems experienced by undocumented maids, for example, stem more from differences in culture than from prejudice and bigotry. One student described her family's maid, for example, as being excessively shy. "She always looks down when she talks to us," she says. "My mom has talked to her about it, but it's a hard habit for her to break." The family apparently does not realize that in many parts of Mexico, looking down when addressing a person of higher rank is considered the correct way to show respect.

Cultural bias is very similar to ethnocentrism. It arises when members of one cultural group have to live by, and be judged in accordance with, the cultural rules and conventions of another. As a result, those not familiar with the subtleties of the other culture are at a disadvantage. One migrant worker experienced this as a boy when he enrolled in an Iowa first grade while his parents worked in the fields. "It was really hard," he says, "because I didn't know much English. I survived by imitating the other kids. Sometimes that didn't work. I waited in line for the cafeteria, for example, only to be told they couldn't serve me because I hadn't paid in the classroom. I learned to pay the teacher, but I didn't like the strange food they served. I was also embarrassed at nap time because I took a pillow from the pile, only to have it yanked away by the owner."

Cultural bias gives indirect advantages to the group whose culture is dominant in society. It is like playing a game when you are not familiar with the rules. In such situations, if you are a member of the nondominant culture, you will probably lose, no matter how fair the referee might be. Bigotry, in contrast, is like having a biased referee who breaks the rules to make sure you lose. Bigotry involves intentional harm based on biased personal beliefs, while cultural bias involves indirect harm based on unfamiliarity with the culture of the dominant group. While a bigot thus has a distorted view of what a group is like, culturally biased individuals tend to judge more evenly, though with standards that favor their own group. Bigotry, for example, causes a person to reject minorities as inferior, while cultural bias applies standards that put them at a disadvantage.

Cultural bias also keeps minorities from advancing by marking them as lower class. People in Mexico judge the Spanish spoken by South

Texas residents, for example, to be inferior. And Mexican Spanish is judged inferior to the forms spoken in Spain. Groups in a more powerful class position often manage to identify their culture with education and refinement—standards that always relegate others to an inferior position.[14]

Occasionally, Anglos on the border find themselves at a cultural disadvantage, though they usually have the power to make the results less harmful. One U.S. maquila supervisor, for example, discovered the great importance Mexicans put on "saving face" after he corrected workers in front of others. "I didn't yell at them," he says. "I have always believed in being frank and correcting problems when and where I see them. I never had any real complaints in our U.S. plants. Here, however, the workers sent a representative in to talk to me. He told me, 'You have an office with a door and a lock. We Mexicans strongly believe that workers need to be respected. We can put up with the low pay, but not with you not respecting us.'"

Nonetheless, much of the domination and discrimination suffered by minorities is related less to attitudes and cultural beliefs than to the way relationships are structured. As indicated earlier, the main thing keeping the poor on both sides of the border from "moving up" is their relative powerlessness in the structure, or the established social arrangements, of society. This happens in two ways that we will call exploitation and structural bias. Exploitation, like bigotry, is a direct and intentional form of domination in which the powerful use their position to take advantage of those with less power.

A farmer who deliberately attempts to keep his workers uneducated to maintain them as a cheap source of labor would provide an example of exploitation of workers. Octavio experienced this one summer when he was working in Colorado. "It rained a lot that summer," he says. "Some of us thought we could attend some classes in adult basic education on the days we weren't working. The local community college even set it up for us to learn English or work toward a GED certificate. The growers gave them hell at the college, though. They claimed they might need us at a moment's notice. One farmer flatly refused to let us go, stating, 'Education ruins a good picker.'"

In this and preceding chapters, we have seen examples of exploitation. Farmers or crew leaders who cheat poorly educated Mexican workers are guilty of exploitation, as are land developers who sell flood-prone colonia land without putting in the required water lines or drainage. The employer who would not let her undocumented maid go to a party also exploited her if it was to keep her from getting married and legalizing her status.

There is considerable debate, however, about whether treatment of workers by the maquila industry is exploitation. Low pay, by itself, is not the issue. Some analysts argue that maquilas owned by U.S. companies pay better than their Mexican counterparts.[15] They also point out that U.S. companies pay workers almost 110 percent more in noncash benefits and wages than do similar Mexican companies.

From the opposite point of view, some writers contend that multinational corporations exploit the situation of corrupt unions, economic mismanagement, and a glut of workers to get away with paying less than a living wage.[16] Using this point of view, if it is exploitation for merchants to sharply raise prices during a natural disaster, for example, then taking advantage of Mexico's economic crisis to pay less than a living wage could also be considered exploitation.

Another important aspect of both bigotry and exploitation involves practices now considered illegitimate. It is considered wrong to harm someone because you are prejudiced against their race, class, religion, or sex (bigotry). It is also considered wrong to manipulate structural arrangements to hold someone down so that you can take advantage of them (exploitation). The problem, though, is that definitions of what is legitimate change over time and can be manipulated. In early U.S. history, slave owners were not seen as bigots or exploiters because social definitions of the time held that slaves were inferior (racism) and that slavery was actually a favor ("White man's burden"). Today we find such beliefs patently absurd.

Something similar happens with the groups we have been discussing. Paying maquila workers less than a living wage is considered "legitimate" if we are helping the Mexican economy or if jobs in Mexico are scarce. Migrant farmworkers can "legitimately" be housed in primitive conditions and paid poverty wages if they are illegal, uneducated, and cannot speak English. Colonia residents can be blamed for their problems if they buy land without improvements and do not even register to vote. We similarly legitimize the exploitation of undocumented maids if we label them "illegal aliens." Indeed, this term legitimizes both bigotry and exploita-

MEXICAN WOMEN ON BOTH SIDES OF THE BORDER ARE FREQUENT VICTIMS OF EXPLOITATION.

tion. In essence, it says that people who break the law (illegal) do not deserve protection. It also says that those who do not belong (aliens) cannot expect equal treatment.

This example illustrates another point. One structural advantage of higher-class positions is the ability to shape definitions of legitimacy. Employers who hire undocumented maids are also breaking the law, but editorials in local newspapers excoriating "illegal aliens" seldom condemn their employers. Similarly, when the peso devaluation lowered labor costs for maquila plants, news organizations and local chambers of commerce made no apparent effort to urge U.S. companies to keep the salaries of Mexican workers tied to the value of the dollar. This is particularly significant, considering that to have done so would have improved retail sales on the Texas border. Mexican workers are not going to come across to buy electronic equipment if they can no longer pay the rent or buy enough to eat.

As damaging as the three preceding types of domination might be, the fourth type, structural bias, is arguably the main impediment to breaking out of poverty today. Structural bias happens when the normal operation of arrangements and relationships produces harmful side effects to powerless groups and individuals. Job security, for example, is often based on seniority. That means that the last people hired will also be the first ones fired when layoffs occur. When civil rights laws broke down bigoted employment barriers, minorities finally started to get well-paying jobs. They were lowest in seniority, however, so the normal working of the system meant that they were the first ones fired when the economy turned bad or jobs went overseas. Thus, a structural arrangement, rather than bigotry, caused workers harm. Because such treatment is unintentional, however, it is often considered legitimate.

Other forms of structural bias were presented in previous chapters. Colonia residents have a fraction of the police protection of people in the cities because the sheriff's department lacks a taxation system that would provide equitable financing. The children of farmworkers fall behind in school because their migration takes them out of class early and moves them from district to district. Maquila workers have their wages cut in half because U.S. companies use the peso, rather than the dollar, as the basis for calculating wages.

There are many other forms of structural bias that affect minorities on the South Texas border. Basing school funding on property values, for example, creates an educational system that gives predominantly Hispanic school districts in South Texas about half the dollars per child that "property rich" districts farther north enjoy. Similarly, following state

Table 4.1 — Types of Domination (or Discrimination)

Source of Harm	Degree of Intentionality	
	Direct and intentional	Indirect and unintentional
Culture (attitudes and beliefs)	1. Bigotry	2. Cultural bias
Structure (structural systems and arrangements)	3. Exploitation	4. Structural bias

guidelines and formulas gives border universities more students per faculty and less than half the per capita state appropriations available to universities in nonborder counties.[17]

Table 4.1 summarizes the four types of discrimination: bigotry, cultural bias, exploitation, and structural bias. It compares these types of domination (also discrimination) in terms of the source of harm (biased attitudes versus structural arrangements) and the intentionality of the harm (direct and intentional harm, as opposed to harm that is indirect and unintentional).[18]

As the table indicates, bigotry and cultural bias are both the result of attitudes and beliefs. Exploitation and structural bias, on the other hand, are the result of inequities in the structural arrangements and systems of society. Exploitation involves the intentional use of these inequitable systems to harm powerless groups or individuals, though for reasons of personal gain, rather than prejudice. Structural bias, on the other hand, is indirect and unintentional, resulting from systems and structural arrangements that produce harmful side effects for powerless groups. As we have discussed, the two on the left are generally regarded as illegitimate, at least in today's society. In contrast, the two on the right are often seen as legitimate forms of treatment, since no harm is intended.

Using this perspective, we should consider treatment by maquiladoras as a form of exploitation only if they deliberately manipulate the system to take unfair advantage of workers. If maquila managers systematically bribed government or union leaders, for example, to prevent workers from gaining better pay or working conditions, a good case could be made for exploitation. Since most U.S. maquila managers avoid any payment of *mordidas* (bribes), however, little evidence exists to support such a claim.

Still there is little doubt that some exploitation does take place. Some U.S. managers do pressure Mexican female workers into sexual liaisons, for example, with threats or with offers of special favors.¹⁹ Similarly, some maquila associations hold meetings on U.S. soil to hold down pay increases. Such practices might be considered collusion to set wages if the workplaces were not outside the United States. Similarly, a few U.S. manufacturers have taken plants to Mexico to avoid more strict environmental and labor law enforcement. To the extent that systems are manipulated to take unfair advantage of workers, such practices would also be considered exploitation.

Though some exploitation of maquila workers does take place, however, it may be more the exception than the rule. Many maquila plants provide more than the required benefits, and most U.S. supervisors seem to treat their workers with respect. U.S. managers also generally try to maintain high standards of health and safety. The harm suffered by most maquila workers may be more the result of structural bias than exploitation. Nevertheless, this is little consolation to poorly paid workers. When a truck runs over you, it helps only a little to find out it was unintentional.

Biased cultural and structural arrangements today cause much of the harm suffered by minorities on the border. Nevertheless, since systems and culture have no will of their own, culture and structure should also occasionally work to the advantage of minorities. One farmworker, for example, described an experience in school that illustrates cultural bias in favor of migrant children. "One day," he says, "an Anglo child asked me if I knew where pickles come from. Since I had worked with my family picking cucumbers, I told him that they made pickles from cucumbers. He wasn't sure whether to believe me, so he asked the teacher. When she gave him the same answer I had, he thought I was pretty smart."

Likewise, since South Texas borders on Mexico, and since Spanish is their first language, Mexican Americans should experience a positive form of cultural bias. They should get an "easy A" in Spanish classes, for example, and should have preference in jobs dealing with Mexican customers or clients.

Though Mexican Americans do experience some occasional advantages, cultural and structural bias generally work against them. Because English is considered the dominant language in the school system, for example, children whose native language is Spanish find themselves at a disadvantage in English-speaking schools. Then when they become bilingual, their ability to speak Spanish is often denigrated as border Spanish or Tex-Mex. Likewise, Spanish classes are geared to writing, rather than conversational, skills, so much of the advantage disappears. The University of Texas–Pan American bars native Spanish speakers from enrolling in regular Spanish classes, insisting that they enroll in special Spanish for Native Speakers—classes that emphasize grammar and writing over conversational skills. In addition, Texas legislators have mandated that university classes must be in "plain English." This effectively bars University of Texas–Pan American students, 90 percent of whom speak Spanish, from having visiting professors from Mexico or Latin America who are not proficient in English.

To make matters worse, Mexicans who visit the area call local Hispanics *pochos*, an unflattering reference to their inability to speak standard Spanish. It is not just the mixing of Spanish and English that bothers the Mexicans. It is the use of archaic expressions and nonstandard grammar. "It drives me crazy," reports one Mexican student, "to hear educated people here in South Texas say 'mi mueble' [loosely, 'my movable property'] instead of 'mi carro' [my car], or 'asina' [archaic form of *así*] instead of 'así' [so]." This student would probably be shocked to discover that in Spain those who say "carro" instead of "coche" would also be regarded as uneducated.

It illustrates, however, why cultural and structural biases seldom work to the advantage of minorities. Those with more power can block situations that might hurt them and promote cultural or structural situations more to their advantage. The Spanish invaders of Mexico rendered the Aztec and Mayan cultures meaningless, and even managed to label them as savage. Similarly, early in South Texas the culture and language of local Hispanics were labeled inferior. Until the mid 1970s, many schools severely punished children for speaking Spanish.

Ludi remembers what it was like. "When I started school," she says, "I didn't speak any English. The only people I ever came in contact with were folks on the ranch, and they all spoke Spanish. One day I went up to the teacher and asked her in Spanish if I could go to the bathroom. She paddled me for speaking Spanish. I remember standing there, tears running down my face, and not knowing what I had done wrong. I felt so embarrassed, so ashamed and hurt. My parents couldn't understand why it was so terrible to speak Spanish. They said, 'If we are not ashamed of our language and our background, why should they take it away from us?'"

This is the whole point. Minorities become powerless when others make them ashamed of their culture and reinforce their class position with stereotypes and power inequality. Structural inequality leads to inequality of culture, which in turn leads to internalized feelings that add to the inability to break out of the "vicious circle." As we will see in the next chapter, Valley schools have played a key role in perpetuating the class structure of South Texas.

The Pain of Gain: Fifty Years of Anglo-Hispanic Relations in South Texas Schools

Chapter 5

WITH MARÍA OLIVIA VILLARREAL-SOLANO

There was a place on the playground with benches and an outdoor stage where the poor Mexicanos usually ate their lunch. Every day, you could see them with the bolsas de papel, todas arrugadas [wrinkled paper bags]. You know, they had to use the same bag all week long. They would pull just enough of the taco out for one bite, and then they would hide it back in the sack. Some would even try to cover it with their hand. Of course, everybody knew they were eating bean or potato tacos. We made them feel like their food wasn't as good as a peanut butter and jelly sandwich.

MARTIN VILLARREAL,
1990

Martin, like many Mexican Americans educated in South Texas schools, uses the Anglo pronunciation of his name (MAR-tin, rather than Mar-TEEN).[1] At an early age, he distanced himself from the low-income Mexicanos. He lived close enough to the school to walk home for lunch. Also, his parents were not farmworkers. When he went away to a private school, he realized he had sided with the Anglos in discriminating against the low-income Mexicanos.

Martin attended school in the 1960s. Twenty years earlier, few Mexican Americans attended South Texas schools, and fewer still had Anglo classmates. Ethnic struggles in South Texas schools are part of the larger struggle of Mexican American and Anglo relations covering the last 150 years. These relations, documented by such historians as Oscar Martínez[2] and David Montejano,[3] reveal a pattern of continuous interethnic conflict, with occasional periods of accommodation. Our concern in this chapter is with the period of gradual integration of Mexican Americans and Anglos in South Texas schools from 1945 to 1994.

The Research

The topic of ethnic relations in South Texas schools was examined through the Former Students Exploratory Interviews and the Former Students Survey. This topic has been a favorite for students conducting exploratory interviews for the Borderlife Project. Many found, however, that the topic is highly sensitive among those they interviewed. One student who interviewed her mother, for example, was told at the end of the interview to destroy the tape. "When I asked her why," she relates, "she said she didn't want outsiders to know that, because of her father's ideas, she was uneducated. Her father used to tell her that boys needed education to write their names and not get cheated. According to him, girls should drop out of school because their husbands would support them."

People who were strangers before the exploratory interview were often hesitant to talk about painful school experiences. One interviewer, for example, talked to some women attending an adult education class in Donna. "They were favorable to the interview," she reports, "until we got down to particulars. Three of them would only answer yes or no and were reluctant to give details about their experiences. They appeared too angry or hurt to discuss what had happened to them. They would only nod their heads to agree with what others said. After I left their table, they continued the discussion. I heard them confirm the harsh experiences shared earlier by others."

Because of the sensitivity of the topic, we did not randomize the selection of subjects for the Former Students Survey (Appendix B, no. 5). We did try, however, to include all segments of the Valley population. We conducted 90 percent of the survey interviews with subjects previously known to the interviewers. This approach fostered trust and openness, something that randomized interviews would not have achieved. We developed questions for the survey from patterns identified in the Former Students Exploratory Interviews. In the survey, we successfully administered the standardized closed-response interview guide to 243 respondents. Each interviewer found and interviewed 5 individuals—one from each of five distinct time periods discussed below.

In a third strategy, we compared data from the two preceding components with data extracted from high school yearbooks. In this yearbook subproject, we counted the number of Hispanics in a variety of categories of high school activities, showing changes in their proportional representation over the years. These three sources allowed us to identify and describe patterns of interethnic relations in Valley schools from the end of World War II to the present.

The Historical Context

Until the end of World War II, the social dominance of Anglos over Mexican Americans was so deeply ingrained throughout Texas that Anglos only occasionally needed force to sustain it.[4] As a result, many

Mexican Americans did not believe that they were victimized. One woman who attended school during this time, for example, said she could not recall a time when an Anglo teacher treated her badly. "As for Anglo students," she says, "I couldn't say because I never associated with them. I vividly remember my tenth-grade English teacher. She was a wonderful person who inspired me to be the best that I could be. She would tell me that just because I was a 'brownie' didn't mean I wasn't intelligent."

Neither the fact that many Mexican Americans were segregated from Anglo students, nor her teacher's paternalistic reference to them as "brownies," registered as discrimination to this woman. Many student interviewers reported similar reactions. More than half the individuals who were of school age in the 1940s and 1950s said that they experienced no discrimination. Much of the evidence now available suggests that the culture of the period so thoroughly legitimized the segregation and castelike treatment that a person could easily believe they were not discriminatory.

One man, for example, described an incident in 1930 when he was only five years old. "We were living in Los Indios, Texas," he says. "One day, an Anglo man came to our house looking for my father. We rarely had visitors at our house, much less Anglo visitors, so when my mother realized who it was, she immediately put her head down and kept her eyes on the floor. I remember seeing her do this, and I followed her example. We both stared at his muddy boots while he asked, in Spanish, to see my father. At that point, my father appeared. I could tell at once that he was very upset with us, but he dismissed us until he finished talking to the Anglo. Then he demanded an explanation from my mother. He told her that the visitor was only a man, not a saint. She said, 'but Chago (my father's nickname), he is an Anglo.' My mother had been made to feel that she was a guest in her own birth country."

The structure and the content of public schools taught this lesson of Hispanic inferiority.[5] "Mexican" schools were physically inferior. Mexican American children used textbooks discarded by Anglo schools. The Anglo children learned that Mexicans were impure and had to be kept in their place. Mexican children were taught and shown that they were dirty and could not become clean.[6]

María Sánchez, who attended a "Mexican" school in the 1940s, for example, recalls this process. "Though we were careful about personal hygiene," she says, "the teachers had a weekly ritual of checking our hair for lice. Every Monday morning, they would line us up and use two pencils to search for head lice. I can still remember the feeling of embarrassment."

An Edinburg "Mexican school" with its Anglo principal, about 1910
(photo courtesy of Hidalgo County Historical Museum).

Paula attended a small "Mexican" school briefly in the early 1940s. As with many Mexican Americans of the time, economics, rather than segregation, caused her to drop out of school altogether. "Sometimes Mother wouldn't have money for new shoes," she says, "so she cut cardboard to put inside the old ones to make them last. I didn't learn to read or write while I was young. The Anglos were the only ones in school back then. Most of us Mexican Americans were picking their fields and cleaning their homes, struggling just to make it to the next day."

We will consider the progress of their struggle by briefly examining four distinct periods of post–World War II Mexican American history.[7] We can then examine how particular forms of treatment in the schools of South Texas have changed during these periods.

1945–1954: Remnants of the Old Segregation

World War II did more to change the character of Mexican Americans than any other event.[8] First, it drew massive numbers of Mexican workers to the United States during the labor shortage created by the war. When the war ended, the flow of workers, now largely undocumented, continued. Meier and Rivera point out the impact this immigration had on South Texas. "Because of this increased *mojado* ['wetback'] influx," they say, "the Lower Rio Grande Valley became a great labor reservoir into which legal and illegal immigrants moved because of easy accessibility and cultural affinity."[9]

Second, more than 375,000 Mexican American military personnel came home changed by the war. They received more medals of honor than any other racial or ethnic group. Mexican American veterans, among them officers who had commanded Anglo troops, began to confront Anglos who wished to return to the old segregationist caste system. One recently returned veteran, for example, described entering a Valley restaurant with his mother. A waitress arrived and politely told him that they did not serve Mexicans. "I told her we just wanted hamburgers," he says, "and that I didn't understand how they could refuse service to an American in the country he had just served. It was clear she was uncomfortable, but it made no difference. So we just left."

A little farther north, in Three Rivers, a funeral parlor refused to bury a highly decorated hero of the war, Felix Longoria. In protest, Mexican American servicemen from South Texas founded the GI Forum. They were able to generate considerable opposition to the decision. Eventually, Longoria was buried in Arlington National Cemetery. Within a few months, a hundred chapters of the GI Forum were formed.

These veterans and their allies recognized that education was essential to changing the caste position of Mexican Americans. The GI Bill made it possible for them to further their education and to get home loans. As they began to press for change, segregation based on race or ethnicity began to give way to a new segregation based on residence and social class. In 1948 a favorable decision in the *Delgado v. Bastrop Independent School District* case mandated an end to the segregation of Mexican Americans in Texas schools. Economic pressures also contributed to the end of ethnic segregation. Small South Texas communities could scarcely afford separate high schools. Increasingly, Mexican Americans were admitted into previously all-Anglo schools.

Yet Mexican American students who attended Anglo high schools seldom graduated. They not only dropped out but blamed themselves for their failure. "I often went without shoes," recalls one man, "and had only one set of clothes. Each day I had to go without lunch. Still, to this day, I am embarrassed that I didn't finish school. I often wonder how things would be today if I had graduated. Nobody could have stopped me. I would have gotten a good job and gone to college at night. I would have figured out a way. But look at me now. Me quedé de pendejo [I've remained an idiot]."

1955–1964: The Civil Rights Era

By 1954 political and economic interests outside the Valley were complaining loudly about the continued influx of legal and undocumented Mexican immigrants. In June 1954, the attorney general of the United States ordered the deportation of all undocumented Mexican workers in an action called Operation Wetback. More than 1 million Mexicans, many of them parents of Mexican American children, were rounded up and deported to Mexico. Overnight, growers in Texas were forced to pay higher wages to farmworkers. Undaunted, they fought back and managed to gain increases in the number of temporary farmworkers, or *braceros*, from Mexico. This battle continued until the authorization for the Bracero Program expired in 1964.

The Civil Rights era was also a time of massive changes in the schools of the United States. In 1954 the U.S. Supreme Court issued its famous Brown decision, officially overruling all laws supporting school segregation in the United States. From 1954 to 1965, southern states did all they could to nullify the effects of the Brown decision. Nevertheless, with the passage of the Voting Rights Act in 1965, Congress validated the prohibition of racial discrimination set forth in the Brown decision. During this ten-year period, Mexican American civil rights organizations struggled to end segregation. Like many Black civil rights organizations, they tried to reassure Anglos that they were nonviolent and only wanted to be "better" (i.e., more Anglicized) citizens.[10]

During this period, Anglo officials grudgingly began to admit Mexican Americans into public facilities, though they made it clear that Mexican Americans were not equals. Concha remembers an incident in 1958 when her father took the family to see a movie. "While Dad was paying for the tickets and getting us drinks," she recalls, "we went immediately to the balcony where Mexicans and colored people were admitted. Dad didn't see where we had gone. Because it was his first time there, and because he couldn't read, he went into the Anglo section. From where we were, we could see him enter. We knew that something would happen, though we never imagined that they would scream ugly names at him and hit him. We ran down as fast as we could, but they had already thrown him out. We wanted to do something, but we knew we couldn't. We went home very depressed. That night, at one o'clock in the morning, I heard my father crying outside. As I listened, I started to cry. He had always been so strong to us. I knew he was ashamed because he hadn't done anything but take the abuse from them."

1965–1974: THE CHICANO MOVEMENT

The year 1965 stands out as a time when many minorities decided to confront such abuse with something besides passive resistance. The Watts riot in Los Angeles that year sparked riots in other major cities. According to Meier and Rivera, "beginning about 1966, a new sense of ethnic worth manifested itself among Chicano youths."[11] Possibly, some of this was related to César Chávez and the Delano grape strike in 1965. Almost simultaneously, Rodolfo "Corky" González, author of the epic poem "I Am Joaquín," founded the Denver-based Crusade for Justice. Closer to home, in Crystal City, Texas, José Angel Gutiérrez and others were beginning to set in motion a new political party, La Raza Unida, to demand equality and political change. In 1968 Chicano students in San Antonio demanded and won an end to the no-Spanish rule there. They also won public recognition of the abysmal quality of predominantly Hispanic schools.

In November of the same year, 140 students walked out of Edcouch-Elsa High School in eastern Hidalgo County. Initially, they supported two students who had been expelled for refusing to cut their hair. One woman who participated in the walkout remembers that it soon escalated to other issues. "The worst problem," she says, "was the no-Spanish rule. At school the teachers would make fun of us or punish us for the way we pronounced words. It got to the point that I was ashamed of my parents because they could not speak English.

"When we walked out," she continues, "all of us were scared. Some of us were going against our parents' wishes. Organizations like MAYO [Mexican American Youth Organization] and Raza Unida kept reminding us that they had a lawyer ready to take our case. When they arrested and sent some of us to juvenile detention, it seemed that things couldn't get any worse. We were wrong. The school refused to readmit us. Because they labeled us troublemakers, other districts believed we might give ideas to their students. Finally the La Joya district let us in. It was a long drive every day, but we stuck it out. When Edcouch-Elsa finally let us back in, they didn't let our pictures appear in the yearbook. Also, they told the seniors who had participated in the walkout not to attend the graduation ceremonies—that they would mail their diplomas to them."

In spite of such retribution, the walkout was successful. Many parents who had previously put up with bigotry now supported the walkout. National media showed just how appalling school conditions were for Hispanic students. Elsewhere, students organized other walkouts. Perhaps the most important result came when a federal judge in 1969 finally put an end to the no-Spanish rule in Texas schools.[12]

A year earlier, in 1968, federal legislators had authorized funds for bilingual education demonstration projects. Within two years, bilingual education became a symbol of Chicano activism. In 1970 the largely voluntary programs became mandatory for districts with a Hispanic enrollment of 5 percent or greater. In 1974 the Supreme Court upheld the mandates for bilingual education, declaring that non-English-speaking children had a constitutional right to special language programs. Thus, in less than ten years, schools that had prohibited Spanish on school property were now teaching Mexican American children in their native language.

1975–1994: The New Assimilation

Despite these victories, by 1975 Chicano activism had lost much of its momentum. When Chicanos joined antiwar protesters to oppose U.S. involvement in Vietnam, they alienated many Mexican American veterans of World War II and Korea. The violent tone of some protests alienated others. In addition, the symbol of Chicano victory, bilingual education, began to meet with considerable skepticism among Mexican American parents.

Much of their skepticism may be related to the competing philosophies wrapped in the same program bundle. Chicano activists generally saw bilingual education as a way to raise self-esteem among Chicano children by teaching them to value their own culture. This goal is part of the broader philosophy of cultural pluralism.

Those favoring an assimilation (or "Anglo conformity") philosophy, in contrast, saw it as a transitional bridge between Mexican American and Anglo cultures. In this view, children would receive early lessons in the three Rs in Spanish only until their mastery of English allowed them to join the English-speaking "mainstream." Still others thought it should produce true bilingualism among all groups, making Anglo children as fluent in Spanish as Hispanic children were in English.

Advocates of the latter view were disappointed that few bilingual programs ever included Anglo children. When research suggested that schools were not achieving the transitional purposes of bilingual education, assimilationists also became disillusioned. In 1977, for example, the American Institute for Research showed that while bilingual programs produced gains in reading Spanish, their students scored worse in English than Hispanic students in other programs. They also had less mastery of other basic subjects, and their measures of self-esteem were not much better than students in conventional programs. In addition, the researchers reported that most program directors were keeping students in bilingual classes long after they had learned English. This led many assimilationists to doubt the transitional nature of the program. Though other studies sometimes had more favorable results, cultural pluralists increasingly found themselves as the lone defenders of the program.

By the 1990s, many Mexican Americans in South Texas were manifesting strong sentiments in favor of educational assimilation. One McAllen father, for example, said he did not want his two daughters enrolled in bilingual programs, believing that they promoted a form of paternalism. "These programs tell our children they need special concessions other students don't need," he complained. A 1988 study by the Educational Testing Service confirmed the extent of such opposition, though for other reasons. Seventy-eight percent of Mexican American parents opposed teaching in Spanish if it meant less time for English.[13]

Such results, however, do not mean that Mexican Americans in South Texas are ready to give up their language or their culture. Most of them want their children to speak both languages fluently. Indeed, South Texans of Mexican origin who do not speak Spanish are often shunned and chastised for not knowing it. David is one of them. His father was a migrant worker in his youth but found a factory job in Michigan, where he met David's mother. They raised their children in an all-English environment, so, when they moved back to the Valley and he enrolled in UT–Pan American, David knew almost no Spanish. "It was hell when I first came," he says. "I look Mexican American, so people are always saying things to me in Spanish. I've been able to learn some expressions, so I can sometimes fake it. It's always hard to explain that I can't speak Spanish. They either don't believe me, or say I have turned my back on my heritage. Mostly, I just try to avoid situations where it comes up, but that's hard to do around here."

Patterns of Change

Our discussion of the preceding historical periods outlines some general patterns in the relation of Anglos to Mexican Americans in South Texas schools. These school patterns must be seen against the background of the ethnic com-

MEXICAN AMERICAN STUDENTS IN SOUTH TEXAS WHO DO NOT SPEAK SPANISH OFTEN FEEL ISOLATED.

Percent Hispanic

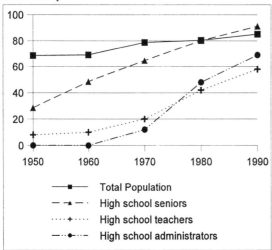

Fig. 5.1. Hispanic representation in four groups in the Rio Grande Valley (Total population figures based on Betts and Slottje, Crisis on the Rio Grande, *Table 1.1;* Borderlife Yearbook Project, *1991–1995*)

position of the Valley during these same periods. We can see just how much Valley schools excluded Mexican Americans by comparing their representation in the Lower Rio Grande Valley population with their representation among the ranks of high school seniors, teachers, and school administrators in the same geographical area. Data for this comparison are presented in Figure 5.1 and come from the U.S. Census [14] and from our study of yearbooks from ten Valley high schools.[15]

The data presented in Figure 5.1 show some discrimination occurring in the periods just described. Though Mexican Americans were in the majority of the population in 1950, for example, they were the numerical minority in many high schools, especially in the early years. Though they were 64 percent of the four-county Valley population in 1950, for example, they made up only 23 percent of the senior class that year. In that same year, only 7 percent of Valley teachers were Mexican American. None of the principals nor the superintendents of the ten schools we examined were Hispanic. Mexican Americans were clearly outsiders and were generally treated as such.

Much has changed since then. According to the data shown in Figure 5.1, Hispanic seniors in 1990 had come to represent a higher percentage in schools than the proportion of Hispanics in the overall Valley population.[16] Enrollment data from the Texas Education Agency [17] reveal that in 1995, over 90 percent of students in Region One (South Texas)[18] were Hispanic. In the following sections, we will examine how the treatment of Mexican American students by other students, by teachers, and by school personnel has changed over the years.

STUDENT-INITIATED DISCRIMINATION

In the 1950s, not all Anglos were segregated from Mexican Americans. Frank's parents were Anglo, but because they were poor, he lived on the Hispanic side of McAllen. "My brother and I were the only Anglos in our neighborhood," he says. "The rest were all Hispanics. We grew up with them, played with them, and became good friends. At least that's what we believed. As we got older, things began to change. One day, a group of us went for a swim at Cascade Pool. When we got there, they told us only Whites were allowed in the pool. So my brother and I went for a swim while the Hispanic kids waited for us. Bad choice. They called us every name in the book, including 'White trash' and 'traitors.' From then on, we were enemies. One day I was walking home from a football game. One of the kids I grew up with beat me up. It was crazy. The Hispanics didn't want us because we were gringos, and the Anglos didn't like us because we lived with the 'Mexicans.' We were outcasts. It's something I never got over."

The saddest part of Frank's story, one that he says little about, is how the system of segregation put kids at odds with each other, forcing them to choose sides. This system included segregated neighborhoods, swimming pools, and schools. Such systems make enemies out of childhood friends. In such situations, name calling and fights frequently erupt. As the name "White trash" suggests, some of the hostility is based as much on class as on race or ethnicity. Olga, for example, remembers feeling inferior because of her clothes. "My mother made all my clothes for me," she says. "One day, I wore a dress I loved and the rich *gringas* laughed and made fun of me. They continually asked me, 'Why are all your dresses homemade? Can't you afford to buy them?' I felt so ashamed and embarrassed. Looking back at it now, though my clothes weren't new or store bought, my mother always made sure I looked nice. Siempre me mandaba bien almidonada [She always sent me looking very prim and proper]. When you think about it, I had my own personal seamstress."

In the earlier periods, Anglo students also frequently ridiculed Mexican food. Often, however, Mexican Americans who made fun of each other had internalized the negative connotations. María Gaetán remembers one Mexican American boy who wanted to be accepted by the Anglos. "One day," she says, "he was making fun of a girl because she was eating a tortilla. While he was laughing at her, some tortillas fell out of his own lunch box. He was really embarrassed because everyone could see he was in the same situation."

As time went on, however, Mexican food ceased being the object of

Percent Saying "Frequently"

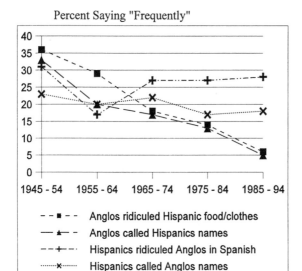

Fig. 5.2. Cross-ethnic discrimination in Rio Grande Valley schools, as reported by former students (Former Students Survey, 1994)

extreme embarrassment. Antonio remembers how this changed from when he and the other Mexican American children had to hide their homemade tacos. "One day," he says, "some Anglo kids saw my tacos and asked me to trade a taste of their lunch for one of mine. From then on, we traded lunch every day. I'd get a ham and cheese sandwich, and they'd get homemade tacos. Those ham and cheese sandwiches on white bread weren't all that great, but that's what I wanted to be seen eating."

The name calling, of course, went both ways. One Anglo who went to school in the 1970s remembers how he acquired a new Mexican American friend. "One day," he says, "Joe saw some kids calling me names in Spanish that I didn't understand, such as 'güero sucio' [dirty Anglo], 'gringo,' 'cochino' [pig; filthy person], and so on. He came over and told them something in Spanish. After that, they left me alone. Joe has been my friend ever since."

In the Former Students Survey, we asked the 40 to 50 individuals from each time period how often Anglos made fun of Mexican American food or clothes, and how frequently Anglos called them names. Similarly, we asked how frequently Mexican Americans made fun of Anglos (in Spanish), and how often Mexican Americans called Anglos names. The results presented in Figure 5.2 show how such practices, as remembered by respondents, have changed over the years.

It is interesting to note that the two forms of Anglo-initiated discrimination, which in the 1945–1954 period were the highest, had be-

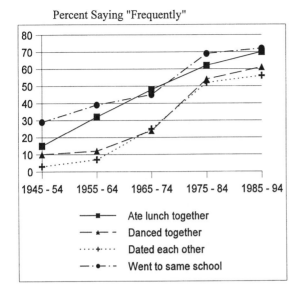

Percent Saying "Frequently"

Fig. 5.3. Cross-ethnic student interaction in the Rio Grande Valley, as reported by former students (Former Students Survey, 1994)

come the lowest by the 1985–1994 period. In contrast, name calling and ridicule by Mexican Americans was reported at virtually the same levels in the last period as it was in the 1945–1954 period. The explanation is probably largely demographic. Anglos had become a minority in the schools by the latter period. In fact, in some high schools, especially those in smaller towns, it was hard to find many Anglos by 1994. This is reflected in an interview with a recent graduate of PSJA (Pharr–San Juan–Alamo) High School. "When I was in high school," he says, "many of us Mexican students didn't like the Anglos. If they weren't smart enough to enroll somewhere else, some of us would pick a fight with them. Most eventually moved to different schools. We had only four Anglos in a senior class of 404 students."

Though Anglos do experience hostility in some Valley high schools, they do not experience it to the same degree, nor in the same forms, that Mexican Americans did in the early years. The ethnic segregation in the early years has been largely replaced by class-based interaction. In fact, interethnic mixing has become rather common, as the survey data presented in Figure 5.3 show. This figure, based on recollections of high school students in each of five time periods, reveals a pronounced pattern of increased interaction across ethnic lines. Though all forms of mixing have greatly increased, the most personal forms, dancing together and dating, have remained somewhat below the less personal forms.

Only if we understand the extent of segregated relations in the earlier periods can we appreciate the magnitude of this change. Dating between Anglos and Mexican Americans in the earlier periods, for example, was a common taboo. Mr. Casárez remembers a girl from Indiana in his English class. "I asked her for a date," he remembers, "and she said she'd go out with me. Two or three days later, she told me she couldn't. When I asked why, she flat out said, 'My friends told me they couldn't be my friends if I go out with you.' I said, 'Okay, that's your decision.'"

Often the patterns of exclusion carry over into adulthood. Polly Torres remembers the school dances in the 1950s in high school. "Usually the only time we got together," she says, "was at a prom or some other social event. We went because it was a school activity. Still, the Anglos didn't dance with us. It's funny, but now, at our reunions, the Anglos stay on one side of the room and we're on the other. They were civil to us back then, but that was all. That's just the way it was then."

In the early years, segregation was not limited to dances and dating. Mary remembers an Anglo friend who rode with her on the same school bus. "One day," she recalls, "my friend asked me to sit with her. I got up from the back of the bus where we Mexicans were and sat down by her. The bus driver saw us together in his rearview mirror. He stopped the bus and ordered me to get back where I belonged. Humiliated, I went to the back of the bus. I never pulled that stunt again."

Something similar happened in many classrooms during the 1945–1954 time period. Alma recalls how teachers in the elementary schools would seat the Mexican American students in the back of the room at the beginning of the school year. She says, "They expected us to remain quiet during class if we wanted to pass. Many of those teachers thought we only came to school to waste time and that we didn't want to learn."

Yet Figures 5.2 and 5.3 show that some Mexican Americans were included in various forms of interaction in the earlier periods. Nevertheless, such cross-ethnic mixing then was almost always between Anglos and Mexican Americans considered "higher class." Sam, for example, is a light-complected Mexican American who attended McAllen High School in the 1955–1964 period. "I joined the varsity football team," he says, "and soon became popular with the jocks. I was once almost crowned Prom King. I lost by a couple of votes. I felt sorry for the other Mexican Americans. I wanted to be friendly with them, but if I had, my Anglo friends would have ridiculed me. I wish I had done it anyway. A few years ago, I went to a class reunion. I felt like a hypocrite because I was the only Hispanic there. I left after a couple of minutes."

One striking aspect of many of the stories of exclusion from the earlier periods is the resignation with which many accepted it. Charlie

Martínez, for example, says, "You always had a couple of Hispanics in groups like student council. But most of the time the Anglos had all the positions. They could communicate better and had more confidence. Things were just like that."

Frances Garza also learned to take for granted the exclusion of Mexican American students. "The social situation then," she says, "was just accepted by everyone. The club officers were mostly Anglos. We never really thought much about it. We just thought that's the way it was supposed to be. The first time I really thought about it was when my sister was in band. My parents and all of us went to the Pigskin Jubilee. I remember how shocked we were when we heard 'Here comes the La Joya Band' and their drum major had a Mexican last name. We said, 'La Joya's drum major is a Mexicana?' It was funny to me. It was like I just didn't expect it. I don't know."

Not all exclusion of Hispanics from school organizations in the early periods was bigotry. Some of it, for example, was based on cultural ideas, including definitions about gender roles. Sonia remembers how her parents discouraged her participation in school organizations. "My parents," she recalls, "wanted me to graduate from high school, find a husband, and have children. My teachers reinforced that belief. I wanted to join band and play the saxophone, but my parents and my teachers said the best organization for me was Future Homemakers—that it would teach me tasks I would be doing for the rest of my life. I really hated it and wasn't the only one. They also discouraged many of my friends from joining organizations. They thought we were stupid and needed the time to learn our subjects. Hogwash! We were smart, but the gringos made us feel like dumb Mexicans. In the classrooms, the *gabachos* [Whites] always had the right answers. We didn't."

Linda remembers always trying to impress the Anglo girls. "I even tried out for cheerleading," she says. "This was in 1958. On the day of the tryouts, I noticed I was the only Hispanic girl with dark legs. I ran out of there and never tried out for anything again." Mrs. de la Garza, a junior at McAllen High School during the same time, also attempted to become a cheerleader. "When I went to the tryouts," she says, "everyone looked at me like I was weird. Finally, someone came over and told me they didn't need someone with a Mexican accent ruining their cheers. I felt so bad. I just walked out."

Anglos who engaged in such discrimination were thus able to see themselves as something besides bigots. Though they rejected Mexican Americans, it was for a bad accent, dark complexion, poor performance in academic subjects, and so forth. The fact that *some* Mexican Americans were allowed to participate made the exclusion seem legitimate. "If you can only be like the good Hispanics," they seemed to say, "we would be happy to accept you."

Those unable to look "higher class," however, were not only excluded but blamed for not trying. Tom, an Anglo who grew up with Mexican American friends, for example, blamed them, though he had few prejudices. "My father was a farmer," he says, "and would hire them to work for him. Sometimes he made fun of them, but he never told me not to mingle with them. Sometimes he even invited them for dinner. This one Anglo hated them. He would call me 'Mexican lover.' It didn't bother me, but it aggravated me to know that they did not want the Mexican Americans. In high school, the few who joined the clubs were just 'tokens.' They didn't even look Hispanic. But they never got to be officers of any clubs. They didn't try because they knew they wouldn't win. That's one thing I never understood about them. Too many of them give up without even trying."

As time went on, more Mexican Americans were accepted on the football teams and in student organizations. In part, it was because Mexican Americans were gaining political power in their communities. Some were even elected to school boards. David's experience illustrates this. "In my last year of high school," he says, "I really wanted to be student council president. I campaigned for two months. My Anglo opponent was the son of a highly respected school board member. When the time came to count the votes, I had obviously won. When my opponent's father heard the news, he came to the high school to demand a recount. When that didn't change the results, he insisted on another election. Lucky for me, my father's best friend was the only Mexican American board member. He talked to other board members. They agreed that the election had been fair, and that the office of student council president was rightfully mine."

The extent and the pace of the change are reflected in Figure 5.4, which shows how often subjects in the Former Students Survey from each period recall Mexican Americans frequently occupying key student positions. To check the accuracy of their recollections, we compared these responses with an actual count of Hispanics in key positions, as found in the yearbook study. The results from the two studies are quite similar. In 1950, for example, 12 percent of cheerleaders in the ten high schools examined were Hispanic. By 1990, this figure had risen to 80 percent, in increments much like the curve shown in Figure 5.4. Similarly, in 1950, only 10 percent of student council officers were Hispanic, with the figure rising to 80 percent by 1990. The similarity of such data

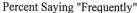

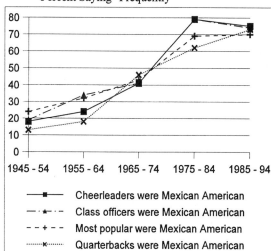

Fig. 5.4. Inclusion of Mexican Americans in student activities in Rio Grande Valley schools, as reported by former students (Former Students Survey, 1994)

to those shown in Figure 5.4 supports recollections of survey respondents as a means of describing ethnic relations in South Texas from 1945 to 1994.

TEACHER-INITIATED DISCRIMINATION

We asked students from each period to describe how teachers and other school personnel treated Mexican American students. Not all accounts, of course, were negative. Omar, for example, remembers getting home from school one afternoon in the early 1960s and finding his mother very ill. He knew she had stomach cancer, but that day she felt really sick. "She had run out of medicine," he recalls. "We were so poor that we couldn't afford a car, and the nearest drugstore was several miles away in Weslaco. I was really worried and didn't know what to do. The next day, I told my coach about it. Though he was sometimes a mean person, like all other Whites we knew, he offered to take me to Weslaco to buy my mother's medication. Though my mother passed away a short time later, I have never forgotten his kind act."

We asked respondents in the Former Students Survey how common it was for teachers to go out of their way to help students who spoke almost no English. For each of the first three decades, approximately 20 percent of respondents said it frequently happened. In the 1975–1984 period, 27 percent said it was frequent, and in the 1985–1994 period, the percent of "frequent" responses rose to 46 percent.

Anastacio also remembers a kind third-grade teacher. "I had an Anglo teacher," he says, "who really helped me. She encouraged me to go to summer school because I was doing well in all my subjects except math. She even came to my home and talked to my parents about sending me to summer school. I have never forgotten her." Juan Martínez also remembers a teacher who would go to students' houses if they missed school to see if they were okay. "She would bring my family food and fresh fruit," he recalls. "Once she took me and other Mexican students to a used-clothes store after school. She bought us all clothes. I was very happy because any clothes were like brand new for me. I will never forget her."

On some occasions, giving things to students was not handled so well. Antonia Morales, for example, still gets upset when she remembers an incident in the second grade. "My teacher brought me her daughter's old clothes and gave them to me in front of the class," she recalls. "She then said something like, 'I thought you needed them more than my daughter.' I then ran home crying to my mother, but she wouldn't do anything about it."

More than kindness or abuse, most of the personal accounts of treatment by teachers deal with neglect. Dr. Miller, a retired history professor from UT–Pan American, recalls an invitation he received in the 1960s to visit a local school district to talk about Mexican American culture. "I looked around at the teachers in that room," he says, "and saw only one who was Hispanic. The Anglos didn't want to hear anything about Mexican American heritage, the historical background of their students, or of Mexican cultural values. I got the impression from them, 'Why bother about them because they're going to work out in the fields anyway?' That was their mentality back then."

Respondents from the Former Students Exploratory Interviews often spoke of how difficult it was to get teachers to pay attention to them. "We needed help," says Juan Narváez, "but most of the time we got none. So in time, we learned to stay quiet." Estela Almendárez, a sixty-year-old woman living in Pharr, agrees. "Back then," she says, "the Mexican American was in limbo in the school. Unless you were having a fit, they wouldn't recognize you. They were trying to reach the Anglos. They were constantly hinting to us, the Mexican Americans, that we weren't the equal of the Anglos."

George Mendoza agrees that being recognized was difficult. He disagrees, though, that it was necessary to keep quiet. "I wouldn't let them ignore me," he says. "Once I was the only one who knew the answer to the question, and the teacher wouldn't call on me, though I had my hand raised. So I stood on my desk and yelled out the answer."

Sometimes the message of inferiority was unspoken. Robert recalls the time he was called to the board to do some math problems. "I don't think any of us had seen these problems before," he says. "I couldn't do them. Everyone laughed, and the teacher simply told me to sit down. He never did explain the problems to me. Trying to get help was an almost useless task."

There were other subtle ways of conveying Anglo "superiority." Julio remembers when his teacher talked about health and nutrition. "She asked me, 'Julius, what did you have for breakfast this morning?' Shocked by the question, I simply replied, 'Miss, I had a cup of coffee with tacos.' I could tell the answer was wrong by the grin on her face, the shaking of her head in disappointment, and the laughter of my class-mates. She proceeded to ask another student the same question. 'Steve, what did you have for breakfast this morning?' Steve proudly replied, 'Ma'am, I had cereal, milk, two eggs, toast, and orange juice for break-fast.' She smiled in approval and said, 'Now class, that's a nutritional breakfast.' From that moment on, I got smart. Whenever some teacher would ask what I had for breakfast, I'd answer, 'Ma'am, I had cereal, milk, two eggs, toast, and orange juice!'"

Some individuals recall harsher treatment by teachers. Emma re-members her class practicing the Gettysburg Address in the auditorium. "I knew it well," she says, "and Mrs. Pryor knew I did. When I got on-stage, however, I froze and I couldn't remember it. She laughed sarcasti-cally and said, 'Mental block, huh, you dumb Mexican!' I told her, 'If you'll give me a hint, I can do it.' She had a good laugh and then asked one of the students to help me."

Mexican American students in the 1950s often found themselves un-able to fight such treatment without suffering severe consequences. Car-los Alaniz remembers a history teacher who was often cruel toward His-panics. "I didn't like going to his class," he says. "One day he called on me to answer a question from our workbook. I didn't know what to say. I started to sweat. Then I replied, 'I don't know, sir.' He said, 'You dumb Mexican. You will never amount to anything.' I was so angry. I wanted to hit him. Instead, I threw a book at him. I knew that would get me in trouble, so I ran out of the class. Later I learned I was expelled from school."

Many former students remember the inequality of treatment be-tween Hispanic and Anglo students more than the severity of their pun-ishment. Jesús "Jessie" Contreras remembers high school as a time when he was blamed whenever something went wrong. "One day," he recalls, "a fire started in the school and I happened to be close by. Since I was known as 'el malillo' [the bad one], they blamed me for it. Weeks later,

Percent Saying "Frequently"

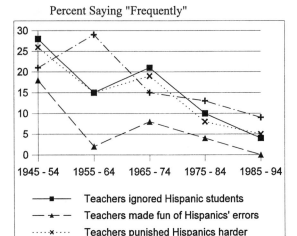

Fig. 5.5. Teacher discrimination against Mexican American students in Rio Grande Valley schools, as reported by former students (Former Students Survey, 1994)

the son of a teacher confessed to starting the fire. They did almost nothing to him and expelled me from school, even after they found out I was innocent."

The situation for many Hispanic students did not improve much when the schools began to hire Mexican American teachers and principals. Mayra Chapa had a teacher who would always pick on the Mexican American students in class. "He was a Mexican teacher, too," she says. "He gave us a quiz one day, and in the quiz he inserted a brainteaser. He said that he would award ten points to anyone who answered the question correctly. I was just an average student in class and very quiet. I didn't know the answer, so I guessed. The next day when he had graded our quiz he came into the room and started by saying, 'There was only one person who answered the question right, and it was her!' He pointed to me in anger. He asked, 'Did you know the answer or did you guess?' I didn't want to lie, so I told him I had guessed. 'I knew it,' he said, 'You'll get no extra credit.' He didn't even give me credit for the quiz."

In the Former Students Survey, we asked respondents from each period how often teachers ignored Hispanic students, made fun of their errors, or punished them more harshly than Anglo students. We also asked how often, when they were in school, Mexican American teachers treated Hispanic students more harshly than did the Anglo teachers. The results, by ten-year periods, are presented in Figure 5.5.

All forms of teacher discrimination except that by Mexican American teachers follow a similar pattern. That is, less discrimination from the first period to the second, and then a resurgence in the third, followed by a continuing decline in the fourth and fifth periods. The increase in the third period, we suspect, was a backlash against the Chicano movement that characterized this period. Many former students report, for example, that efforts by Chicano students to assert their rights were met by increased harshness from teachers and administrators. Only after they had established these rights, and increasing numbers of Mexican Americans remained in school, did the negative treatment decline.

One Anglo teacher described an encounter in the 1970s with the new Chicano assertiveness. "I was walking out to my car after school when about five of my male students surrounded me to complain about their grades," she says. "I told them if they really wanted to talk about it, we should go back inside. They said they wanted to talk about it right there. One of them stepped forward and asked why they all had failed and all of the 'Whities' in the class had passed. He said I thought a 'wetback' couldn't do as well as a White person. I assured them that they all got the grade they deserved and said, 'All you need to do is try a little harder.' This enraged them. One of them grabbed me from behind. Just then, a police officer driving by saw the tussle and stopped. The boys moved back, but they didn't run. The officer asked if anything was wrong, but I said no and covered for them. After he left, one of them said I was just afraid to face them later. He was sure no White person, teacher or not, would ever help a 'wetback.' Four of them never showed up for class the rest of the year. The one that did worked hard and pulled off a C. Just before summer, he asked why I hadn't turned them in. I told him that all of them could have passed and only needed encouragement to live good lives. He didn't quite understand but said he would try to go on like I thought he could."

The somewhat different pattern of discrimination by Mexican American teachers shown in Figure 5.5 requires a different explanation. Why did it increase from the first to the second period? Also, why did it decline from the second to the third period, while other forms of teacher discrimination were increasing? Two factors seem important. First, Hispanic teachers in the early period were the first ones allowed into the all-Anglo teaching ranks. No doubt they were carefully screened to assure they had the "proper" view of things. Likewise, they knew the Anglos were watching them for any leniency toward Mexican American students. In such an atmosphere, Hispanic teachers might bend over backward to show no favoritism.

Olga learned this the hard way in high school. "On my way to class," she says, "a group of Anglo boys started picking on me, chanting, 'Dirty, stinky Mexican!' I tried to keep walking, but they wouldn't let me out of their circle. I looked around for a teacher and saw Mr. González. He saw them, but he just kept walking. I felt stabbed in the back by one of my own people. Just then Mr. Smith stepped in and stopped the boys. He made them apologize and dragged them to the principal's office. I was grateful for his help but could never understand why Mr. González wouldn't help me."

Some Hispanic teachers seem to have mentally distanced themselves from ordinary Mexican Americans. Indeed, many of them preferred to be called "Latin Americans" or avoided any labels that would identify them as something other than a regular American. Patricia Saenz remembers a Hispanic typing teacher who did not think of herself as Hispanic. "In class," she says, "she was always laughing and talking with the Anglos. The only thing she'd say to us was, 'Get to work!' or 'No talking!' She sat us Mexican Americans in the back. During tests, she stayed back there to make sure we didn't cheat. She never said anything bad to us, but it was the cold treatment that hurt. We couldn't even laugh when she or the girls in the front said something funny. If we did, they would turn around and look at us until we'd stop and get back to work."

THE GREAT DIVIDE

Even after schools were desegregated, many classrooms, like that just described by Patricia, remained divided. Increasingly, Mexican Americans of light complexion who could speak English without an accent were included with the Anglos. The message was clear: 'Start looking and talking like us and we'll accept you—almost.' Ana Valencia was one of those allowed to cross over. She recalls how it felt. "My first-grade teacher liked me," she recalls, "and gave me lots of attention. My parents taught us English before we started school. She treated me nicer than the kids who were dark complected and didn't speak English. She hardly paid any attention to them. One day, she divided the classroom into two groups. On her left side, she put the darker Mexican Americans. On her right were the White students. I was Hispanic, but she put me with the White students. Then she said, 'I've divided you so I can remember the ones that need the most help.' After that, everyone stayed with their group, on the playground or in the classroom. Our group could roam around for 'free time,' and she was always more helpful to us. For a while, I began to think I was White."

In the first period of our study, from 1945 to 1954, classes were often divided. Alicia remembers having to sit in the back of the classroom in the third grade because that was where the "Mexicans" belonged. "We were never to speak Spanish at any time," she recalls. "One day I got caught speaking Spanish to my friend because I hardly knew any English. The teacher came up to me and slapped me across the face and told me never to speak Spanish in her class again. So the rest of the year, I kept quiet and never said a word in class again. The following year, I just quit going to school completely. I haven't set foot in a classroom since."

Some students during these earlier years received little encouragement to stay in school. Eusebio López remembers when his mother passed away. "My dad sat me down," he says, "and told me I had to help support my younger brothers and sisters. I agreed because I was the oldest. Right before I did though, my White advisor had a talk with me. For a moment, I thought he would try to talk me out of it. But he only encouraged me to do what my dad had asked. I was disappointed, but what could a thirteen-year-old do? I worked for a gasoline station for years. I always encouraged my brothers and sisters to stay in school, but only two of them ever graduated. I taught myself to read and write, and now I own several gas stations."

Tomás Ramírez experienced more direct pressure to quit school. "One day when I was a sophomore," he says, "a counselor stopped me to ask if I had a license to drive my truck. When I said yes, he said, 'Well, isn't your father a labor contractor?' I answered yes, he was. So he asked, 'Then why don't you quit school and help him work?' I didn't understand why he wanted me to quit school. I wanted to graduate. They were very degrading toward Mexicans. They tried their best to encourage us to quit school."

During the 1965 to 1974 period, more Hispanic students made it through high school to graduation. Still, few were encouraged to go on to college. Roberto Salinas, as a senior in high school, made the all-district football team and was elected captain. Also, he played baseball. "One day," he says, "I went to the coach's office to talk about where to go to college. He said, 'Now, Roberto, son, you're a damn good hitter, but that's all you'll ever be. Join the service where they need men like you, or find a good vocational school that will accept you. But forget about college. It's too hard for you.' I couldn't accept that, so I went to a counselor for advice. He told me the same thing! I did join the service, but afterward I graduated from college."

Often the discouragement was more subtle. Chuck Limón remembers when a teacher asked each person in class about their college plans. "When she came to an Anglo," he recalls, "she would ask, 'What college are you planning to go to?' But when she came to a Hispanic student, she would ask, 'Are you going to college?' That wasn't very encouraging."

Starting in the 1965 to 1974 period, teachers had to be more careful about blatant discrimination. Some of them, however, maintained the old beliefs about Hispanics being best suited for field work and the like. Mónica remembers her sophomore year when one of her sisters dropped out. "My Anglo counselor called me in," she says, "to find out if I also planned to drop out. I told her I wanted to graduate and go on to become a nurse. She didn't like the idea. She suggested I should drop out 'temporarily' to help my family. I got angry and asked her why she wanted to keep me from what I wanted to do. I told her my grades were very good and I never gave my teachers a hard time. I demanded to know why she wanted me to drop. I raised my voice to her, so she got upset and yelled back, 'Because you Mexi—' I don't know why she didn't finish her statement. I just left. I finished school, went to college, and became a nurse!"

Often school officials encouraged Mexican American males to join the military. Leo Soto remembers a career day in his high school. "We were all walking around the gym," he says, "trying to decide which university representative we wanted to talk to. We walked up to a representative of a major university. Well there was a long line of Anglos, and he was giving them a big pitch about his university. When we Mexican Americans got there, though, he just gave us a brochure and said, 'You boys look like you would be good for our country's military.' I threw the brochure on his table and walked off."

In the Former Students Survey, we asked about the ways Mexican American students were tracked away from college. We asked respondents from each period, for example, how often during their school years teachers, counselors, or principals discouraged Mexican Americans from going to college. We also asked how often counselors encouraged Mexican Americans to join the military or get a job in unskilled labor. Finally, we asked how often college prep courses were mainly for Anglos and vocational courses were mainly for Mexican Americans. The percentages from each period who answered "frequently" are shown in Figure 5.6.

These responses reveal a pattern strikingly similar to the one regarding treatment by teachers (Figure 5.5). There, as here, the percentage of "frequent" responses on each item declined from the first to the second period, went back up in the third period, and then declined for the fourth period. Two items continued the decline in the final period, while two remained essentially unchanged during this last period.

Again demographics and political change may explain much of this pattern. By the 1956–1964 period, the few Hispanics who made it to

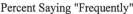

Percent Saying "Frequently"

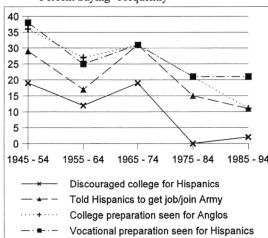

Fig. 5.6. Forms of administrative tracking of Mexican American students in Rio Grande Valley schools, as reported by former students (Former Students Survey, 1994)

high school were usually light skinned and well assimilated. They probably did not experience much discrimination. Desegregation brought many others in the third period, though, who had to be admitted, but were still regarded as unsuited for college. By the fourth period, politics made such bigotry unacceptable. In addition, by this time, Hispanic students far outnumbered Anglos in the high schools. But even in the last period, more than 20 percent of respondents believed that Mexican Americans were being tracked into vocational courses.

Additional forms of tracking have emerged in recent years. Some of them are designed to help Hispanic students. In 1980 Mary Lozano went to register her daughter in kindergarten. School officials wanted to test the child to determine how much English she knew. "I informed them," she says, "that my daughter was more comfortable with English. I asked if they were testing all students, and they told me that only Spanish-surname children would take the exam. I refused to let them test her. Still they put her in the all-day class for monolingual Spanish-speaking children. We filed a complaint with the principal and the school district. Even the teacher recognized that it was hard on the few children who were not fluent in Spanish. She had them retested, and finally they were placed in the half-day, all-English class."

A more subtle form of tracking has come about in recent years because of state-mandated tests. Texas has an accountability rating system for public school districts that is based on exams given to children, starting in the third grade. If more than 30 percent of students in a district fail the exam, the district receives an unacceptable rating. Because children categorized as special education students are not required to take the exam, however, districts officials are tempted to place many at-risk students in this category. In 1995, 9.1 percent of Hispanic students in the South Texas border region were categorized as special education students.

In addition, until recently, limited English proficiency (LEP) children were not required to take the exam. The temptation to exempt LEP children from the exam is especially great in South Texas, since almost half the children start the first grade with little or no knowledge of English. Nevertheless, in 1995 a Spanish version was finally available for third-grade students. Each year, another grade will be included. School districts struggling to avoid the unacceptable rating will no longer be able to exempt children from the exam because of limited English. They will either take the scores as they come, or place additional children in the special education category to avoid having them tested.

Many such programs pose a threat of reduced expectations. One woman whose husband is a melon farmer goes north to Pearsall, Texas, each season. "Government migrant programs were just beginning in our little community north of Edinburg," she says. "Some of our workers asked us to register our children as migrants so they'd have enough families to qualify for the program. We had no problem with that and filled out all the necessary papers. About that time, our eighth-grade son took an achievement test. His math teacher showed me his scores and said, 'He blew the top off the scores!' When he entered high school, however, they placed him in a general math course. I talked to his counselor who told me that all migrant students were in general math because it was easier for them to pass. Boy was I mad! I went straight to the president of the school board. If this could happen to my son, I knew that they had given others the same treatment with no regard to their capabilities. Finally, they put my son and a few migrant students into more challenging math and English classes."

The issue of bilingual education as a separate track, of course, is far too complex to deal with justly here. Many educators believe it tends to "dumb down" the expectations of limited English proficiency children. It becomes a slow track with general math offered instead of algebra and a curriculum that leaves children unprepared for college preparatory classes in high school.

Not every district has fallen prey to reduced expectations. La Joya and Pharr–San Juan–Alamo, for example, have bilingual education for all children. While LEP children are taking English classes, limited

Spanish proficiency (LSP) students are learning Spanish. They thus avoid the trap of considering monolingual Spanish students as "handicapped." Unfortunately, the enrollment of Anglo students is so low in these two districts as to barely affect bilingual education for Anglos in the Valley.

Sink or Swim?

Some opponents of bilingual education long for the days when Spanish was prohibited on school grounds. They claim the sink or swim method actually helped children become bilingual faster than today's programs. A few of the people we interviewed said they were glad the teachers let them speak only English. "If they hadn't pushed us, who would have?" remarks one man who went through the English-only system. As to whether Hispanics were made to feel like dunces, he responds, "Not all the teachers were harsh and mean. Some actually cared, and that's why we never quit."

Nonetheless, in the early periods, when the English-only rule was in force, punishments were often extreme. Thirty-eight percent of respondents from the first period said that violations of the rule were frequently punished with physical force, and another 32 percent said physical force was occasionally used. Martha Salazar remembers what these punishments were like. "When I was in grade school," she says, "the only girl I could talk to was my friend Nelda. At school, we were punished if we spoke any Spanish. We were both embarrassed to speak English, though, because we couldn't speak it well. So we would talk quietly to each other in Spanish. One day, some girls heard us talking Spanish. They said they were going to tell the teacher. A few minutes later, our teacher approached us. She sent us to the office, and we each got a spanking. When we got back to our classroom, she made us face different corners. Then we had to write, 'I will not speak in Spanish' five hundred times."

Sometimes, the no-Spanish rule was used as a cloak for bigotry. Minerva remembers when she was in fourth grade. "Our principal hated us Mexican Americans," she says. "One day a new boy came to our school. His English was very bad, so he was speaking in Spanish when the principal passed by. He reached out and grabbed the new boy and shook him very hard. Then he got a paddle and hit this boy, over and over, until the boy fainted. Then he turned to the rest of us and said the same thing would happen to us if he caught any of us speaking Spanish. The new boy never came back to school, and I never spoke Spanish in school again."

Some forms of punishment served only to humiliate Spanish speakers. "The entire faculty in my elementary school were Anglos," recalls Juan Rodríguez. "They put all of us Mexican American children in the same classes and told us not to talk to each other in Spanish. Those who did were reported and punished. Every day, the children and teachers all met before classes in the auditorium. They called any child who had spoken Spanish on the school grounds onstage and swatted them in front of everyone. It worked for some, but others just dropped out."

Another consequence of the English-only system was to turn Hispanic children against each other. Carlos Contreras remembers when his friends dared him to say something in Spanish. "At first," he says, "I told them no. Then they started calling me chicken, so I gave in. Sure enough, I got caught and was given several 'licks' on my hand with a ruler. I'll never forget my friends' faces when the teacher hit me. It was hard enough speaking Spanish without letting the teacher find out, but it was even harder when friends started telling on each other. One boy, who really wanted to get on the teacher's good side, was always looking for someone to report. One day, he told the teacher, 'Look, Miss, he's laughing in Spanish.' The teacher just laughed at his comment, and he felt hurt. Some kids would try anything to be a teacher's pet, even if it meant telling on their friends."

Perhaps worse was that the English-only rule deprived children of the means to communicate even basic information, leading to confusion and serious injustices. Lupe remembers when a boy who sat next to him had to go to the bathroom. "Neither of us knew how to ask in English," he says, "but the Anglo kids always said, 'May I be excused?' All I could remember was *be-skuse* because I thought that was the English word for bathroom. We weren't allowed to talk in class so I was whispering it to him. He kept telling me, 'No entiendo [I don't understand],' so I repeated it louder until our teacher came over and reprimanded both of us. I was upset so I stood up and pointed to Toño, my friend, and said, 'Be-skuse, be-skuse.' It was evident she didn't understand, so I tried telling her in Spanish. Then she got even more upset. So we both got in trouble and Toño ended up wetting his pants. Until junior high, I thought the English name for restroom was *be-skuse*."

Ricky Alameda remembers being spanked for not understanding all that they said to him. One day on the playground, he and another boy accidentally ran into a little girl. The teacher asked them if they had done it on purpose. The boys looked at each other asking, "¿Qué es *purlpus?*" (What is *purlpus?*). "We shrugged our shoulders," he says, "and nodded our heads yes. They promptly took us to the office and spanked us for hitting someone. The lesson was well learned. We never again admitted hitting anyone else 'on purlpus.'"

Even after the no-Spanish rule was banned in Texas, problems continued for several years. Pablo Arredondo remembers his freshman year at McAllen High School. "I was a quiet student," he says, "and kept to myself. During my algebra class, I remember turning back and asking my classmate, in Spanish, to return my eraser. When I turned back around, my teacher, who was Anglo, said, 'If you want to speak Spanish, go back to Mexico.' Well, I wasn't from Mexico. My family has been here for three generations. At home we speak both Spanish and English. He sent me to the principal's office. They called my parents and told me that I could stay in my algebra class only if I would apologize to my teacher in front of the class. Since I refused, I was dropped from the class and was placed in the lowest math class available."

Having teachers who did not understand Spanish created other problems, even when students were no longer punished for speaking Spanish. Mike is thirty years old, the son of migrant farmworkers. One day, he arrived late for his eighth-grade class. As he sat down, he remembered that he had left his homework at home. Angry and talking to himself, he said, "Sonso! [Dummy!]" aloud. The teacher thought he had said a bad word and sent him to the office. The teacher sent a note to the principal saying he had used abusive language in class. "So the principal spanked me," he says. "He also called my parents. Since they were working and could not come to pick me up, he just sent me back to class. The teacher didn't like that. She made me write, 'I will not use abusive language in class,' one hundred times. After that incident, I never spoke another word of Spanish again because they might again misinterpret my words."

Today almost no students report being punished for speaking Spanish. Bilingual education programs even encourage speaking Spanish. Because of migration and higher birth rates among Hispanics, more than 90 percent of students in South Texas schools are Mexican American. The percentage of Hispanics among teachers and administrators, while not equal to that of the student population, has increased dramatically over the years. Mexican Americans are chosen in student-life organizations in about equal proportion to their representation in the schools.

MANY MIGRANT CHILDREN FIND IT DIFFICULT TO KEEP UP WHEN MIGRATING TAKES THEM AWAY FROM SCHOOL DURING MAJOR PORTIONS OF THE SCHOOL YEAR.

Yet many old problems remain. Fifty-eight percent of Hispanic adults twenty-five years of age and older in border counties dropped out of school prior to graduation.[19] Bilingual education and migrant programs often fail to prepare Mexican American students for full participation in college track classes. Standardized test scores for Hispanic high school students are frequently among the lowest in the state. In 1996, for example, only 35 percent of Hispanic eighth-grade students in South Texas met minimum expectations on the statewide Texas Assessment of Academic Skills (TAAS) exam. For Black students, the figure was 43 percent, while 73 percent of Anglo eighth graders met these expectations.[20] The gains made over five decades in South Texas schools seem to fade like a mirage in light of these depressing facts. Much has changed in Valley schools, but they remain the same in what matters most: inequality of educational attainment.

One other depressing fact remains. Race still matters. Dark complexion still labels many Hispanic children as "low class" and "better suited for field labor." Recently, a researcher at UT–Pan American did an experiment with a high school class of Hispanic children. He showed them pictures of students from another high school, cut out of the school's yearbook, and asked them to categorize the students based solely on their pictures. The Hispanic children showed a high degree of consensus, putting about half the pictures into a pile of those they called "cholos," a word for low-income Hispanics seen as troublemakers. As the professor and others examined the pile, they could determine no other basis for this selection than the obviously darker complexion of the students.

Few Hispanics with a lighter complexion, however, seem to want to be Anglos. Many have developed pride in their roots and an ability to stand up to the occasional forms of bigotry that still exist. Gloria is one of them. "Because of my fair skin and blue eyes," she says, "they often mistake me for an Anglo. Once in a cafeteria line at a public restaurant, an elderly Anglo man, a Winter Texan, leaned over to me and whispered, while pointing to a Mexican family that had just entered, 'Don't you hate dirty Mexicans like that?' I leaned over and whispered back, 'No, I'm Mexican, so I hate bigots like you.' His bottom lip fell to the floor. He said, 'But you look Anglo.' I smiled, 'Surprise!'"

From Mexicanos to Mexican Americans

Chapter 6

*My family moved to
Detroit when I was just
starting school. The Anglo
kids there didn't like having
us Mexican Americans on
the bus with them, so they
made life miserable for us.
They teased me because of
my color, my accent, and the
way I dressed. My parents
didn't think it was important, but it got so bad I
wanted to quit school. I
begged them to move back
to Mexico. Instead they
moved us here to the Valley
to be with relatives. I felt a
lot better because the people
here are mostly Hispanic.
But my parents couldn't
stand the way Mexican
Americans here had changed
their language and their
culture to be more like the
Anglos. It didn't bother me
because I felt we were all
just trying to fit in. So I
assimilated into the Anglo
culture and raised my children in Anglo ways. Lately,
I've come to realize that
I've lost something.*

TINA MORALES, 1991

Tina's experience is both normal and unique.
It is normal in that she, like many immigrant
children, experienced teasing, isolation, and discrimination. Like many immigrants, she also
missed her home and longed to return. Her situation is unique, however, because she under-
went the assimilation process of going from
Mexican to Mexican American to just American
in a single generation.[1] In the process, she discovered she had left something valuable behind.

Tina also discovered certain difficulties in
the relationship between Mexicanos and Mexican Americans in South Texas. Both speak
Spanish, though certain linguistic differences
divide and inflame.[2] In addition, the deep loyalties that some Mexican immigrants feel toward
Mexico irritate those Mexican Americans who
feel strong allegiances to the United States.
Furthermore, Mexican Americans often dislike
the class bias of well-to-do Mexicans, while
these same Mexicans deplore the distortions of
Mexican culture by *pochos* (anglicized Mexican
Americans). As a result, unity is often strained
when both groups are struggling to climb the
same ladder.[3]

Paula is another immigrant who now con-
siders herself a Mexican American. The strained
relation between Mexicans and Mexican Americans surprised her when she arrived in the
United States at the age of nine. "It was very
hard to adjust," she says. "I didn't know a word
of English. I remember that first day of class. I
had always been in the same class with my sister, but they would not allow sisters to be in the

same class. I felt so alone. All the children looked at me. When they spoke, it was always in English. Even the Mexican American children made fun of me. After class I ran out crying. The teacher later sat me down and explained what they had discussed that day. I felt such relief when she spoke to me in Spanish. I missed home desperately and wanted to go back to Mexico."

Some immigrants do return to Mexico, but most hang on and eventually adjust.[4] Then when they have children, they see disturbing signs that signal they cannot control what culture is retained or which traits will replace it. These families begin the age-old process of Americanization, though in an environment quite unlike that faced by the waves of immigrants who passed through Ellis Island. In this chapter, we will hear them describe their own experience, taking their accounts from several Borderlife interview projects.

Few topics attract the attention of our student interviewers like that of immigration to the United States from Mexico. Many UT–Pan American students are themselves immigrants. Others have parents or grandparents who came from Mexico. Most have some relatives still living in Mexico. Many students work in stores or restaurants where almost every other customer is Mexican. As a result, UT–Pan American students often choose to conduct interviews on topics such as the *bracero* experience, undocumented workers, immigration officials, diverse cultural orientations, and the relationship between Mexicans and Mexican Americans.

These topics inform the Mexican Immigrant Exploratory Interviews reported in this chapter. They also helped us design two additional survey interview projects that provide quantifiable measures of key variables. One is the Mexican Immigrants Survey, a survey of 324 Mexican immigrants living in South Texas (Appendix B, no. 6). The other is the Multiethnic Culture Survey, a survey of 532 respondents designed to compare the cultural orientations of Mexican Americans (282 respondents), Anglos (165 respondents), and Mexican immigrants (85 respondents) in the Rio Grande Valley (Appendix B, no. 10). Because each survey included both documented and undocumented immigrants, we used a sample of respondents easily accessible to (and trusting of) student interviewers, rather than a random sample.

The Immigration Experience

Because of the proximity of Mexico to the United States, the immigration experience is often a drawn-out process that does not start with a single decision to migrate. Instead, immigrants make many decisions along the way, change their reasons for coming, make occasional trips back to Mexico, and frequently change their plans.

José's experience illustrates this complexity. Like many Mexican immigrants, he came to the United States as a child. He and two brothers, Raúl and Antonio, were born in San Luis Potosí. Their aunt raised them while their mother worked in McAllen as a waitress. "She would send money to my aunt," he remembers, "to feed us and buy us clothes. My aunt had a large family of her own, so the money didn't go far. Sometimes we went to bed without supper. Whenever my aunt bought *bolillos* [bread rolls] or tortillas, we'd sneak some and hide them under our pillows so we could eat them in the dark. We tried selling *chicles* [chewing gum] and newspapers on the streets, but got a bad case of *granos* [boils] that covered our bodies. Every time my aunt bathed us, we cried because the *granos* would burst. She took us to a doctor, but he never found a medicine that worked. They kicked us out of school because we had a contagious disease. When my mother heard we were not attending school, she decided to bring us to the United States.

"We were happy to be in the United States with our mom. She found a doctor who cured the *granos*. We lived in a very small house because it was all we could afford. During this time, my mother was still seeing my dad and got pregnant. But when my sister was born, he left the five of us in a house with no bathroom or kitchen. Fortunately, the neighbors let us use theirs. After eight months, we moved to a larger house on the same lot.

"When school started, they put me in the fifth grade. I was happy to attend school, but I felt like I was in another world. We had little money for clothes, so I had to wear the same thing every day. I didn't understand English, so I thought the other kids were always talking about me. My friends laughed at me because I couldn't understand the English they used. Once, one of them told me pencils were like money—that each was worth a nickel and that I could buy candy with them. Gathering all my pencils, I went to the school store and told the lady I wanted some candies. She looked at me and laughed. My friends called me Nickel from then on. I learned English my first year in school. My teacher even wrote on my report card, 'José está aprendiendo inglés muy bien [José is learning English very well].' My mom was so proud of me when she read that.

"One day, my mother heard that illegal aliens were getting kicked out of the schools. Of the three of us boys, only Antonio was discovered. She sent him back to Mexico for a time, but he came back and enrolled again. When he did, he brought a cousin who could take care of us while my mother was working.

"One day, we saw a green Migra [Border Patrol] van drive up with some agents and our mom in it. We got scared and told our cousin, 'Escóndete debajo de la cama [Hide under the bed].' The Migra saw her trying to hide and got her too. They sent her and my mom back to Mexico. We were scared that they would come back for us, and we could not stand to think of going back to live with my aunt, so we frequently changed houses. While I was in school, we lived in a total of eleven or twelve houses in the Pharr area.

"After I graduated from high school, I wanted to go to college, but I had to register as a nonresident. That meant I had to pay out-of-state tuition, and my mother couldn't afford it. I wanted to work, but I didn't have a social security number. I did yard work for a while and helped members of my church in order to earn money. I got tired of that real quick. I wanted a steady job, so Mom went to *la pulga* [the flea market] and found someone who made me a Social Security card using my little sister's number. I soon got a job as a courtesy clerk in a grocery store. Since we were then living in a federal housing project, I had to go to a friend's house to change clothes so the project director where we lived wouldn't find out I was working and raise the rent.

"Every day, I went to work afraid that the Migra would pick me up. After three years, I quit because many of my Mexican American co-workers told me I was breaking the law. A few months later the Migra got my brother Ramón and processed him for deportation. They gave him thirty days to leave the United States. My mother got a lawyer who sent us to the immigration office in Harlingen. We were able to get everything straight, and I finally got my own Social Security card. I thank God because though we faced many problems we managed to come through. My mother has raised all of us all by herself. Now I can work freely anywhere I want without being afraid of La Migra. After all I have gone through, I can tell a person from any other country that life in the United States is not as easy as it looks in the movies. A person really has to work hard at it."

Why They Come

José's situation illustrates the difficulty of determining why Mexicans migrate to the United States.[5] He came to be with his mother, yet he also wanted to escape a bad situation with his aunt. His mother wanted him here, so he could go to school and get medical attention. She also needed his help in earning income for the family.

In the Mexican Immigrants Survey, we asked respondents to stipulate the main reason they had come to the United States. The results pre-

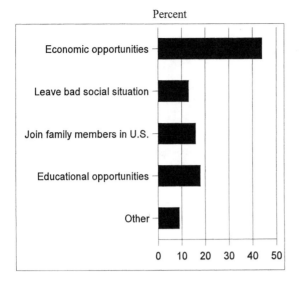

Percent

Fig. 6.1. Reasons for coming to the United States reported by Mexican immigrants in South Texas (Mexican Immigrants Survey, 1995)

sented in Figure 6.1 show that economic factors are most commonly expressed as the main reason for coming. Indeed, 70 percent of respondents reported that their income had increased following their immigration to the United States. However, many respondents expressed concern at having to name a main reason, since so many factors had influenced their decision to come.

Often the motivation for economic advancement is based on distorted information. Carlos remembers growing up in a small *aldea* (village) in southern Mexico. He recalls that life was very hard. "We were eight children growing up in a small two-bedroom home," he says. "Although we were poor, my father always provided food on the table for us to eat, and my mother kept our humble home neat and tidy. One day a neighbor family came back to visit us after having gone to the United States about a year earlier. They drove up in a new car, wearing nice clothes and fancy jewelry. We were really impressed. They seemed so rich and had once been poor just like us. So we came back with them to the Valley. I can see now that they weren't really that much better off than when they left, yet the impression was enough to get us to move here."

Many returning migrants try to show off new wealth, even when it is more imagined than real. This gives many Mexicans a distorted vision of life in the United States. Gustavo recalls when he first came to the United States in the 1950s as a *bracero*. "When the train from Monterrey made a short stop in Monclova," he recalls, "I got down and begged for food. I didn't even have money to buy a taco. On my way back, however, I stopped in Falfurrias [Texas] to buy things to show off to the people from my village. I even bought cigarettes, though I didn't smoke. I guess I just wanted them to believe I was successful, though I really didn't earn all that much money."

For some immigrants, social and cultural concerns are more important than economic considerations. When Hortencia was twelve years old, she thought she was going to get married just like every other girl in her small *pueblo* (town). "My father did not send me to school," she says, "because he believed that I would soon get married. My mother told me that my father would soon be looking for a suitable husband for me. I asked if I could look on my own, but my mother warned me that men would begin to look at me differently after I turned twelve. One night at a fiesta, I met an eighteen-year-old boy. I didn't realize what was happening, and he raped me. After a couple of days, they caught and sent him to jail. My parents decided that staying in our pueblo was not wise. My father sold what little we had and we left. That's how we came. I have a little boy now. I have no regrets. I really don't remember much."

HIGHER-INCOME IMMIGRANTS

Both poor and well-to-do Mexican immigrants experience difficult adjustments when they come to the United States, but the nature of the adjustment is different for each group. Well-to-do Mexican immigrants experience not only cultural shock but also frequently encounter class-related conflicts. "When I first attended a public school in the United States," says Juan Molina, "I couldn't believe what I was seeing. Though it was a good school, academically speaking, almost 90 percent of the students in my first class were lower-class people. They had bad taste in clothing, smelled bad, and they all were dark. When I heard them speak Spanish, I was horrified. I seriously wanted to cry."

Such class bias obviously causes serious conflict. María Valencia, for example, experienced a strong reaction from her classmates one day when her mother sent their maid with a change of clothes. "I waited for our maid near the gate to the playing field," she says. "My mother wanted me to have a change of clothes after the PE class. When the girls saw what was happening, they all started laughing and calling me 'muñequita de pastel' [little cake doll]. One of them even threw a rock at me, but it hit Olga, our maid. I ran after the girl who did it and knocked her down. My mother was really upset when she found out what had happened. She decided to put me in a private school with a lot of Anglos. It's funny, because I got along great with the Anglos."

Juan Molina's account describes another point of conflict, especially with educated Mexicans, and that is the way Spanish is spoken. Teresa remembered her first days in school. "They all laughed at me," she says, "because I would say 'ahí' [there; pronounced "ah-EE"] rather than 'ay' [Valley pronunciation of *ahí*; pronounced "AYE"] and 'silla' [chair; pronounced "SEE-ya"] instead of 'sia' [Valley pronunciation of *silla*; pronounced "SEE-ah"]. One day, one of them asked why I spoke so weird. Making friends with them seemed impossible. When I could see that they wouldn't change, I spoke to my father. He told me, 'You are better than they are and you don't need them.' From then on, I called them *nacos* [lowlifes] and found other friends."

René also comes from a well-to-do Mexican family. His parents insisted that he come to the United States for a few years to learn English and to get a U.S. education. He misses his family and the life he once led. He can scarcely wait to return to Mexico. He has almost nothing positive to say about the United States but will go on for hours about how much he loves Mexico. "Over here," he says, "your laws are too strict, your schools are too easy, and the people are too serious." He says he could never get accustomed to U.S. culture, claiming it really is not a culture at all but just a cheap copy of other cultures. He is a bright student, but his resentment toward the United States causes conflict with local students. He believes that English is an important language, so he will master it before returning to Mexico. Then he plans to work in his family's business.

In the Mexican Immigrants Survey, only 8 percent reported family incomes of more than fifty thousand dollars a year. In contrast, 42 percent reported yearly family incomes of less than thirteen thousand dollars (and approximately the same percentage reported completing six or fewer years of education). These figures may underrepresent well-to-do Mexican immigrants in the Valley because they were harder for student interviewers to find. In addition, few interviewers had previously established relationships with wealthy Mexican immigrants, making it difficult to gain the trust needed for interviews. For these reasons, we will focus primarily on lower- and middle-income immigrants, though we will refer to incidents and data reported by the wealthier ones.[6]

LEGAL VERSUS ILLEGAL ENTRY

Since 1929 legal immigration from Mexico has not been easy. In 1977 it became worse. Mexicans were limited to a quota of only twenty thousand resident visas a year. Though family reunification was the main criterion for granting residency, Mexicans, who have many relatives in the United

States, were allowed no more visas than people from other countries in the Western Hemisphere.[7]

Wealthy Mexicans with money to invest have a much easier time adjusting to a new environment than those who can offer only their labor. Catrina's family is among the better-off immigrant families. They own businesses in Nuevo Progreso, Mexico. She came to the United States with her family so that she and her sister could attend high school. They have a house in La Feria, Texas. Nevertheless, most of her friends are from Mexico. She spends most of her weekends with them, often in Mexico. "Once," she remembers, "the 'in-crowd' at my high school invited me to go with them to a party. Since none of my friends wanted to go, we ended up going to Mexico as we do every weekend."

Antonio Flores also came eight years ago as a legal immigrant. Like many first-generation immigrants who come as adults, he still has a strong allegiance to Mexico. He told his interviewer, "I miss life in Mexico a lot. When I was a bit younger than you, my father would take me to a friend's ranch to show me how to ride a horse. I was scared, but he kept encouraging me until I could ride well. He also took me to the *palenques* [cockfights] quite often. When we'd get back home, he'd show me how to prepare the roosters for battle. I was very close to my father. He's now eighty-two, and I feel really bad that I can't be with him in his final years. Here I never do anything quite as exciting as those things that I used to do with my father. The people here are nice, but not as nice as people in Mexico. It's sad, but you Mexican Americans have lost your identity. You don't know what it means to be a Mexican. You're not all like this, but a lot of you have lost your way. For example, my nephew is a delinquent. He dresses sloppily and listens to wild music. When I see him doing stupid things with his friends, I feel sorry for him. People in Mexico are not like that. I guess that's why I love Mexico so much more."

For many, the affinity to the home country is so strong that they end up returning.[8] María de la Luz is one of them. Contacted for an interview while visiting her family here, she spoke of her earlier experience as an immigrant. "I came to the U.S. legally," she says, "because my brother petitioned the government for me. He thought I could get a better job and my sons could get a good education. When I first came to Texas, we had to live with him because I had no job and no house. The only job I could find was as a maid. The good jobs required experience and education. My sons liked school here and did well. I regretted having come, but I knew my sons would get a better education here. I had seen that my brother and his family were very happy, had a nice house, and dressed well. I didn't stop to think that they had been living here for a long time and that they had gone through a lot of trouble to get where they were. I finally went back to Mexico, but I left my sons with my brother so they could finish school. When I got back to Mexico, it was hard to find a job like my old one. Now my sons have graduated and have good jobs. They keep asking me to come back to the U.S. with them, but I don't want to make the same mistake again. I'll come for visits, but I'll live in Mexico until I die."

Mexican immigrants who come illegally do not have the same degree of choice that María had. Getting into the United States can be such a traumatic experience that few want to risk it with multiple entries. Carlos Ortiz, for example, was robbed by *bandidos* who threatened to kill him if he did not give them all his belongings. "They had rocks in their hands," he says, "and demanded all my money. They even made me give them my shoes. After that, when I tried to find work, nobody would hire me. The employers said that they could be fined ten thousand dollars. When I couldn't find work, I decided to return to Mexico. I stopped a Border Patrol officer and asked him to take me back to Mexico. He laughed and asked why I wanted to be deported. I told him what had happened, and he took me to the bridge. The next time I came, some friends helped me cross, and I've been able to get occasional work. Some day I hope to be able to apply for residency."

Gabi entered the United States about five years ago. She recalls the horrible experience she and two other women had when they crossed the river. "We came across the river with the help of a coyote," she says. "He took us across on a tube. He told us the water was very dangerous and to hold on tight to the tube. He did that just to scare us. On the way across, he had his hands all over us. When we got to the other side, we were crying because we were so angry and embarrassed."

Illegal entry has other harsh outcomes for Mexican immigrants, including exploitation and family problems. Israel Cano experienced both of them. "Everyone expects too much from undocumented workers," he says. "We are hardworking people with families to support in Mexico. When I worked in the fields, my boss expected me to start working at four in the morning and work till dark, with only a short lunch break. He also paid me less than the other workers. The one thing that kept me going was my wife and children in Mexico. Months would pass before I could get back to see them. It was very lonely here without them. Unfortunately, I began messing around with other women who were field workers, and my wife found out. She moved to another city in Mexico with the children, and they don't want anything to do with me. I wish I had never come to the United States. I'm worse off than I was before."

Many Mexican immigrants use a mica *to cross the border legally, but lack authorization to work*
(photo courtesy of George C. McLemore).

Many Mexican immigrants who come to the Valley enter without legal authorization to work. Some of these have since become legal by marrying legal residents and U.S. citizens. Others have close relatives who have requested legal residency for them. Many more have gained legal status through the Amnesty Program of the 1986 Immigration Reform and Control Act (IRCA). This law allowed all persons residing continuously in the United States since 1982 (or who had worked at least ninety days in agriculture during 1980) to legalize their status. By some estimates, approximately one-half of Mexicans living illegally in the United States in 1990 would eventually gain legalized status through the amnesty program.[9]

Arturo is one immigrant who was able to gain legal status through the amnesty program. "I came to the U.S. to work," he says, "and to find a better life for my seven children. I wanted them to get a better education in the U.S. and to learn English. Here in the Valley, making a living is very difficult. This is the reason I have to migrate up north. We do dirty, dangerous work that nobody wants to do. Also, here in the Valley, people report undocumented workers just for nothing. I got tired of people turning me in or threatening to call the Migra for the slightest disagreement. Now, because of the amnesty program, I can live without fear and defend myself and my family from these people and from unscrupulous farmers. I want to live in the U.S. for the rest of my life. Also I want my children to find better jobs and to retire from the fields."

The amnesty program helped people at other socioeconomic levels as well. Blanca is a fifty-year-old woman who was born, raised, and educated in Reynosa, Mexico. Blanca completed her education and obtained certification so she could work as a nurse in Mexico. Her husband was working illegally in the Valley but living in Mexico. "One day," she remembers, "my husband was caught and was forced to make a decision of either losing his crossing card or claiming amnesty. If he claimed amnesty, I would have to move to the Valley. It was hard to leave my work and my circle of friends, but he wanted us to have the opportunity. After getting amnesty, I was able to get a job in a small laboratory. I have friends in the Valley, but it has not been easy. I still cross regularly to be with my social circle in Mexico. It's hard to fit in with the Mexican Americans here. Their values are so different from ours."

Adjusting to Life in the United States

Like Blanca, many Mexicans are able to cross the border frequently and to maintain regular contact with family and friends. Those who come from places farther inside Mexico often feel more cut off and isolated. Sixty-three percent of Mexican immigrant respondents in the Multiethnic Culture Survey, for example, said they maintain frequent contact with family and friends in Mexico. With each generation, however, this contact apparently declines. Only 18 percent of Mexican American respondents in the same survey claimed frequent contact with family and friends in Mexico. Because they live so close to Mexico, Mexicans find the adjustment process quite different from what it is for immigrants from other countries.

Many immigrants we interviewed said they prefer the lifestyle of Mexico to that of the United States. Benito Arredondo, for example, expressed a strong preference for the lifestyle of Mexico. "What I really miss," he says, "is always finding people in the streets. In Mexico people are always out in the streets buying and selling things. People mingle in their neighborhoods. I may be poor in Mexico, but there's always something going on. I just can't get used to how people keep to themselves here."

Adriana agrees. "I come from a small town," she says. "People were always doing things together. Here I can't go anywhere or do anything

The strong sense of tradition of many elderly Mexican immigrants may clash with the Americanized lifestyle of their children and grandchildren
(photo courtesy of George C. McLemore).

without getting in a car. I feel like a prisoner, always kept in isolation." Socorro, who comes from a city just across the border, has similar feelings. "In Rio Bravo," she says, "I feel like I'm somebody. I can go down the street and talk to anyone. Here I just keep to myself because I hardly see the neighbors."

Many immigrants also find it hard to accept the way young people in the United States treat their elders. Juanita, a Mexican mother who came to the United States with her husband many years ago, states, "Kids here are very disrespectful to everyone—their aunts, uncles, even to their grandparents. They think they don't have to answer to anyone. My parents were very strict when I was a child. If I was being spanked with a *faja* [belt], and I looked at my father like I was mad or upset, it was more reason to get it harder."

While doing the interview, Juanita's husband, Rogelio, walked in. The student interviewer comments, "The children, who were sitting around listening to us, quickly dispersed. The quick departure of the children seemed to show that the age-old tradition of a dominant father still exists in this home. Rogelio is a commanding figure who expects and demands the ultimate in respect. He says that his father controlled every aspect of their family life as did his grandfather before him. This type of machismo is a tradition that is still carried on in some Mexican American households."

Some Mexican immigrants lament the loss of traditional Mexican ways they see among Mexican Americans. Maribel, for example, came to the United States shortly after her marriage. She still prefers the old ways. "To get married," she says, "Roel, the man who is now my husband, had to ask my father for my hand in marriage. My father was a very stubborn man and was hard to please. So to get approval, Roel bought my father a horse. He didn't really have to do this, but to get married in rural Mexico, a gentleman has to have the permission of the future bride's father. The only way to get my father to approve of us getting married was if he liked Roel enough to say yes. We were really nervous because if my father said no, then it was no! We simply would have had to respect his wishes. We also needed his blessings for a good future. Fortunately, my father said yes. If he hadn't, I'd probably be married to someone else."

This respect for the authority of older males causes considerable conflict for those not raised in Mexico. Sandra remembers a problem with her grandfather. "I planned to go out, just myself and my date," she says. "It turned into a huge argument with my grandfather. He told me as I was leaving with my date, '¡Si te vas, no vuelvas! Las mujeres que salen con pelados así no más son unas cualquieras. [If you go, don't come back! Women who go out with bums like that are no more than street women.]'" He was extremely angry when he told me this. I went anyway. When I came back home, he told me I had to marry my date because he knew I had done something wrong. That was my first and only date."

The problem, of course, is not only having different ideas about authority and sex roles, but how being alone with someone of the opposite sex is interpreted in each country. Jesica is from Mexico City. She finds things in the Valley very different from Mexico. "Here," she says, "people date in couples. In Mexico we go out in groups. The other day, this guy invited me to the movies, and I said yes. But when he came to pick me up, he was by himself. I thought that was strange because I'm used to going out in groups. So I told him to invite more people. He got upset and we never went anywhere."

Though the emphasis on respect for one's elders is strong in many households, both Mexican and Mexican American, assimilation sometimes confuses the specifics. Tencha, for example, now a young adult, was born in the United States to Mexican parents. She remembers an occasion when, as a young girl, she needed to leave the room where some adults were gathered. Her parents had taught her always to ask permission to leave, but she had trouble remembering the phrase they had taught her to excuse herself. "The phrase I was searching for," she says, "was 'Con permiso [With your permission].' Since the appropriate phrase would not come to me, I said instead, 'Dios los bendiga [God bless you].' This caused my parents to stare at me in bewilderment and my sisters to burst into giggles."

Maintaining old traditions in a new land is difficult. Catalina moved to the United States when her children were adolescents. "Each day," she says, "a new problem came up. My daughters wondered why they were not allowed to do the things their friends were doing, such as dating and other liberties. I am sorry, but having lived in both countries, I can tell you that Mexico's morals and values are far superior to those in the U.S. In the U.S., there is no vision of unity and closeness in the family. In Mexico 'La familia es primero [Family comes first].' It was hard for my kids to understand that at first. Now they never tire of thanking me for raising them the way I did. Now they're glad I didn't let them do what their friends were allowed to do."

Often the old ways are less tangible, like the care given to the preparation of food. Josefina, for example, believes that U.S. mothers put too many things ahead of making a nice meal for their families. "In the first place," she says, "I hate the food. Hamburgers and pizza is what everyone eats here. U.S. food has no flavor, and everything tastes the same. There is too much fast food. Mothers should worry more about what their families eat and not give them frozen food cooked in a microwave most of the time."

It is hard to exaggerate the importance of food and the work that goes into preparing it in Mexican culture. Yolanda Gaona remembers her childhood in Mexico. "When I was very young," she says, "my mother and aunts would wake up long before dawn to begin making tamales. Usually they were made of pork, so we would kill one of our pigs for the occasion. One of my aunts would make the *masa* [dough], while others would prepare the meat. Then, we'd all sit with a pile of corn leaves at our side and begin spreading the dough on the corn leaves. Then we'd make the filling. Finally, we'd place them in the oven. Making each *tamal* didn't take much time, but we'd make such large quantities that it took us until about two in the afternoon. Then we'd share them with friends and neighbors. Though all the women of the town made tamales, we'd

Many Mexican immigrants long to return to Mexico and prefer the lifestyle of Mexico (photo courtesy of George C. McLemore).

always send some out and get others back—kind of a Mexican version of sending out cookies."

Making tamales and other traditional dishes remains an important practice in many Mexican and Mexican American homes in South Texas. A far greater source of distinction and distraction between the two groups is language.[10] Carlos discovered this recently when he came from Mexico to live with his uncle's family. "Mi tío me dijo que pusiera el mugrero arriba de la troca y después que la aparqueara enfrente de la casa [My uncle told me to load some old stuff on the truck and to park it in front of the house]," he says. "Though he was speaking Spanish, I didn't understand half of what he was saying. So I told him. Then he made fun of me. He said that if I were a true Mexican, I should have understood him. I know English and Spanish, but I didn't know any Tex-Mex. So now I've got the reputation of being a stuck-up Mexican."

Often the reputation of being "stuck up" is occasioned by Mexicans who claim superiority to Mexican Americans because of errors they perceive in local Spanish. Julio is a young business executive who moved to the United States within the last three years. "One thing that's been hard for me to accept," he says, "is the way people here speak. They combine English with Spanish and even misuse many Spanish words. There are times that I've tried to correct them, but they let me know they don't want my help."

Ernesto is another Mexican immigrant who grew up in Reynosa and later moved to the Las Milpas colonia near Pharr. He says, "One of the hardest things that I went through when I came to Las Milpas was getting used to 'Tex-Mex.' I grew up speaking proper Spanish and developed a strong Mexican identity. I can never get used to how the Mexican Americans combine English and Spanish. I can't understand why they want to speak this way. It makes them think they're gringos. It also shows they've rejected their culture and their identity as Mexicans. They refuse to learn about their Mexican culture and language. I still live here in the United States, but when I'm ready to raise a family, I'm going back to Mexico. I want my kids raised in a Mexican environment and to feel proud of it."

In the Multiethnic Culture Survey, we asked Mexican immigrants and Mexican American respondents a series of questions designed to measure affinity for certain cultural traits related to Mexico. The first was, "How well do you like the lifestyle in Mexico?" Figure 6.2 shows the percentage of each group that answered "a lot." We then asked how important it was to their parents, when they were growing up that: (1) they be extremely polite and courteous with adults and respect the elderly; (2) they observe the customs and traditions of Mexico; and (3) they speak correct Spanish. Figure 6.2 shows the percentage of each group, Mexicans and Mexican Americans, who answered "very important." As a check on our samples, we included some of the same questions in the Mexican Immigrants Survey. Responses by both samples of Mexicans were within 2 percentage points of each other on each of the last three questions shown in Figure 6.2.

Several conclusions are apparent from these results. First, there was a substantial difference between Mexicans and Mexican Americans on each item except the importance of being polite to adults and respecting the elderly. Mexicans had approximately double the percentages of Mexican Americans agreeing that Mexican customs are important and that it was important to their parents that they speak good Spanish. Both items suggest a source of contention between the groups. Indeed, in the inter-

Percent Who Agree

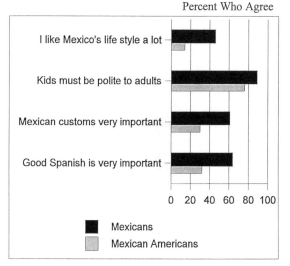

Fig. 6.2. Agreement of Mexican immigrants and Mexican Americans on key items supporting Mexican culture (Multiethnic Culture Survey, 1996)

views, Mexicans often commented that Mexican Americans have turned their backs on their heritage. Mexican Americans, by comparison, expressed the sentiment that Mexicans need to remember they are no longer in Mexico.

Second, we should comment that a very small percentage of Mexican Americans (14 percent) said they liked the lifestyle of Mexico "a lot." Indeed, 32 percent of Mexican Americans said that they did not care at all for the lifestyle of Mexico (compared to only 8 percent of Mexicans and 38 percent of Anglos with this opinion). Here again, the exploratory interviews revealed a pattern of suspicion and hostility between the two groups. Mexicans tend to think of the lifestyle of Mexico in terms of cultural warmth and family solidarity, while Mexican Americans think of it in terms of political corruption and poverty.[11]

A third observation we can make is that politeness with one's elders was clearly important to the parents of both groups. Indeed, it seems somewhat universal across cultures, since 69 percent of the Anglos surveyed also said their parents felt it was very important to be courteous and to respect the elderly. Though there is near agreement on the importance of this element of culture, many Mexicans revealed a belief that respect for elders will be lost by living in the United States.

One immigrant, for example, compared his children with those of his brother who stayed on their father's farm and raised his family in Mexico. "I am very disillusioned," he says, "with living in the United States. We moved here because we thought we would improve our lives. Instead, all our sons are in trouble with the law. Our family has fallen apart. Not my brother's family, though. His children got an education and have good jobs. His two daughters married well. His two sons are still on the farm and are modernizing it. All of his children have a great deal of respect in the community and are very respectful toward everyone. The atmosphere in America is not very conducive toward family closeness. Instead, individualism is the way of life here and morality is very low. The laws call parents 'abusive' if they spank their children. Permissiveness is causing these problems. In Mexico, permissiveness is not so prevalent. The schools are much more strict. Parents work with the teachers to make the children behave and follow their parents' wishes. I really believe that if this were done in the United States, our problems with our children would greatly decrease."

Many Mexican immigrants expressed similar worries about how life in the United States would affect their children. They worry particularly about permissiveness and the breakdown of the family. Elva and her husband moved from Veracruz to Chicago when their children were twelve and fourteen. "My kids were excited about living in a different country," she says. "When they started school, I noticed changes in their behavior. They started to ask questions about sex and drugs. After that, things just got worse, and we decided that it was not a proper place to raise children. Soon after that, we looked for ways to be transferred back to Mexico."

Mexican parents are often appalled at the sexual standards of the United States. Mónica remembers how her mother helped her maintain her standards in the face of peer pressure. "I was dating a college guy," she says, "and he wanted to have sex with me. When I said no, he just got up and left. I felt so alone, but felt I had made the right choice. My friends all told me I was crazy. They said having sex was the 'in thing' to do. One day, I told my mom about it and told her how they were always making fun of me. I'll never forget what she told me. She said I could always be like them, if I wanted, but now none of them could ever be like me—a virgin."

As implied by the foregoing examples, many Mexican immigrants fear that life in the United States will break down the strong bonds of family so important in Mexican culture.[12] Imelda, a second-generation college student, discovered this concern of her parents. "It was my second year at St. Mary's University," she says. "Almost all my friends were going somewhere other than home for spring break. They wanted to include me in their plans, so I decided I'd go with them. So I called my parents at home in Mexico and explained my plan. They said no. They didn't even think about it or ask any questions. They just came right out and said no. I was upset that they were being so close-minded about it."

Mexican–Mexican American Relations

Worse than the conflict between generations are those that cross ethnic and class lines. Angélica is a biology major at UT–Pan American. She was born in Mexico, but her parents moved to the Valley when she was nine years old. They felt she would have a better future in the United States. They worked hard in the fields so she could have a chance to attend school. "They never imagined," she says, "that anyone would mistreat me because I was Mexican. After all, 95 percent of the kids who attended my school were Mexican American. They too had Mexican blood.

"On the first day of school," she says, "they sent me to a classroom for fifth graders who could not speak English. Our class was known as the language development class, or LD. As we sat and listened to our teacher, I heard loud banging on the classroom door. I was frightened, but then a student told me that those were just the other kids who hated the LDs. A few days later, they beat up some of my classmates. They went around calling us names like 'wetbacks' and 'aliens.' They told us to go back to Mexico where we belonged. I couldn't understand this, since they too were Mexicans and all had Mexican names such as Pablo, José, or Jorge. I managed to blend in as the years went on and graduated at the top of my class in high school. As for the mean kids, many of them didn't even graduate."

How widespread is such antagonism, and what is happening to bring it about? Apparently these are not isolated incidents; others report similar confrontations.[13] One Mexican immigrant, now in her twenties, also reported hostility from the Mexican Americans during her junior high years. "They would throw their food at us during lunch time," she said. "They would also take our things. The teachers just told us to avoid them."

Apparently, it is also a problem among older age groups and even among the better educated. Javier, also a university student from Mexico, feels hostility from some Mexican American professors. "Once I took an evening course," he says, "because an Anglo was teaching it during the day and a Mexican American at night. I thought I'd learn more from the Mexican American, but I was wrong. The Mexican American professor took every opportunity he could to ridicule and criticize Mexicans and Mexico. He knew that at least two of us students were Mexican. After three weeks of humiliation, I decided to drop the class. From then on, I haven't bothered to find out whether a professor is Anglo or Mexican American."

Mexican Americans also experience harsh treatment from some

Mexicans. Eugenio "Gene" Garza works at a large shoe store in McAllen. He was raised in North Texas and never really learned much Spanish. This sometimes causes problems because his employer gets many customers from Mexico. One day, while Gene was talking to some Anglo customers, a dignified-looking man from Mexico came up to him and asked regarding some shoes. "I really couldn't answer him," he says, "because he had asked in Spanish, and I really couldn't make it out. He repeated his question, but in an angry tone that made me feel embarrassed. When he saw I really couldn't speak much Spanish, he switched to English. He looked around and said, loud enough for everyone to hear, 'I'm embarrassed that they let a damn Mexican American who can't speak Spanish work in a place like this.' So I told him he was in America now, and he should speak English. He looked at his friends and said, again in English so that everyone could hear, 'These Mexicans here in the United States have not only lost their mother tongue, but also their courtesy.' It was then that I decided I was glad I had adopted the American way of life. I feel nothing at all in common with Mexico."

Mexican Americans also experience occasional problems when they visit Mexico. One Mission High School senior employed in a McAllen hotel, for example, decided to party with a friend in Mexico one evening after work. "We had already been drinking before we arrived in Reynosa," he says. "We went from one nightclub to another to make as much of Friday night as we could. As we left one nightclub, heading for our car, two Mexican police officers stopped us. They accused us of being drunk and illegally parking the car. One of them demanded ten dollars to drop the charges. I turned to him and in my usual slang said, 'Oye, bato, no me hagas eso [Hey, guy, don't do that to me].' They grabbed both of us, threw us against the police car, and handcuffed our hands behind our backs. They said they didn't like Mexican Americans who couldn't speak proper Spanish. They took us to a filthy jail where they placed us in the large cell with about thirty other guys. A removable block in the floor covered the sewer line. That was the bathroom. After two days of nothing to eat but bread, and water from a faucet, I paid a guard to call my parents. They had to pay an even larger amount to get us out. I lost five pounds from that ordeal and still have nightmares about it."

Living on the border greatly increases the contacts between Mexicans and Mexican Americans. South Texas Mexican Americans who find employment in establishments that cater to Mexican customers especially have intense contact. Frequently such experiences are not pleasant, especially for those with well-to-do Mexican customers. "They try to make us feel as though we're beneath them," says one. "They know we have to be nice to get our sales, but they take advantage of us. Last week, for example, a Mexican woman asked me where something was. It wasn't in my department, so I told her where she could find it. Her husband started yelling at me, saying I should have left my department and gone after it for her."

The exploratory interviews suggest several sources of conflict between Mexicans and Mexican Americans. Those most frequently mentioned are language differences, class-related differences, divided national loyalties, citizenship status, and other cultural disparities. Of these, language is perhaps the most prevalent and aggravating. For Mexicans, the ability to speak Spanish well is a sign of education and national pride. They use the term *pocho* to signify their resentment of Hispanics who speak a nonstandard dialect of Spanish that not only includes many English words but also numerous archaic Spanish words. Most Mexicans are unaware of the English-only period of Texas education, so they fail to comprehend that much of the loss of standard Spanish was forced. They also fail to see the importance of Tex-Mex as a form of cultural identity for those who see themselves as neither fully Mexican nor American.

In class-conscious Mexico, language is also a mark of social position. Educated Mexicans go to great lengths to ensure that their children learn "proper" Spanish, well aware that it is an essential gateway to economic and social opportunities. When they hear Mexican Americans using archaic expressions (*asina* instead of *así*, for example), they interpret it as a sign of poor upbringing or low character.

Juan Puente immigrated to the United States from Durango. He remembers his initial impressions of Mexican Americans. "I thought they were *cholos* [delinquents] and ignorant people," he says. "My mother was so shocked she even wanted to pull me out of the public school. She assumed all the Mexican American students were lower class. I finally convinced her that I could get a good American education in spite of anyone's social class. My father still thinks that Mexican Americans in the Valley are lazy. He says they depend too much on government welfare and just want food stamps. He tells me, 'If I can work hard and provide the best for my kids, including a car, why can't these Mexican Americans do the same?'"

Another cause of resentment between the two groups is divided national loyalties. Mexican immigrants often maintain a loyalty to Mexico and think Mexican Americans should also. We can see the intensity of this loyalty to Mexico in Carmen's case. She and her husband left Mexico twenty-five years ago. "It took nineteen years," she says, "before my father acknowledged my existence and forgave me for having left. All of my brothers and sisters stayed in Mexico with my parents. My father gave them each a piece of land from our family ranch nearby so that they could make their living doing the same thing he did. Yet my husband and I had a dream of living in America. My father saw our leaving as a betrayal. His last words were, 'The minute you step off this ranch, you will never be welcomed back.' The rest of the family had no choice but to go along with my father."

Mexican Americans, on the other hand, believe that if immigrants cannot find a loyalty to their new country, they should return to Mexico. Juan Heredia remembers a negative reaction to Mexico from a Hispanic teacher. "One day I walked into class wearing a shirt from the Mexican soccer team," he remembers. "The Hispanic teacher asked me if I liked the Mexican soccer team, and then if I liked Mexico. To both questions I answered yes. Out of the blue, he said, 'If you like Mexico so much, why don't you go back?'"

Of related concern is the issue of citizenship. Some Mexican Americans believe that, as citizens, they should have preference over immigrants who are only legal residents. For example, Carla, who is a recent immigrant, recently got a job in a food store in Mission. "They hired me as a sacker," she says. "One day at the beginning of my first week on the job, two of my coworkers, both Hispanics, started giving me angry looks and saying something to each other. Finally, one of them came up to me and said, 'My sister applied for your job. She's an American citizen, and you are only a Mexican. How come you got the job?' I guess she thought that because her sister was born here, she had more right to the job than me. I told her that the management is in charge of such decisions and I hoped her sister could get a job there too."

When undocumented Mexican residents get into such situations, they may get more than pointed questions. Mónico Moreno describes a conflict he had in 1967. "I was working in a restaurant here in the Valley," he says. "They hired me though I didn't have any papers. I started as a waiter because I didn't have the requirements to be a cook or a cashier. The owner of the restaurant didn't pay me much, but he did give me a place to live and paid some of my bills. After six months of working hard, he promoted me to assistant manager. This, of course, made me very happy because I was going to be able to send more money to my family in Mexico. The next day one of the young Mexican American waiters, who had more time working in the restaurant, became very angry. He said he was more fit for the job than I was and could speak English better. He asked the owner, 'How could you put that stupid Mexican as assistant manager when I'm more qualified?' The owner wouldn't change his mind and that made him even more angry. The next day, as I came out of the office, he came up to me and told me that I should be careful from now on because I could end up back in Mexico. I didn't pay much attention to him because I had the boss's support. Two weeks later, two immigration officers came into the restaurant and asked to speak to the assistant manager. I got scared and ran out the back door. I never even went back for my paycheck."

Many Mexican Americans refuse to use such tactics, even when it would be to their economic advantage to do so. They, more than Anglos, however, find themselves in competition with undocumented Mexican immigrants. Many have struggled to get out of poverty and have families of their own to support. The whole immigration situation in South Texas frequently pits them against each other as they struggle for scarce jobs and other benefits. This, by itself, accounts for much of the resentment against Mexican immigrants, especially against those who are undocumented.

One additional source of conflict should be mentioned—that of ignorance of Mexico's historical and cultural heritage. Paula Lara, for example, was shocked while attending a Valley high school to see how little local Hispanics knew about Mexico. "In my Spanish class," she says, "the teacher asked if anybody knew the significance of El Cinco de Mayo and El Dieciséis de Septiembre [May 5 and September 16—holidays to celebrate Mexico's defeat of Maximilian's army and Mexican independence, respectively]. Nobody knew! I felt ashamed of all those students who live in the Valley, so close to Mexico, and have Mexican blood. They have no idea of what these historic dates mean. I wanted to stand up and tell them they should know more about their heritage and culture. Some of them have never even heard of Hidalgo or Villa. Instead they embrace rap music and fast cars. Somehow I think they are ashamed of their Mexican origin."

Not all the stories, of course, are negative. Some Mexican immigrants experience very positive relations with Mexican Americans. When we interviewed Humberto, for example, he had just arrived from Mexico, had no money, and did not speak much English. "I had to find a job," he remembers. "I stopped at a house to see if they had work. The old man and his wife said they had work, but not much money. They fed me three meals a day and treated me like a member of their family. They did not pay me much, but I had never been treated that well before. The main reason was that they were Mexican Americans, rather than Anglos."

Relations between Anglos and Mexicans

Mexican immigrants have an interesting relationship with Anglos in South Texas. Some feel more comfortable around Anglos, while others

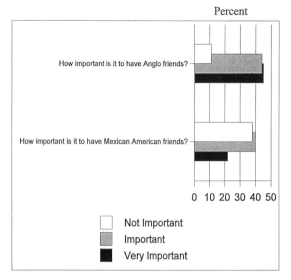

Fig. 6.3. Importance
Mexican immigrants give
to friendships with Mexican
Americans and with Anglos
(Mexican Immigrants
Survey, 1995)

feel rejection and bigotry. Much, of course, depends on the social class, immigration status, and English abilities of the immigrants.

Jorge Ortiz comes from a background of poverty and little education. "We worked on their lawns, pools, and houses," he says. "To me, they are nice friendly people, but becoming friends was impossible for us." Ana agrees. Her employers are a very friendly Anglo family. "I see them only as my employers," she says. "To them I am an employee. They treat me nice, but our relationship has never been much more than business."

In the Mexican Immigrants Survey, we asked respondents how important it was for them to establish close personal relationships with Mexican Americans and with Anglos. Figure 6.3 shows that nearly 40 percent of respondents said that friendships with Anglos were not important. Only 11 percent found friendships with Mexican Americans not important.

This result, most likely, is related to the class status of Mexican immigrants. Mexicans from upper-income levels often find themselves more accepted by Anglos than by Mexican Americans. Olivia is one of them. "On the first day of high school," she says, "it was kinda scary. People were saying hi to their friends and talking about their summer. I made some new friends and started getting more comfortable. I realized that most of the people I met were Anglos. They were people with money and were very popular. I guess they started hanging with me because I had money and a cool car. We would go to the mall and shop at the expensive stores. I was also invited to popular parties, to which they invited only certain people. Moving here made me realize that McAllen wasn't that different from back home."

Some find, however, that having money is not enough. Carla Maldonado, for example, is a young Mexican immigrant whose family first moved to a city in Central Texas. "I started attending an Anglo Catholic church," she says. "Sunday after Sunday I attended, but each time I would walk in alone and leave alone. None of the young people tried to make friends with me or involve me in their activities or group. It seemed to me like they had their cliques, and no one could get in. I really wanted them to accept me so I bought some new clothes and tried to dress like them. I avoided talking Spanish around them. Even when I went to college, they did not accept me."

When rejection comes because of Anglo ethnocentrism, learning English and adopting other aspects of Anglo culture generally speeds the acceptance of immigrants among Anglos. If the problem for Anglos is bigotry, however, they will not regard Mexicans as equals, even when income or mastery of English is high.

Francisco "Frank" Cano remembers many years ago, before he moved to the Valley. He and his family had just come from Mexico and lived in Austin. "This one guy, Robert Hayward, always gave me problems. Every day after school, I had to walk home, and every day he'd follow me on his new bike, teasing me. I told my parents about it, but they just told me to ignore him. Well, I did for as long as I could. One day, I just got fed up with him. The next time he called me names, I stuck a stick in the spokes of his front wheel. Robert and his bike did a flip in the air and landed on the ground. His bike was all messed up, and he cried louder than anyone I've ever heard. I thought it was pretty funny, but I knew I was in trouble for doing something to one of the richest White boys in town. I ran home hoping I could hide behind my parents because I knew the Haywards would come and make a big *escándalo* [uproar] about it.

"Sure enough, Robert and his parents came to our front door and started yelling about what I had done. To top it all off, Robert told my parents that I always teased him and made fun of him. Because they were who they were, my father sided with them. He hit me with a belt right there in front of them. I cried, not because it hurt, but because I was so embarrassed. I was sure that of all people, my dad would understand. I was sent to my room. When the Haywards left, my father came into my room to talk to me. He kept apologizing to me. He told me that he didn't want to hit me, but he did it because he was afraid of what Mr. Hayward could do to our family. We were new there, and we were Mexicans."

Many Mexican immigrants avoid conflict by keeping their contact with Anglos to a minimum, especially contact of a personal nature. Sometimes, however, that is not possible. When Hortencia moved here from Mexico, she learned English quickly and did well in school. She even ended up in the top 10 percent of her class. She got a scholarship to a major university. "I was terrified," she says. "I thought things would be all right if I could just meet some new friends. Well, the first day at my dorm I was unpacking when a blond-haired girl walked into the room. She took one look at me and said, 'Oh my gosh, there's no way I'm going to share a room with a bean-eating Mexican.' She left and I never saw her again. I guess she moved in with someone else."

Much of the bigotry Mexicans encounter is related to the stereotypes Anglos have of Mexico and everything Mexican. José lived for several years in the United States before returning to Mexico. A cousin who talked to him in Monterrey interviewed him. "In the United States," he says, "if something bad happens and there is a Mexican around, they'll blame the Mexican—tenemos fama de rateros y malvados [we're known as thieves and bad people]." He continues, "Los gringos nos ven inferiores a ellos sólo por ser morenos [The gringos think we're inferior to them just because we're brown]." José had worked at a convenience store. The owner found some money and items missing. Without any proof, he blamed José for everything, though an Anglo clerk had been on duty when the items were taken. When José asked why it could not have been the Anglo clerk, the owner said, "Because all of you Mexicans are thieves and can't be trusted!" Shortly after that, José returned to Mexico. He says, "No regresaría a los Estados Unidos aunque me pagaran [I wouldn't return to the United States even if they paid me]."

Though outright bigotry is less common today, it has not disappeared. Margarita remembers an incident eleven years ago soon after she had moved to the Valley. "I wanted to buy some clothing," she remembers. "Without thinking, I entered a very elegant store in the mall. The Anglo clerks stared at me as if I were some sort of animal. I saw a beautiful blouse on a mannequin and asked if I could try it on. They told me it wouldn't fit and that it was out of my 'price range.' Before I left, I looked at the price tag. It wasn't really that much. They just didn't want me there because I wasn't wearing expensive clothing."

Though class and race issues still cause some problems, the biggest obstacle between Mexican immigrants and Anglos is the language barrier. Arturo, for example, recently entered a bookstore looking for a particular book. "I looked around," he says, "and all I could see were two Anglo clerks. One of them came over. I assumed he was asking if I needed help. Since I didn't understand English, though, we both just got frustrated. I left the store without my book."

Nevertheless, the language barrier is more imagined than real for some. When Luisa and her husband moved to the Valley six years ago, for example, they decided to fly to Houston to visit her mother-in-law. "On the plane," she says, "we took seats near the exit door. Since we had been conversing in Spanish, the Anglo stewardess assumed we couldn't understand English. She told a Hispanic lady across the aisle from us to tell us to move because we were next to the exit door and wouldn't understand what to do in an emergency. I understood every word she said, but we were so embarrassed that we just moved to avoid any other problems."

Some Anglos react more to the immigration status than to the ethnic or racial characteristics of Mexicans. Juan worked for an Anglo employer in Willacy County, not far from the checkpoint near Sarita. One morning his employer needed him to take some equipment north of the checkpoint. Since Juan did not carry his immigration papers with him, he asked if he could get them from home. "He thought I was kidding," says Juan. "Then he said, 'You mean you're not an American citizen?' I said, 'No sir, I'm not.' He then said, 'Well, you can't work here until you become one!' That same year, on my wife's birthday, I was naturalized. When I went back for my job, he had given it to someone else."

Anglo and Mexican American Treatment Compared

In the Mexican Immigrants Survey, we asked four questions that allowed us to compare how Mexicans perceived they were treated by Anglos with how they perceived they were treated by Mexican Americans. Specifically, we asked Mexican immigrants which group, Anglos or Mexican Americans, was more likely to (1) have many stereotypes about Mexico; (2) invite Mexicans of their social class into their homes for social visits; (3) act superior to Mexicans of their social class; and (4) use prejudiced remarks about people from Mexico. Respondents had four choices for their answer: "Mexican Americans"; "Anglos"; "neither"; and "about the same." On the first question, 10 percent said "neither," and for each of the remaining three questions, 13 percent also had this response. The remaining responses are summarized in Figure 6.4.

These results show that among the Mexican immigrants surveyed, twice as many believed that Anglos, rather than Mexican Americans, will have stereotypes about Mexico and would be more likely to act superior

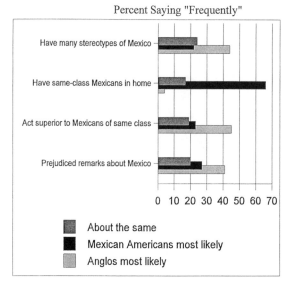

Percent Saying "Frequently"

Have many stereotypes of Mexico

Have same-class Mexicans in home

Act superior to Mexicans of same class

Prejudiced remarks about Mexico

0 10 20 30 40 50 60 70

■ About the same
■ Mexican Americans most likely
□ Anglos most likely

Fig. 6.4. Social behavior of Mexican Americans and Anglos encountered by Mexican immigrants (Mexican Immigrants Survey, 1995)

to Mexicans of the same social class. Significantly more also believed that Anglos are more likely to make prejudiced remarks about Mexico. Nonetheless, the greatest difference is on the item related to who would most likely invite Mexicans of the same social class into their homes. Only 4 percent said "Anglos," while 67 percent said "Mexican Americans" and 17 percent said "about the same." Thus, though many Mexican immigrants report some difficulties with Mexican Americans, they feel more acceptance and less prejudice from them than from Anglos, at least according to these measures.

Nevertheless, we need to emphasize that these responses are closely related to social class. Wealthy Mexican immigrants are much less likely to report prejudice and discrimination from Anglos than are lower-income Mexicans. Class remains one of the most significant variables in the process of adjusting to Anglo society.

The great social distance of many Mexican immigrants and their children from Anglos may be a mixed blessing for those who wish to preserve Hispanic culture. Beth Ann Treviño, for example, lost much of her identity as a Mexican American. Her parents came to the United States when she was just a baby. "My Anglo friends started calling me Beth Ann," she says, "and I grew up with that name. My dad was a systems analyst, but I had friends whose fathers were socially and professionally near the top of the ladder. For my fifteenth birthday, my parents said I could have my friends over for a party and an overnight stay. My parents and I made such great plans. After handing out the invitations, though,

Though some conflicts divide Mexican immigrants and Mexican Americans, their similar economic and political interests often give them more in common with each other than either group feels with Anglos (photo courtesy of George C. McLemore).

my friends quickly let me know they couldn't come. In fact, I realized that I had gone to their homes often, but they always had excuses for not coming to mine. My father was very upset, but he knew we couldn't do anything to change our social status or our ethnic background. 'We are what we are,' he said, 'and we should be proud of that.'

"We were still friends, though, and I soon forgot the birthday incident. I came to like the Anglo music my friends liked and couldn't stand the Mexican and salsa music my parents enjoyed. When my parents and their Mexican club invited us to celebrate Cinco de Mayo and Dieciséis de Septiembre, my friends and I went for the dinner. When the music and dancing began, though, we left. I guess I like Anglo culture better. At times I wish I was Anglo. They seem to have it all."

Many of the Mexicans we talked to do not agree. Natalia is one of them. "I would never change the way I have been raised," she says. "I will never anglicize my name or lower the respect I feel for my parents. They taught me to respect my family and to have strong moral values. I won't change any of my traditions or customs either. For example, my father doesn't allow me to bring any male friends into our house unless the guy comes to ask for my hand in marriage. Another tradition that is important is that I must get married being a virgin. That is what the white dress symbolizes. He expects my brothers to follow the same principle with the girls they see. We know that whoever we marry must be of our same social class. For my father, that leaves out all the Mexican Americans."

Somewhere between these extremes are the Mexicans who become Mexican Americans. Like many waves of immigrants before them, they and their children keep some of Mexico, take some Anglo culture, reject a lot more, and come up with some of their own. Neither Mexican nor Anglo, they have carved out a cultural niche that is unique in United States society—Mexican American, while being neither Mexican nor fully American.

"¡Ahí Viene el Bolillo!": Anglo Newcomers to South Texas

Chapter 7

When we were working in the fields, sometimes the only chance we'd have to rest was a water break. On a really hot day, we'd sit for just of couple of minutes to enjoy the water and the break. Occasionally, in the fields, we'd get a sudden surprise of shade when a stray cloud would cover the sun. We'd pause for just a moment to enjoy the cooling shade. Then suddenly we'd hear, "¡Ahí viene el bolillo!" It meant the gringo boss was coming, and we'd better get back to work.

RUBY ALVAREZ, 1988

When Ruby related this, the *bolillo* she and other farmworkers had in mind was the Anglo farmer. Actually, a *bolillo* is a white bread roll produced by Mexican bakeries. Its use as a synonym for Anglos is a gentle form of humor along both sides of the U.S.-Mexico border.

In recent years, the expression "¡Ahí viene el bolillo!" (Here comes the *bolillo!*) has taken on new meaning. The growth of tourism, the expanding maquila industry, and the need to recruit professionals for the expanding job market have brought a new wave of *bolillos* into South Texas. What is it like for them when almost 90 percent of the local population is Hispanic? [1]

The adjustment is more severe for some than for others. So it was for one Border Patrol agent who was transferred to the Valley from Arizona. He was driving a U-Haul truck, with his wife following in the car behind him. As they passed through Roma and Rio Grande City, his wife started flashing her lights, signaling him to pull over. "When I got out of the truck," he says, "she was really upset. She accused me of having crossed into Mexico without telling her. It took me some time to convince her that we were still in the United States."

Dr. Margaret Ross, currently a school administrator in the Valley, also had a difficult time adjusting to Texas. She was driving to McAllen from her home state of Oregon. "I had been driving for four days," she says, "two of them on Texas highways. I could not believe the vastness of the state. None of my friends knew where the Valley was. I had never driven this far south before. Then, late at night, I hit a very lonely two-lane stretch of road between George West and Alice. I had been on the road all day and was really exhausted. It was raining, and this car in front of me kept slowing down and pulling over on the shoulder of the road. I knew nothing about the Texas custom of pulling onto the shoulder to let someone pass. I thought the guy was drunk, so I didn't pass him until we came to the divided highway. By then, I was so upset I was crying. I stopped at the first motel I saw. I didn't even stop to consider why the rate was only sixteen dollars a night. It was the original 'no-tell motel.' I stacked all the furniture that wasn't nailed to the floor against the door. I lay on the bed until dawn. The next day I began the final leg to the Valley, not realizing that my adjustment was just beginning."

One of the most difficult aspects of the adjustment is becoming accustomed to seeing so many Hispanic people and hearing Spanish spoken. When Todd, a high school teacher, first came to the area, he and his wife went to a retail store for supplies. "Everywhere we went," he says, "people were talking Spanish. I'd never even spoken to a Mexican before. I asked a clerk for help, and she answered me in Spanish. I couldn't believe it. Suddenly I had become a minority just by moving down here."

The fact that most Anglos make the adjustment, and even come to enjoy living in South Texas, is illustrated by Ken, a technician with five years' residence in the Valley. "I love the people in the Valley," says Ken. "They're warm and caring. Now I even have my own *compadres* [close buddies]. Recently, I went back to West Virginia. I went to a Wal-Mart to do some shopping. That's when it occurred to me that there wasn't even one Hispanic person in the store. I felt homesick for the Valley. I guess I hadn't realized how accustomed I had become."

Though some Anglo newcomers immediately love the Valley and its people, most go through an adjustment process spanning months or even years. Many, like Ken, learn to enjoy the area and its people. Others feel condemned to a very difficult existence and count the days until they can leave. In this chapter, we will describe this adjustment process and examine some factors that help determine whether the outcome is positive or negative.

We collected the data and life incidents for this chapter from several Borderlife projects. The personal accounts come primarily from the Anglo Newcomers Exploratory Interviews, conducted with 192 Anglos who moved to the Valley as adults. We also drew from 45 exploratory interviews we have conducted with Anglos who attended Valley schools where Anglos were less than 5 percent of the student population, although we have not yet developed a formal project that includes these. In addition, we conducted the Anglo Newcomers Survey, comprised of 224 persons born outside the Valley, of which about half had lived here for less than five years (Appendix B, no. 7). We also examined the responses of 165 Anglos who had been interviewed in the Multiethnic Culture Survey; approximately half of these were raised in the Valley (Appendix B, no. 10). Finally, we did the Winter Texans Exploratory Interviews with 288 retired persons who migrate annually to the Valley. We followed this up with our Winter Texans Survey of 326 respondents (Appendix B, no. 8).

Having to Adjust

When we asked Anglos to describe their initial impressions of the Valley, most, like Todd, expressed surprise and dismay at being a minority. Mike, for example, is twenty years old and moved here from Indiana four years ago. His initial view of the Valley? "I thought it was hell," he says. "I couldn't seem to grasp the culture down here. I was being discriminated against because I was White and couldn't speak Spanish. When I tried to get a job, everyone asked me if I was bilingual. I finally started going out with a Mexican American girl, but her parents didn't like me because I was White. Now I think I know how Black people must have felt when I was growing up. I guess that's a blessing from God to make me open my eyes."

For most respondents, language may be a much larger obstacle than race or ethnicity. Many Anglos report feeling excluded when Hispanics start speaking Spanish in a group setting.[2] Patricia, for example, remembers such a conversation soon after she moved to the Valley. "I was at the office," she says, "talking with a friend of mine. Then another employee came in. He walked up to the other guy and began speaking Spanish. In less than ten seconds I was completely isolated from the conversation. I got up and left the room."

Such occurrences seem to happen most frequently in work settings when informal conversations take place. Often Hispanics do not even realize that they have begun speaking Spanish, since Tex-Mex involves frequent switching between languages. Hilda, for example, is a speech teacher. "Not long ago," she says, "I was eating lunch with four other teachers, all of them bilingual Hispanics. We were discussing our students when one of them switched to Spanish. She must have said something very amusing, since they all seemed to enjoy their laughter. Though they probably didn't even think about it, I felt totally excluded."

When Anglos attempt to mix with Hispanics in social settings, similar problems often occur. Karl, a UT–Pan American student, for example, remembers a Christmas Eve party at a friend's house. "I figured that this would be a party like all others," he says. "I was wrong. I never expected to be the only Anglo there. Still, I tried to make the best of it. The only two people speaking English were my friend Joe and his brother Gabriel. When I was not following them around, I was eating something and saying, 'Bueno, bueno.' I was trying to say 'The food is good,' or 'I'm having a great time.' That made me really want to be bilingual, so I could have more friends."

Monolingual Anglos often feel that the Spanish spoken around them is directed against them. Many assume others are talking about them, especially when they know the group can speak English. Sarah is a technician, the only Anglo working in the X-ray department of a hospital. She feels that Mexican Americans say things about her in Spanish and then laugh about it. "One day," she says, "I ordered lunch at the hospital cafeteria. I told the line worker I wanted certain things on my sandwich, and she started babbling words in Spanish. I knew they were all laughing at what she had said about me. When I asked others around me what she had said, no one would admit anything."

Another concern of many Anglos is the confusion they feel when Hispanics begin speaking directly to them in Spanish. Cindy describes how she felt the second day she was here and went shopping at K-Mart. "I felt like I was in a foreign country," she says. "Everyone was speaking Spanish. When I went to the checkout, another customer said something to me like 'Permiso.' I didn't know what she wanted me to do, so I went in front of her. Evidently she wanted to pass by me. She got angry and bumped me with her cart. Not long after that, I was helping my daughter's Girl Scout troop sell cookies downtown. Someone told me to shout '¡Galletas!' [Cookies!]. I did the best I could, but a man stopped to inform me that I sounded like I was telling people '¡Cállate!' [Shut up!]."

Monolingual Anglos may also feel discriminated against in employment situations.[3] Arthur, for example, described a job search he had recently experienced. "I had heard about a good-paying job in sales," he says. "Since I've been in sales for more than five years, I thought I had a good shot at it. When I went in for an interview, the manager and I hit it off really well. When he gave me an application to fill out, I noticed a question in big bold letters, 'Are you bilingual?' I didn't pay much attention to it. When I gave it to the manager, he glanced at it and said, 'You don't speak Spanish?' I answered, 'No.' Then he said, 'Well, I'm sorry. There's no use in even talking further about the job.' I just said, 'I thought we were in the United States' and got up and walked out."

Though many Anglos who do not speak Spanish feel like such treatment is discrimination, many others recognize that it is not. When Mary Hudson applied for a job teaching second grade in a Valley school, her employers asked whether she was bilingual. "I had to tell them I wasn't," she says. "I got the job anyway. Don't ask me how. I came down here thinking that I should allow only English to be spoken in my classroom. After the first week, though, I clearly had to learn Spanish or my students would suffer. Many of them used Spanish phrases I simply couldn't understand. I was always having to ask other students to translate. So I got my husband's parents to teach me Spanish. I feel sorry for my students from that year. I didn't do nearly as well with them as I have with my classes since I learned Spanish."

Kevin MacDonald also recognizes that knowing Spanish is a legitimate requirement for his job. He works at a nice restaurant that frequently gets customers from Mexico. "Last week during rush hour," he says, "I was working fast to take care of my customers. Two ladies who spoke no English called me over. I think they were from Mexico. They kept asking something in Spanish, pointing at the menu, and getting upset that I couldn't answer them. In such cases, I usually look around for someone who can take Mexican customers, but everyone was really busy. Finally, a customer at a nearby table saw how lost I was and translated for me. I took their order and did the best I could with his help. Nevertheless, I knew they were unhappy and were making comments about me in Spanish."

Janice is a nursing student who has decided she must either learn Spanish or find work outside the Valley. "When I started working here," she says, "an elderly lady asked for 'el pato.' I knew enough Spanish to know that a *pato* is a duck, but that didn't make sense. Then I thought she was saying the name of a Mexican restaurant, El Pato, and that maybe she was hungry. She kept slapping the bed and saying, '¡El pato, el pato!' I went and got my supervisor and he asked her what she needed. Then he had me feel the bed and said, 'She asked for a bedpan, but now just change the sheets.'"

We wanted to learn how frequently Anglos in South Texas feel discriminated against in relation to their inability to speak and understand Spanish, so we included several questions on this topic in the Anglo Newcomers Survey. Newcomers were defined as Anglos who were raised elsewhere but had since moved to the Valley.[4] We also included the same questions in the Multiethnic Culture Survey, to which seventy-seven Anglos who had been raised in the Valley responded. In the first question we asked, "How common is it for Anglos to feel isolated from friendship

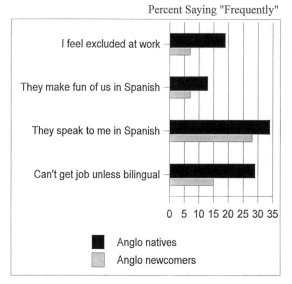

Fig. 7.1. Language-related problems experienced by Anglo newcomers and Anglo natives (Anglo Newcomers Survey, 1996; Multiethnic Culture Survey, 1996)

circles at work because they are not Hispanic?" Next we asked, "How often do Hispanics here make fun of you or your race (in Spanish)?" Then we asked, "How common is it for local people to start talking to you in Spanish and for you not to understand?" Finally, we included the question, "How common is it for Anglos and others who do not speak Spanish not to get hired because they are not bilingual?" The percentages of each group, Anglo newcomers and Anglos raised in the Valley, who answered "frequently" are shown in Figure 7.1.

These data show a pronounced difference between Anglos raised in the Valley and those who have moved here later in life. On all four measures, long-term residents were more likely to answer "frequently" than newcomers. The greatest difference can be seen in the first item, on which long-term residents were much more likely to say they felt excluded than newcomers did. A similar difference can be found on the item asking how often Anglos are unable to get a job because they are not bilingual. Again, long-term residents were much more likely to report frequent difficulty.

Two factors may be responsible for these results. First, Anglos who move to the Valley are frequently recruited to come here because of a scarcity of local people with the education and experience to fill managerial and technical positions. These newcomers face much less competition for their job from local Hispanics.[5] Once here, many of them associate with highly educated people who speak more English than Spanish. As a result, the language factor would not seem as important to them as it would to those who were raised here, many of whom have to compete with bilingual Hispanics for lower-level positions.

Second, Anglos who grew up in the Valley, especially those who never learned Spanish, were exposed to much of the prejudice against Mexicans and against the Spanish language so common thirty to forty years ago (see Chapter 5). As a result, many feel highly insulted when they cannot get a job because they are not bilingual. Martin, for example, was raised in the Valley. He does not have happy memories of his school years. "I never had friends when I was growing up," he says, "because I didn't speak Spanish and I couldn't even understand it. One day, for example, I was on the bus and some kids were talking in Spanish, pointing at me and laughing. I remember feeling so helpless. I told them, 'If you can't speak English, go back to where you came from.'"

Beth is another long-term resident. She still has some feelings of bitterness toward employers in the Valley who insist on having Spanish-speaking employees. "Speaking Spanish is not really necessary," she says, "and those who require it are violating the law of equal opportunity for employment. Mexicans who come to America should learn English and not expect English-speaking Americans to speak Spanish."

Bilingual Anglos

In contrast to the resentment expressed by monolingual Anglos, those who are bilingual generally report much greater acceptance by Hispanics in South Texas. Dora, for example, is a forty-five-year-old woman who has lived in the Valley all of her life. "I don't remember when I learned Spanish," she says, "but it must have been when I was two or three years old. I was brought up on a farm and the only children I had to play with were the daughters of the Mexican workers that lived in the house behind ours. It's helped me a lot over the years, and I have many Mexican friends and enjoy Mexican culture."

Anglo owners of local farms and businesses, however, often reported exclusion and discrimination in the exploratory interviews. They have learned what is sometimes called farm Spanish. Although they know enough basic Spanish to talk with their workers, they are not completely fluent but can get by. Such individuals often seem to have negative feelings about their interactions with Hispanics in South Texas.[6] This is perhaps because, rather than interacting as equals, these Anglos interact from a position of higher social standing, as the employers of Mexicans and Mexican Americans. Many researchers have concluded that frequent cross-ethnic interaction among social unequals tends to increase the prejudice of those in a higher social status against those of lower social rank.[7]

In contrast, bilingual Anglos who frequently interact with Hispanics on an equal-status basis seem to enjoy warm personal friendships. We found very few Anglos in such relationships who felt that Hispanics discriminated against them. Furthermore, they doubted that Hispanics go around talking about Anglos in Spanish. They said that even in situations where Hispanics did not know they understood Spanish, overhearing Hispanics talking about them was very rare.

Thus bilingual Anglos who interact as equals with Hispanics seldom feel discriminated against or excluded. Their experience with Hispanics is vastly different from that of monolingual Anglos. The experience of the two groups with Hispanics is so different that it is hard to believe that they are talking about the same people. Bilingual Anglos usually report that Hispanics are warm and accepting. Darlene, for example, moved here as a young girl more than twenty years ago. She also knew some Spanish and has become more fluent over the years. "I immediately felt at home here in the Valley," she says. "I never felt isolated by Hispanics. They are so friendly and accept you almost as a member of their family."

So how is it possible that many monolingual Anglos believe that Hispanics are talking about them, while bilingual Anglos report that it almost never happens? When Hispanics switch to Spanish and look at someone and laugh, it is easy for the person to feel like the target of the laughter. Craig, for example, is an executive at an electronics firm. He is convinced his workers are talking about him whenever he walks through the warehouse at his company. "Every time I walk past a group of workers," he says, "they give me funny looks and begin to speak about me in Spanish. Often, not long after I pass, I hear them laughing."

While Latinos may use Spanish on occasion to talk about a particular Anglo, it is doubtful that it happens nearly as often as monolingual Anglos like Craig assume. Bilingual Anglos that we talked to, for example, reported that such experiences almost never happen to them. It is possible, of course, that Hispanics make comments in Spanish to each other only about Anglos that they know do not understand Spanish. Since 53 percent of Hispanics surveyed said they thought it was very important for everyone here to learn Spanish, some may talk about Anglos as a form of pressure to get them to learn Spanish. Chris remembers the pressure from his years in a Valley high school. "In school," he says, "people would talk in Spanish when I was around just so I wouldn't understand. Some guys would even tell me off in Spanish and then laugh because I didn't know I was being insulted. As a result, I learned Spanish and now enjoy living here."

Lone Anglo Students

The pressures to learn Spanish and adopt some aspects of Hispanic culture are particularly strong in Valley high schools that enroll few Anglo students. James is one of a handful of Anglos attending Los Fresnos High School. When he started school, he showed little interest in school and had problems with handwriting. So administrators there placed him where they usually placed students with problems—English as a Second Language (ESL). As a result, he grew up with other ESL students, soon becoming one of them. "Some other kids used to call me 'mojado' ["wet-back"]," he says, "because they associated me with the Mexicano students. It got to where everyone would forget that I was White. Once, for example, we were playing Port Isabel, a school with many Anglos. Anyway, we were losing and one of the guys said, 'Let's beat up the gringos really bad after the game.' I went over to him and said, 'Hey, what do you mean beat up the gringos? I'm a gringo!' He just looked at me and said, 'Shut up. You're Mexican just like the rest of us.'"

Crystal, an Anglo, has undergone a similar cultural transformation. Her friends in high school were all Hispanic. She has dated one Anglo male and says that one is enough. "He was one of the few Anglo guys at my school," she says. "He asked me out to a movie and then out to eat afterward. He asked me to stop by the theater and get the tickets before they sold out, saying he would pay me back when he picked me up. When he picked me up, he didn't pay me back and didn't open the car door for me. When we got to the movie, he didn't even ask me if I wanted something to eat or drink. At the restaurant, he didn't open the door for me or pull the chair out for me like all the other guys I dated. Worse yet, he had no table manners and really grossed me out. Then, to top it all off, he said he forgot his wallet. So I ended up paying for everything when he was the one who asked me out. From that day on, I decided that I was never going to date another Anglo."

Not all Anglos, of course, cross over. Ann remembers her high school graduation. "There were only eight Anglos out of two hundred students," she says. "I never could understand the Hispanics. They were always talking about us in Spanish or behind our backs. I left the Valley for Houston as soon as I finished high school."

Those who learn to fit in appear to make two important adjustments.

First, they learn some Spanish. Second, they learn how to use humor to their advantage, especially to take teasing without becoming offended. Keith remembers when he was the only Anglo on his high school basketball team. "They'd call me 'Cornflake' or 'Wonder Bread,'" he says. "One night when we came out for a big game, a bunch of the students had a big banner that said 'Cornflake.' They had a few other banners for some of the other guys. Actually, I think the kidding showed they liked you. When they'd start kidding and using nicknames, I'd always joke back and laugh so they'd know I wasn't offended."

The name-calling is not always good-natured. Karen remembers walking down the hallway at school and hearing mean comments. "Sometimes," she says, "they wouldn't even bother saying them in Spanish. Even if they did, I had lived in the Valley long enough to pick up basics of the Spanish language. I was always in trouble because I never put up with much from rude or mean people. I'm not fat, but I am heavy boned and I can handle myself. One day, when I was a sophomore, we were all sitting in the gym, since we couldn't go outside because it had rained the day before. Well, this guy started saying things like I was 'easy White trash' and 'a blond airhead.' Needless to say, I got up and started beating up on him. I really did a work on his face. After a few minutes, the coaches separated us. They suspended us for a week, but it was worth it since he's never dared to speak to me again."

When Tom Graham's family moved to the Valley, he felt that all the students stared at him in class. "It made me wonder if I had something on my face," he says, "because they'd stare and no one would talk to me. Little by little, I made friends. At first, the guys would play jokes on me. One day, for example, they told me to call one girl 'mamacita' [promiscuous girl]. When I did, she gave me an ugly stare. Lucky for me, she knew I didn't speak any Spanish and suspected they had set me up. Now when I remind her about that incident, we both laugh."

LONE ANGLO STUDENTS
FREQUENTLY LEARN TO
ADOPT MUCH OF THE
CULTURE OF HISPANICS.

Those who are unable to accept teasing and the use of ethnic nicknames often have a very difficult adjustment. Almost every Anglo in the Valley, for example, has been called *güero* or *güera* (Anglo; fair-complexioned person) at one time or another. Usually, no animosity is intended. When Harold heard himself referred to as a "güero," however, he thought offense was intended. "I was only twelve when my mother, brother, and sister all moved to McAllen," he says. "My parents had just divorced, and I was already quite depressed. When I started school, I tried to fit in and get along. I became friends with two Mexican Americans. I thought we were getting along fine until I found out they were calling me 'güero.' I tried not to let it get to me, but I hated them always calling attention to the fact that I am White. Since then, I have a hard time not feeling bitter toward Mexicans."

Andy, on the other hand, learned to put up with, if not enjoy, the ethnic teasing. "There weren't many Anglos at Weslaco High," he says, "and the Hispanics often called me names like 'Hick' or 'Farmer Boy.' As the years went on, I noticed that the name calling was gentler. The grudges also disappeared. Although I was still one of the very few Anglos, the Hispanics and I had somehow managed to end up good friends. Everything turned out okay."

Adjusting to Hispanic Culture

For most Anglos, the adjustment does turn out all right. In fact, most come to appreciate the Hispanic culture of South Texas. Of the 224 Anglo newcomers asked how they liked the local culture, for example, 60 percent said either "a lot" or "quite a bit." Only 1 percent said "not at all." This 1 percent and another 12 percent who said they liked the culture only "a little" often voiced the sentiment that they felt left out and did not understand the local culture. One Anglo employer, for example, says, "I never could understand why my Hispanic employees wanted certain Mexican holidays off. I thought they were just looking for an excuse not to work. Recently, some of my employees came to me and explained what those days mean to them. It helps when they have the confidence to explain things to you."

Karen Barker ran up against unfamiliar customs soon after she moved to the Valley. "Last summer," she says, "another teacher and I went to the dollar movie in Pharr. We were in a long line for tickets, right behind a young girl holding a baby. I was admiring her really adorable child. Suddenly, she thrusts the baby into my arms and yells, 'Here! You might as well hold the baby since you've been staring at her the whole time.' The next day, some Hispanic teachers told me that many people here believe you have to touch any children you admire or they'll get *mal de ojo* [evil eye]. I never expected people to want someone to touch their baby. That's certainly not part of my culture."

For many, the food also takes some getting used to. Several Anglo newcomers reported that they did not know what tortillas were before they came to the Valley. Teri Saunders remembered her first encounter with Mexican food at a company party. "They served tamales," she says, "and I'd never seen one before. I tried to cut it with my knife and thought it was awfully tough. When I looked up, the people at my table had stopped eating and were watching me, smiling. They showed me how to take the husks off first. I laugh about it now, but it was really embarrassing."

John Towers also had a tough time getting used to some local foods. "My coworkers bring some pretty strange things to eat for lunch," he says. "I almost threw up when some of them brought in tacos made of meat from a cow's head and wanted me to share them. The hardest thing to eat, though, was *menudo* [tripe stew]. I'm used to it now, though, and consider it fine cuisine."

Bill James, a twenty-five-year-old marketing director, also has learned to appreciate the Hispanic culture of South Texas. More than the food, he appreciates subtle cultural aspects like the closeness of Hispanic families. "Back in Des Moines," he says, "my family hardly ever had dinner together. We were all so busy that we were almost strangers. When I moved to the Valley, I made friends with a coworker, Ramón. Soon, I was having dinner at his house. I noticed his whole family sat down to eat together. Afterward, they would talk awhile before leaving the table. I thought they were being courteous because I was their guest, so I asked Ramón if they always did that. He looked at me funny and asked, 'Doesn't your family?' I didn't know what to say and was embarrassed. He noticed and quickly said, 'We really don't think about it. It just happens!'"

Ken Anderson also appreciates the importance of family in Mexican culture. His immersion in local culture is a bit more intense than most, since his neighbors are all Hispanic. "At three o'clock one morning," he says, "some beautiful Mexican music awakened me on Mother's Day. I saw a group of mariachis singing at my neighbor's window. They were singing to his mother. I could see that she was so happy she began to cry. I wish I knew what that song was about because it was so beautiful. I wish my people did things like that. We usually just buy our mother a card or take her out to eat."

Family was the aspect of Hispanic culture most admired by Anglo newcomers. Katherine Hill, for example, said that her greatest surprise when she moved to the Valley came as she walked through the mall in McAllen. "I was surprised," she said, "to see how many families were there. Parents and children were often together. It wasn't just young kids, but teens and their parents were doing things together. Most kids up north wouldn't be caught dead at the mall with their parents, and many parents there don't have time for their kids."

Paul, a college professor, expressed surprise at how most of his students continue to live with their families. "Even after getting married," he says, "many of them continue to live with or close to their families. I'm always surprised at the size and closeness of families living in the same household. Where I come from, children are encouraged to go away when they graduate from high school."

Patricia came to South Texas two years ago to run a temporary employment service. "I am constantly amazed," she says, "how older brothers and sisters here take responsibility for younger family members. Also, it's usual to see real affection between a father and his children. It doesn't seem to embarrass Hispanics here to show love for each other."

While most Anglo newcomers we talked with admired the family-centered aspect of Mexican-origin culture, more than a few expressed dismay at the way some Hispanic men treat women.[8] Hilda, a forty-five-year-old housewife who had lived in the Valley for only fourteen months, for example, found the move here from Illinois quite a culture shock. "I see discrimination all the time," she says, "but not against Anglos. Here they discriminate against women. If I call the bank about a payment or loan, they automatically treat me as if I'm incapable of doing or understanding anything. When my husband calls, though, they always return his calls and treat him like a valued customer. I find it difficult to adapt to such a backward society."

Andrea is a single mother with similar sentiments. "The other day," she says, "I took my car to a national chain repair shop. I was having problems with the air-conditioning and asked them to give me an estimate on fixing it and replacing two tires. They assured me they would call me the next day. I heard nothing for several days, so I went to find out what was going on. I really had to have my car. They hadn't even touched the air-conditioning, but they had already put on one tire without my approval. So I demanded my keys. They tried to convince me they had lost them. I threatened legal action and they suddenly 'found' my keys. Had I been a man, I truly doubt they would have tried such a stunt."

Although many Anglo newcomers recognize this issue as a legitimate concern, most Anglo newcomers believe that local Hispanics are very friendly. Fred Aikens says he enjoys South Texas because people here are really caring. "About two years ago," he says, "I worked the evening shift at a convenience store for almost a year. Every day I had people who would stop and chat with me about the weather, life, or the day's happenings. To me, this typifies the Valley's outlook on life. You don't always have to be in a hurry, but should relax, be friendly, and take time with people."

Stephanie Kazen has a similar impression of the Valley. "I have lived here in the Valley for ten years," she says. "We've always had good experiences with the Hispanics here. One day, for example, I was on my way home with my two children when I got a flat tire. I didn't know how to fix a flat, and the kids were crying. I was almost at my wits' end when a Hispanic family pulled over. The man fixed my flat while the woman took my little girl into her arms to comfort her."

Not everyone, of course, likes the close personal treatment. Susan Morgan feels that local Hispanics sometimes do not respect her privacy or personal space. "One Saturday afternoon," she says, "my family and I decided to head down to the beach at South Padre Island. Big mistake. It was so crowded. We took one look at the crowd by the jetties and headed toward the other end of the island. We finally found a little stretch of beach that didn't have too many people around. No sooner had we settled in than people started moving in. I couldn't understand why everyone wanted to be so close together until one day a friend explained that Mexican culture has a different idea of social distance than ours. That also helped me understand why some people from Mexico stand so close to you when they speak."

Culture and Discrimination

Because Anglos and South Texas Hispanics have different cultural backgrounds, some misunderstandings are inevitable. Some bilingual Anglos who come to South Texas, for example, are dismayed when certain local Hispanics refuse to speak Spanish with them. For example, John, a high school teacher, says, "I was excited to be moving to a place where I could practice my Spanish. Whenever I speak it to any of the students, though, they answer back in English. Some even get huffy about it. The same thing happens with some teachers. I know they speak Spanish because I hear them using it among themselves. What good does it do to learn Spanish if Hispanics refuse to speak it with you just because you're Anglo?"

John apparently believes Latinos discriminate against him because many of them refuse to speak Spanish with him. Nevertheless, their reluctance to do so may be understandable. Some of them interpret an Anglo's use of Spanish with them as implying, "I know you can't speak English well, so I'm going to speak to you in Spanish." Others may not want to show that the form of Spanish they speak is not the standard Spanish John probably learned in college—they do not want anyone making fun of their Tex-Mex or calling them "pochos." Still others, particularly younger Mexican Americans, have come to use language as a cultural boundary that distinguishes insiders from outsiders. Because being Mexican American is more than a linguistic distinction, they are not always willing to let an outsider in simply because he or she has learned the language.

Ann Compton, however, finds many Spanish speakers willing to let her use her Spanish. "I have many friends," she says, "who let me speak Spanish. Most of them are older people, particularly those born in Mexico. Mr. Garcia, for example, is our *conserje* [custodian]. We always greet each other in Spanish, and he seems to appreciate it. When I was a new teacher at La Joya, many of the teachers had not received supplies like chalk, erasers, or drawing paper. I went to talk to Mr. Garcia and asked for what I needed. He got them for me right away. Later I discovered that the other Anglo teachers went a couple of days without their supplies because they couldn't communicate with him. Without my Spanish, I'm sure I would have been in the same situation."

Even when language is not a barrier, cultural differences and stereotypes may divide Anglos and Mexican Americans. An Anglo psychology professor at UT–Pan American, for example, remembers an incident that happened ten years ago, soon after he had moved to South Texas. "I went to a Mexican restaurant," he says, "to get some breakfast tacos. I ordered scrambled eggs and *chorizo* [spicy sausage]. On the menu, the order came with flour tortillas, which you could roll into tacos. But when the Mexican woman brought me my order, she had substituted dry, unbuttered toast in place of the tortillas. At first I thought she was trying to tell me that I didn't belong there with all the Mexican customers. Because she was so friendly, however, I guessed that she believed gringos eat toast instead of tortillas and was simply trying to accommodate me. Choosing to believe the latter explanation, I choked down the dry toast and left with a 'Muchas gracias.'"

Sometimes, the stereotypes work to the advantage of Anglos. One of our Hispanic interviewers, for example, reported an incident that he has seen repeated, in one form or another, on many occasions. "I had picked up some groceries," he says, "and was at the checkout. The Anglo guy in front of me paid with a check and all that the clerk, a Hispanic, made him do was to show his driver's license. When it was my turn, I too paid with a check and showed my license. But the cashier wanted more ID. I told her she had not requested any additional ID from the guy ahead of me. She replied that it was store policy. I thought, 'Bull!' I just grabbed my groceries, gave her the check, and left without showing her any other ID."

Raymond Smith observed a similar form of preferential treatment. "One day," he says, "I was coming home from work. I noticed a line of cars stopped by a police blockade. As I waited my turn, I could see the drivers ahead of me showing papers to the police officer. Then it hit me. This was a license and insurance check. At the time, I had neither. The police officer checked every driver ahead of me. When I got there, he just looked at me and said, 'Thanks. Go on through.' When I got home, my wife, who is Hispanic, told me it was probably because most Hispanics in the Valley believe that Whites are all rich, so there's no need to wonder whether a gringo in a nice car has a license or insurance."

Some stereotypes, however, have an opposite effect. Many single Anglo women report that some Hispanic men often stereotype them as "easy." Sandy remembers an incident that happened at the home of her friend María. "We were going to band practice," she says, "so I asked her for a ride. My parents dropped me off at her house. While she was changing for practice, I waited in the game room. Juan, her older brother, saw me and started making passes at me. He even placed his arm around me, so I pushed him away. I told him that those White girls he sees on TV are make-believe and that he needed to face reality."

Sally had a similar experience in 1990 when she found herself the only Anglo first-year student in a local high school. "My younger brothers and sisters were all in grade school," she says, "so I was all alone. The first day was the worst. I got called 'la güera barata' [cheap Anglo] and 'la güera fácil' [easy Anglo]. At first I didn't know what it meant, but it wasn't hard to tell it wasn't something nice. Those first few months were very rough, until people took me for myself and not the goofy image they get of White girls from movies or TV."

Though name-calling like this did happen to younger Anglos in the public schools, most reported that such incidents happened only before they had a chance to make friends. The few Anglo adults reporting bigotry or ethnic comments often overheard them in casual conversations. Katy, for example, was shopping at Sears during her first year of teaching in the Valley. Behind her were two Hispanic women discussing a friend who was apparently engaged to an Anglo. "They were outraged," she says, "that she would marry an Anglo. When I turned around and looked at them, they got a bit sheepish and turned and left."

Most Hispanics who have anti-Anglo sentiments generally voice them in private. Yoli, for example, had no idea her own family harbored anti-Anglo sentiments until she became engaged to one. "I couldn't believe their response," she says. "They made comments such as 'You're really going to marry a hillbilly?' and 'How can you think of bringing White trash into the family?' I couldn't understand how my own family could make such ugly comments. My mother wasn't as harsh, but she brought up the issue of children. 'White people don't have the same morals we do,' she told me. I had never heard such sentiments from any of them before. But then, I guess it's because I never thought I'd marry an Anglo."

In all our exploratory interviews, only one Anglo newcomer reported a flagrant act of bigotry. Edwin Halstrom sells grocery products to local stores. "This job brings me into contact with all kinds of people," he says. "One day, I went to a neighborhood grocery store in Pharr. As I set up a demonstration of my products, the owner walked in. I offered my hand and introduced myself. He just looked at me, saying nothing. So, after a few seconds, I lowered my hand. Then, he said, 'My family owns this store and we don't do business with White trash.' I couldn't believe his unnecessary rudeness. I just packed up my products in silence and left."

Occasionally, we hear reports that some Anglos feel excluded from clubs and social organizations. Nonetheless, in all the exploratory interviews we conducted, only one incident was reported. Martha Richards is a teacher whose family has lived in the Valley for sixteen years. "Because our daughter had become very interested in folkloric dancing when we lived abroad," she says, "we let her join a folkloric dance club here. She really enjoyed it and seemed to fit in well with the other children, all of whom were Hispanic. But whenever we went to a club meeting, the Hispanic parents seemed very cold. None of them ever talked to us, and we felt pretty isolated. They never told us to leave. We just took the hint and quit going."

Most Anglos have quite a different experience. Many report frequent invitations to visit socially with Hispanics. Also, many are invited to attend Hispanic social events such as weddings, *quinceañeras* (coming-out parties for fifteen-year-old girls), and *pachangas* (barbecue parties).

Mary and her husband, Charles, for example, moved to the Valley in 1981 as retirees. They rented an apartment but did not know anyone. One day, only two weeks after they arrived, they took a walk to the pool area of their apartment complex. "We didn't know that someone had rented the recreational building for a wedding reception," she says. "We could hear Mexican music and some very good singing by male voices. In just a few minutes, the bride's parents stepped out and saw us. Without even knowing us, they asked us to come in and join in their celebration.

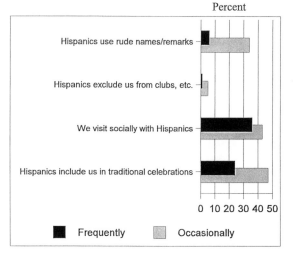

Fig. 7.2. Discriminatory
and inclusive Hispanic
behavior experienced by
Anglo newcomers (Anglo
Newcomers Survey, 1996)

Although we were pleased at their invitation, we weren't dressed prop-
erly. They understood, but a few minutes later they sent the mariachis
outside to sing for us. I'll never forget how special that made me feel."

In the Anglo Newcomers Survey, we included several items designed
to measure how frequently respondents believed they were either discriminated against or made to feel included. The items used to measure
discrimination were (1) "How often do local Hispanics use offensive
or prejudiced remarks about you or your race or ethnic group?" and
(2) "How often do you feel excluded from clubs or civic organizations because of your race or ethnic status?"

Two additional items were selected to measure social inclusion.
These were (1) "How often do you have social visits with friends who
are Hispanic?" and (2) "How often do Hispanics invite you to participate in their traditional customs and celebrations?" Figure 7.2 shows the
percentage of all respondents who answered either "frequently" or
"occasionally."

For both items used to measure perceived discrimination, the percentage of respondents answering "frequently" was very low. Almost no
Anglo newcomers reported any degree of exclusion from clubs and civic
organizations. Though 34 percent said they believed Hispanics occasionally made biased remarks about Anglos, 60 percent (not shown) believed it happened rarely or never.

A much larger proportion of Anglo newcomers expressed the view
that they felt included by Hispanics in social visits or in traditional Hispanic celebrations. The combined percentage saying they were fre-

quently or occasionally included was more than 70 percent on both items. Thus, though some Anglo newcomers perceive discrimination and exclusion, a far larger percentage believes that Hispanics are nondiscriminatory and inclusive in their relationships.

On most of these items, we were unable to compare the responses of Anglo newcomers with those by Anglos raised in South Texas. The second item from the top in Figure 7.2 (how often Hispanics exclude them from clubs and civic organizations), however, was included in the Multiethnic Culture Survey, which included long-term Anglo residents and allowed us to compare Anglo newcomers with long-term residents on this item. In contrast to the figures shown for Anglo newcomers on this item (1 percent "frequently" and 5 percent "occasionally"), 7 percent of long-term residents said they frequently felt excluded, while 20 percent said they occasionally felt left out.

Similar to the results shown in Figure 7.1, long-term Anglo residents seem much more likely than Anglo newcomers to feel excluded and to perceive discriminatory treatment by Hispanics. We believe the explanation for this is similar to the one proposed earlier. That is, many grew up in an age when Anglos were dominant and thus have a hard time adjusting to a world where being Anglo does not automatically confer superior social status. In addition, many long-term Anglo residents are in a less protected social position, having to compete for jobs and status with increasingly mobile middle-income Mexican Americans.

Bolillos Migrantes *(Winter Texans)*

If Anglo newcomers are more protected than long-term residents, Anglo retirees who migrate annually to South Texas are even more so. Every year, approximately ninety thousand of them migrate to the Valley to escape cold winters "up North." Approximately 85 percent of these Winter Texans congregate in recreational vehicle parks, where daily life revolves around recreational activities exclusively for park residents. Even excursions outside the parks to shop or to dine out are usually done in groups. As a result, Winter Texan retirees seldom interact with local people as neighbors, friends, or coworkers.[9]

With little chance to develop close personal relationships, some local residents become resentful of the increased pressure on local facilities. Bill Wilson, a forty-one-year-old resident of many years, comments, "We got out of church one Sunday morning and wanted to eat out for lunch. After a long wait to get in the restaurant, all we could see was a room full of white-haired heads. Winter Texans were all over the place. Many of them acted as if they owned the place, taking all the time in the world to visit long after finishing their meal. They were totally oblivious to the rest of us who were waiting to get in."

Winter Texans are often fully aware of their contribution to the local economy. According to local chambers of commerce, they pay out more than $200 million a year for goods and services. As a result, some feel entitled to extra benefits. Seventy-three percent of the 326 Winter Texans we surveyed, for example, agreed that people in the Valley should be grateful to Winter Texans for their contribution to the local economy. A smaller proportion, 24 percent, believed that local businesses should give them some form of preferential treatment.

To make matters worse, a few Winter Texans do not wait for local people to provide such preference. One produce manager, for example, says he is tired of out-of-state retirees helping themselves to produce at packing sheds and fields and orchards. "I often have to run them off," he says, "and a few can get pretty ugly about leaving. I've had them curse me, and so have farmers who object to them helping themselves. They argue that they have a right to free produce because they're helping our economy. We don't object to giving out a few samples, but they can't understand that there are thousands of them, and we can't afford to let them all help themselves to whatever they care to haul out of our sheds or fields."

In spite of negative perceptions like these, the vast majority of Winter Texans and Valley residents we talked to have generally positive impressions of one another. Many Winter Texans said they had chosen to come to the Valley because they had heard the people were so friendly. One couple said, "In Florida, we saw signs like 'Go Home Snowbird.' We never liked the term *snowbird*. When we came to Texas, we saw signs everywhere saying 'Welcome Winter Texans.' That made us feel like we're really wanted and that we're part Texan."

Marvin Rand, a sixty-eight-year-old retiree from Canada, has similar sentiments. "We had traveled most of the southern United States," he says, "and found nothing but high crime rates and unfriendly people. I had never in my life encountered such rudeness. The young people in Arizona are the worst. They just don't want outsiders in their towns. A friend recommended the Rio Grande Valley, so we decided to give it a try. We've found doctors that take time with us and people on the streets who'll say hello and even stop to visit. For the past three winters, we've been in Winter Texan paradise. Valley residents are by far the friendliest people we have encountered in our six years of travel."

Valley residents we talked to generally have only superficial impressions of Winter Texans because of the very limited contact between the two groups. The RV parks are generally closed to outsiders, so Winter Texans and Valley residents seldom interact, except on the roads and in restaurants, stores, and shops. Arturo Anzaldua, for example, voices a common complaint. "One evening," he says, "I was late for a meeting. I got trapped behind a carload of Winter Texans from Iowa. They were going only twenty-five miles an hour in a thirty-five-mile-an-hour zone. I tried to pass, but I couldn't. They kept looking at everything and slowing down. I finally got around them, but I was late to my meeting because of them."

This response is interesting in light of a complaint commonly voiced by Winter Texans. One respondent said, "Why do people here have to drive so fast and get so impatient to pass? That would be illegal where we come from." Indeed, 57 percent of Winter Texans surveyed agreed with the statement "Local drivers are reckless and impatient." Most Winter Texans come from small towns in midwestern states such as Minnesota, Iowa, and Kansas, and driving habits are undoubtedly quite different in the Valley.

When Valley residents do get to know Winter Texans on a personal basis, friendships can develop and driving habits fade in importance. José and Blanca, for example, live in a mobile home park that, in the winter months, fills with Winter Texans. "We got acquainted with one couple," Blanca says, "and we became close friends. They would frequently babysit for our smallest child, and we would take care of things around their house. When our oldest son married last summer, they made a special trip to be at the wedding. The following summer, we made a trip to see them in Minnesota."

Such friendships, however, are quite rare, not because of bad feelings but because there are few opportunities for interaction as friends and neighbors. When Winter Texans become friendly with local residents, it is usually limited to the customer-clerk relationship. Several Hispanic employees, for example, report that Winter Texans like to be friendly, but usually as customers. Some like to give them advice about life. One beautician says, "I frequently receive free advice from Winter Texan customers. Recently, for example, they've found out I'm engaged. They have lots of advice about marriage, how to save money, how to stay married, etc."

One mechanic says that Winter Texans are constantly giving him advice about how to run his shop. "Obviously," he says, "there are times when their advice doesn't sound applicable. But I don't take it as an insult. I appreciate them taking the time to share their point of view."

Some Winter Texans are equally tolerant and understanding. Ben Frost and his wife describe a recent incident at a local restaurant. "I ordered rice," he says. "In Iowa, that means a bowl of rice cereal. What they gave me here, though, was Spanish rice, with all of the spices and stuff. We laughed about it with the restaurant people. Ever since then, I've learned to specify what kind of rice I want when I'm in the Valley."

Many Winter Texans comment on how polite local young people are. Paul Anderson, for example, is from Minnesota. "I had finished eating at a fast-food place," he says, "when I reached out for my cane. It had rolled out of reach. Immediately a young Hispanic boy got the cane and handed it to me. My friends and I always comment on how much we appreciate the way local kids show respect for age."

Not all young Valley residents are polite, of course. Charles Mathews had one bad incident to relate. "One day in McAllen," he says, "we had a flat tire. While I was fixing it, I noticed many people whizzing by very recklessly. Some of them didn't even try to avoid us. I just ignored it until someone yelled, 'Get off the road, you old geezer!' I was very mad, but I couldn't do anything about it."

In spite of such incidents, Winter Texans generally report that local people treat them very well. Fully 94 percent of respondents in our Winter Texans Survey agreed with the statement "Most Hispanics who work in local businesses are friendly and helpful to Winter Texans." Betty Carlson, for example, says that she and her husband always feel welcome. "We ate out the other day," she says, "and this little Mexican lady came up and asked if she could clean the cracker crumbs from our table. I told her, 'We can do that.' Then she said, 'Oh, but those cracker crumbs give me a job.' They're always like that. When we go somewhere to eat, they go out of their way to make us comfortable."

Local people employed in establishments frequented by Winter Texans generally recognize that their jobs depend on these visitors. As a result, many see them in a positive light. One young woman who works a night shift at Whataburger, a Texas-based fast-food restaurant, says, "Without Winter Texans, business is usually dead. They come in the mornings for breakfast, coffee, or just to read the newspaper. Then they're back for lunch. You'll always see them here. I like the night shift because they come in after their folk dances. They look so cute. The men wear shirts that match their wives' dresses, and the ladies have those short dresses with those puffy slips underneath."

Still, the images that Winter Texans and the local population have of each other are not always so positive. One of our interviewers, for example, was stunned when two of the three couples she interviewed ex-

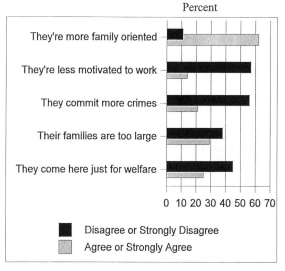

Percent

Fig. 7.3. Agreement of Winter Texans with stereotypes about Hispanics (Winter Texans Survey, 1995)

pressed stereotyped notions about Mexican Americans. One couple, the Masons, said, "The Valley is a perfect place for Hispanics. A lot of labor is needed in the fields, and that's what you people do best." Ellen, the wife of one of the other couples, said she remembers how she used to feel sorry every time she passed a field up north. "I'd see Mexican workers struggling on their hands and knees in heavy rain," she said. "At first, I thought this was kind of cruel. But then I realized that you are all used to working under those conditions, so it's not cruel at all."

We asked the 326 Winter Texans surveyed several questions to measure whether they agree with many common stereotypes about Hispanics. The responses in both the "agree" and "disagree" categories, as shown in Figure 7.3, reveal a general tendency to reject negative stereotypes and to accept positive ones. All but a handful, for example, agree that Hispanics are family oriented. In addition, far more respondents reject negative stereotypes than accept them. Only on the issue of family size do these respondents come close to a generally negative judgment regarding Hispanics.

Perhaps the most frequent complaint by Winter Texans about Hispanics is their use of Spanish. Richard Wolfson, for example, hates to hear Spanish spoken by U.S. citizens. "It bothers me," he says, "for people to call themselves U.S. citizens when they've been here for generations and never learned English. Every person that becomes a U.S. citizen should have to speak English." Still, only 11 percent agreed that Hispanics would be better off if they forgot Spanish and spoke only English.

Thus most seem to take the use of Spanish in stride. Arthur Manning and his wife describe an incident in a store. "We had found some funny shirts," he says, "with things on them about the Valley. We thought they'd be nice to send to our kids. We asked the clerk for the price, and she just smiled. We asked again and she looked at us with the same smile. Then we realized she didn't speak English. We asked another shopper to translate for us, and she was happy to do so. Without further confusion, we bought the shirts and were on our way."

Winter Texans who hear people speaking Spanish around them often suspect that Spanish is being used to talk about them. "A few years back," says Buck Harvey, "I was in a local restaurant on a Saturday night. As we were having dinner, a couple of men were laughing and making a racket in Spanish. We don't speak Spanish, but we knew they were talking about us. It makes us feel left out or like we're not in the United States. They should stick to English."

Like many Hispanics, Paula Zamora thinks Winter Texans should remember that they are in an area where most people speak Spanish as their native language. "My husband and I were going into a store the other day," she says, "just minding our own business. We were talking about some family matters when some Winter Texan came up behind us and said, 'You're in the United States now. You should speak English.' I turned to him and said, 'When you're in Mexico, do you speak Spanish?' My husband didn't want a scene, so he took me by the arm and led me away before I could say anything else."

Few Winter Texans, of course, speak Spanish when they go to Mexico. Still, most manage to get by and enjoy the experience. Forty percent of Winter Texans surveyed said they frequently cross the border to shop or visit, while another 50 percent said they occasionally do so. The Johnsons and their friends are among those who frequently go to Mexico. "There's a restaurant in Monterrey that serves only *cabrito* [young goat meat]," says Mr. Johnson. "We went in and really enjoyed it. The restaurant was beautiful. They didn't speak any English and none of us knew Spanish. We didn't know how to order, so we did our best with sign language. The waiter was really nice. He brought over a diagram of the different parts. When he brought us our food, it was delicious. He also brought a big grinding-stone container of salsa. It was so hot that if there was anything in the *cabrito*, the salsa killed it. We had a lot of fun. We love Monterrey."

When Mr. and Mrs. Luken travel to Mexico, they prefer the border city of Miguel Alemán, across from Roma. "People there are always glad to see us," she says, "even if we don't buy anything. Since the street peddlers don't speak English, I make signs with my hands, and they understand me. We love taking family members over to Mexico. When my daughter and grandson came last year, we took them on the hand-pulled ferry at Los Ebanos [between McAllen and Rio Grande City]. All we did was go across and come right back, but we had a lot of fun. I told my grandson, 'You'll never do this again in your life.' The man on the ferry didn't speak English, so he had a hard time telling me we had to pay both over and back, even though we didn't get off. We really enjoy having Mexico so close."

Because of experiences like these, some Winter Texans develop a fierce loyalty to South Texas and its people. Seventy-two percent of Winter Texans surveyed said they like the customs and lifestyles of Hispanic people in the Valley either "quite a bit" or "a great deal." Bill Fields, for example, is a widower who has been coming to the Valley for many years. "I will continue to drive down for as long as I can," he says. "When I reach the point that I can't drive, my sons have agreed to bring me down and take me back. When I get to where I can't sit in a car for several hours, I'll have them fly me down. The only thing that will keep me away will be if I'm lying helpless in a nursing home."

Sometimes Winter Texans enjoy the Valley to the point that they choose to become year-round residents. The Morgans, for example, decided two years ago to buy a home here rather than stay a few months in an RV park. "The change," says Mr. Morgan, "was drastic but pleasant. I discovered just how friendly people are. One day, for instance, I was cutting my lawn when a neighbor from two houses down offered to help. I was amazed at his eagerness to help, and we soon became close friends. We've learned to overlook our differences in culture and have become like one big family."

According to a recent survey of Winter Texans by business school professors at UT–Pan American, the percentage of Winter Texans living outside the RV parks went from 8 to 17 percent between 1994 and 1995.[10] If this increase represents a stable trend, contact between Anglo retirees and Hispanics will take a new turn. Other Anglo retirees, like the Morgans, will increasingly interact as neighbors with Hispanics.

Volunteer work is another factor that increasingly brings Winter Texans and Hispanics together as equals. Twenty-eight percent of those surveyed said they did some volunteer work on at least half the days they are here. Karen Torgerson, for example, discovered volunteer work soon after her husband died. "After he died," she says, "I really didn't have anything left for me in Illinois. We had been coming here for several years, so I came alone, with just my dog. I got bored playing shuffleboard and cards, so I decided to find out where I could do some good. I've tried many places and enjoy them all, but the hospital has been the most enjoyable. I really enjoy the people I work with there, and I feel like I'm really doing something useful."

Winter Texans who isolate themselves in RV parks, however, seldom come to think of the Valley as home. They find friendly people, but few friends, among the local population. Some of them can identify everyone in their park, but cannot name a single local person with whom they have established a lasting friendship. They admire local culture, but from a distance. Myrtle Adams, for example, says she appreciates the value that Hispanics place on family. "They have a very strong bond of love that holds them together," she says. "The young Hispanic children are the happiest I've ever seen. I think they don't know how to cry, because I've never seen any of them do so." But she has no Hispanic friends.

There are exceptions, of course, to such generalizations. Winter Texans who volunteer in hospitals, museums, and schools often establish close friendships with Hispanics. In fact, though 47 percent of the Winter Texans we surveyed said it was important to them to establish friendships with local residents, only 17 percent said that they frequently did so. Many fail to establish such friendships because they live in exclusive RV parks, rather than homes, apartments, or even regular mobile home parks.

A few manage to become friends with local service people. The Johnsons, for example, had a minor accident in McAllen on their first trip to the Valley in 1983. "At first," says Mr. Johnson, "we thought fate was trying to tell us to go back home. The first week was hell because we didn't know our way around and couldn't find a decent price to fix our RV. We finally found Antonio, a man in his early forties, who did a fine job on it. He came to visit when he finished the job. He even invited us out to eat. We had a pleasant time, and now we always get together every time we're down here. I really appreciate his friendship. We used to keep our distance from people because we didn't want to feel obligated to them if we had something else planned. Now, though, I enjoy just being friends and don't mind being a bit obligated."

Because of experiences like this, some Anglos find South Texas a truly enjoyable place to live. Those who come thinking it will be "Everywhere, U.S.A.," however, often become disillusioned and claim that they are a mistreated minority group. As we have seen, the difference between these two reactions cannot be explained simply by the number of years one spends here or by how well one speaks Spanish. Long-term residents, as we saw, often feel more discriminated against than Anglo newcomers. Similarly, Anglos who know farm Spanish may harbor more old stereotypes than those who know no Spanish. More than anything else, interaction with Hispanics in friendships and other equal-status relations seems to produce the best adjustment.

Mrs. Rose Bork is a Winter Texan who discovered this secret through her volunteer work at a junior high school in Mission. "When I came back to the Valley this year," she says, "I was very uneasy about whether the children would remember me or want me back. When I got there, though, two boys that I had helped a lot last year came running up. They gave me big welcome back hugs and enormous smiles. I really felt appreciated. Now, every time someone says, 'Welcome home,' I feel like I really *have* come home."

Black, Brown, and White: Race and Ethnicity in South Texas

Chapter 8

I went to school in Mission back in the 1940s. Relations between Anglos and Mexicans were very one-sided. Whenever fights would occur, we Mexican kids would always get licks, but the principal would just tell the Anglos to go back to their side of the school grounds. Once, I got in a fight with the only Black kid in our school. The principal called us in and swatted me several times. When he finished with me, the Black kid said, "I hope you're not going to give me licks, sir. We Anglos gotta stick together." The principal laughed and gave him only one lick.

OMAR IZAGUIRRE, 1994

Though quick thinking saved this African American from a few extra swats, a greater problem of identity remained. Where do Blacks in South Texas, who are less than 1 percent of the population, fit in? Since 88 percent of the Valley is Mexican American, and since many Anglos and Hispanics hold traditional stereotypes of Blacks, some confusion about their place in the racial and ethnic makeup of the Valley is understandable.[1]

Rodney Harris became acutely aware of this when his family moved here two years ago. "First," he says, "Whites and Hispanics have lived together in this area a long time and have had a long time to adjust. Many kids in the Valley have never seen a Black except on TV, so they have some pretty weird ideas about us. At first, mixing in was hard and I felt awkward. Once I really got involved in school clubs, though, I started getting many friends. Now I'm just Rod Harris, not Rodney Harris the Black kid. With more Black families moving into the area, I hope that everyone can get over the shock and just see us as people."

Others, like Sharon Johnson, do not want to be just another American. She feels it is very important to maintain her identity as an African American. "It's very hard to maintain your blackness," she says, "when you're surrounded by Mexican culture. If I didn't keep on my kids to remember their roots, they'd soon be acting like little Mexicans. Don't get me wrong, Mexicans have every right to be as proud of their

*Though Blacks have made
important contributions to
Valley history, few African
Americans are natives of
South Texas*
(photo courtesy of
George C. McLemore).

heritage as we Blacks are of ours. But Black people have no business living their life like a Mexican. My boys were tempted many times to hang with those little gangster wanna-bes, but they've held strong. I'm really proud of them."

Mrs. Johnson helps her children maintain their identity by showing them documentaries about Black history and films by Black directors. They also read biographies of influential Black leaders or other inspirational books. In addition, she regularly seeks out other Blacks living in the area. "It's very important for the Black community to bond together," she says, "because we're an extreme minority down here."

Though Blacks have always been a minority in the Valley, they have a long history here.[2] Estevanico was an African shipwrecked with Cabeza de Vaca on the Texas coast in 1529. Together, they wandered through South Texas and up the Rio Grande, before being rescued in the Sonoran desert. Another shipwreck, sometime before 1747, stranded a group of African slaves who intermarried with local Native Americans. The tribe became known as Los Negros and settled somewhere between present-day Reynosa and Matamoros, only to disappear along with other local tribes.[3]

In the early 1850s, John Webber, a White settler in Texas, married Silvia Hector, a former slave. They brought their family to South Texas to escape the extreme prejudices of Texas settlers. Together, they founded El Rancho Viejo on the north side of the Rio Grande, near what is now the Santa Ana Wildlife Refuge. Other racially mixed couples and former slaves joined them. In 1884 this group built the Jackson Ranch Church, probably the oldest Protestant church in Hidalgo County.

After the Civil War, the building of the railroad into South Texas and the assignment of Black troops to military bases here brought in greater numbers of Blacks. A strong community of Blacks developed in Edinburg. They had their own church, school, cafes, and taxi stand. In 1942 the first Black high school opened in Edinburg, the only one available to Blacks in the Valley. With the growing immigration from Mexico, however, Mexican immigrants took jobs traditionally held by Blacks. As a result, many Black families moved north to find work. Only in recent years has another in-migration of Blacks—one whose members are increasingly college-educated—developed. In 1992 long-term residents and Black newcomers worked together to organize the first chapter of the NAACP in South Texas.

Because of the shortage of skilled and professional workers in South Texas, many highly educated Blacks find it fairly easy to obtain employment. From these newcomers and from some long-term residents, we collected exploratory interviews from 85 respondents (the Valley Blacks Exploratory Interviews). We followed these with the small (37 respondents) Valley Blacks Survey to describe the experience of Blacks in South Texas (Appendix B, no. 9).

Though slightly over half (56 percent) of the respondents in the Valley Blacks Survey said they liked the lifestyle and customs of the Valley "a lot" or "quite a bit," most also reported a difficult adjustment. Mrs. Barnes, a Black teacher interviewed by a former student, for example, describes the initial shock. "When I decided to come to the Valley," she says, "I thought that I would fit right in because the Valley is mainly Hispanic, and they, like us, are a minority group. It didn't cross my mind then that minorities can also have prejudices of their own. You remember how strict I am and how much I emphasize discipline and learning. Well, I found that many of my students mistook my concern for hatred. I've overheard conversations in the halls by students who call me 'the witch who hates Hispanics.' They are wrong. I treat all my students the same, whatever their race or creed. I consider myself one of them, but they attempt to separate themselves from me. They always think of my skin color when they don't agree with my teaching methods."

Mary, the student who interviewed Mrs. Barnes, recalls her own initial misinterpretations. "I remember her strict disciplinary tactics," she says. "As a freshman in high school, she once hit my hand with a ruler because she caught me looking at the typewriter keys during dictation. I thought she just wanted to humiliate me. Not even my mother treated me like that. But all of that changed during an awards assembly. When they gave me an academic award, she approached me, hugged me warmly, and told me with genuine tears in her eyes, 'I knew you could accomplish great things. All you needed was a little push.' Then I remembered all those times she'd come to school an hour early to give me extra help. All the hard times were evidence that she really cared. She didn't have to go out of her way for her students, but she always did, and still does. Many students are beginning to appreciate her now."

Students like Mary, who have had little experience with Blacks, may tend to assume that any personal idiosyncrasies of Blacks are racial in nature. A strict Hispanic or Anglo teacher, among the many Hispanic and Anglo teachers such students have already encountered, is accepted simply as a strict teacher. But the lone Black, in a world of limited experience with Blacks, may find much of what he or she does attributed to race.

Emerson Jefferies discovered this when an angry father came storming into his classroom. "He was pissed at me," he says, "because I flunked his kid for cheating on my exam. The next thing I know I'm down in the principal's office face to face with a man who wants to tear my head off. He yelled at me, 'How the hell can you flunk my kid? You Blacks get all the breaks. If it were a Black kid, I'm sure he'd get off with a simple warning.' He demanded that I explain why I was so prejudiced against the Mexicans. I told him if any kid is caught cheating, they're dealt with just as his kid was. That wasn't enough for him. He demanded that the principal reprimand me for my behavior. The principal tried to compromise by telling me to give the kid a new exam. At first, I refused. I explained that I had warned all the kids what would happen if they were caught cheating. The principal made me do it anyway, and the kid passed."

Stereotypes

When Valley residents have limited experience with Blacks, many of them fall back on stereotypes. Jack Anthony remembers the first few weeks after he arrived here as the worst. "I had only been in the Valley three weeks," he says, "and everywhere I went, people stared and gave me strange looks. Sometimes, little kids at the mall would point at me, or say something, only to be corrected by their mothers. Now I don't mind. I'm probably the first Black man they've seen, so I'm happy to talk to them. But I still get some very strange reactions.

"One day, though, I was walking down a dark street in my neighborhood. I had left my watch at home, so I walked up to a man and asked for the time. The next thing I know, he's begging me not to hurt him and giving me his wallet and watch. I told him I only wanted to know what time it was. He apologized and said someone in Houston had robbed him using the same line. Later, I got to know him better and now we're good friends."

Things do not always end so well. Allen Davis remembers going to an electronics store with his mother. "While my mom was in line to pay for some merchandise," he says, "I was checking out some camcorders. As I was checking the price on one, this man came up and stood right beside me. He said, 'Those cameras must be way out of your budget. Besides, I just counted them.' It really made my blood boil."

Gary Anthony finds that some stereotyping is well intentioned, even if it is offensive. "We have this one neighbor," he says, "who makes a point to remember Juneteenth [June 19, the African American holiday that celebrates when word of the emancipation of slaves got to Texas]. Trouble is, he comes by and gives us a big watermelon and a liter of red soda. He seriously thinks he's being respectful to us, so we don't say anything."

Sharon Rogers often runs into problems with stereotyping in her job as a teacher. "One day," she says, "a boy in one of my classes asked if my sons were like those gangsters in *New Jack City* or *Boyz in da Hood*. I got upset and told him he watched too many movies."

Isolation and Discrimination

For many Blacks in South Texas, stereotypes are only part of the problem. Because they are culturally and racially different, some find themselves isolated and discriminated against. Often it is hard to decide whether people are biased because of cultural differences or because of race. When Duane Allen moved here from Dallas, for example, he found himself facing new cultural interpretations and old prejudices. "Everything here is laid back," he says. "The people and the scene are really different from back home, but the racial prejudice is about the same. Some people still think that Blacks should be treated like we were in the 1890s, rather than the 1990s. It's really frustrating at times."

For Martin Ash, cultural differences were the hardest. "My first day on the job was pure hell," he says. "No one spoke to me, though they were always talking to each other in Spanish. Things are a little better now and I have friends, but the feeling of not belonging still lingers."

In our Valley Blacks Survey, 8 percent of Black respondents said local residents frequently make them feel like an outsider. Another 24 percent said local people occasionally treat them this way. Though Anglo newcomers often experience similar isolation, they generally have many other Anglos with whom they can interact. For Blacks, the adjustment can be a long, difficult process. La Tanya Burns, for example, experienced considerable isolation when she began high school in the Valley. "When I first moved here," she says, "everybody seemed cold. Since I had virtually no friends, I concentrated more on my studies. Yet a person needs more. I would go to the football games and pep rallies alone. Finally, some people got accustomed to seeing me and approached me. I'm a very friendly person, but it took several weeks to make any friends here."

Often, the feeling of isolation comes from not understanding the culture of the area. Twenty-five percent of Black respondents surveyed said that they frequently felt isolated from cultural and social events in the Valley. Another 25 percent said they occasionally felt isolated. Nevertheless, 56 percent said they frequently have social visits with Hispanic friends, evidence that friendships eventually develop.

One's choice of friends can also create problems. Bill Washington is friendly by nature, but because he does not know much Spanish, he often finds more friends among the Anglo students at his school. "Sometimes," he says, "Hispanics pull me aside and say, 'Hey, why are you hanging out with those White dudes? You need to hang with us!' They think I should hate Whites, but I don't. I try to look less at color than at the individual."

After the initial adjustment, many Blacks find it easier to fit in. La Tanya, for example, says, "Once I got into the hang of things and made some new friends, I found that I was enjoying myself more. It felt very good to be more than just a stereotype. Sure, occasionally someone slips and says something with racial overtones. But they accept me for what I am, so I can do the same for them."

Nevertheless, such friendships often take a long time to build. "I have been with this school district for more than twenty years," reports one Black school administrator. "I thoroughly enjoy my work. I would be lying, though, if I said that I never experience discrimination here. My color makes me an easy target. But such incidents are very isolated and less common now than in the past. Now my husband and I have many friends. We can truly call the Valley home."

Though our respondents reported that most Mexican Americans here treat them with respect, they say a few are insensitive or racist. Fourteen percent of survey respondents, for example, said local Hispanics frequently make offensive or prejudiced remarks about Blacks. Another 32 percent said they occasionally do so.

Mike Rand described one Hispanic who made his life difficult. "At work," he says, "Yoli, a fellow worker, would constantly tell jokes about Blacks. She told some about Mexican Americans too, so at first I didn't get offended. But every joke used exaggerated stereotypes of Blacks as dumb, lazy, or oversexed. I tried to tell a few jokes of my own, hoping to defuse the situation. After a while, though, I couldn't stand her insensitivity. She never caught on that her tactless jokes really hurt. I really didn't know what to do because my parents had tried to protect me from people like her by sending me to a small private school.

"Finally, Mayra, a coworker, saw what was happening and told her to stop. But then Yoli began making really cutting remarks. One day, in my presence, she asked Mayra if she would ever date a Black man. Before Mayra could answer, Yoli said that she wouldn't even consider it. That was all I could take. Although Yoli's a Mexican American, her skin color is slightly darker than mine. So I spoke up and said, 'I would never date anyone darker than me.' Then I said, 'Mayra has the perfect color of skin. Don't you think so, Yoli?' She never referred to race after that incident."

Perhaps Mike's rejoinder worked because he touched a very sensitive nerve. Among some South Texas Mexicans and Mexican Americans, skin color is an important issue, though it is seldom mentioned directly. One legacy of the Spanish conquest that still lives on in Mexico and elsewhere is the association of light skin with the elite or upper classes. Dark skin is associated with Native Americans and the poor.

Among some Mexican Americans, this aspect of racial stratification still exists. Some of our interviewers, for example, said they have seen Hispanic parents refuse to let a son or daughter date someone darker than themselves. Others reported that family members are often as interested in a newborn's skin tone as they are in its sex.

For single Blacks, dating is another sensitive matter, as Mark Shields, a Black graduate student at UT–Pan American, discovered. "I dated Carmen, a very nice Mexican American woman, for several months," he says, "and we were getting serious. One day, out of the blue, she called to say she couldn't see me anymore. I couldn't leave it like that, so I went to her house to find out what was going on. Her grandmother met me at the door and said that I was no longer welcome there. If I tried to see her granddaughter again, she said, they would disown her. She said that their family was severely split between those who couldn't accept a Black as part of their family and those who thought each person should choose for themselves. I knew how important her family was to Carmen, so, as I thought about it, I decided not to be the cause of any breakup."

In spite of such difficulties, many African Americans in the Valley date Hispanics. In the Valley Blacks Survey, 54 percent of Black respondents said that Blacks frequently date Hispanics. Only 14 percent said Blacks here rarely date Hispanics.[4]

Reactions, of course, are mixed, though often along generational lines. Amparo Garza dated a Black student from UT–Pan American for several months. "We were at a restaurant," she says, "and, as usual, people were staring at us. Since it happens so frequently, we're accustomed to the stares. Two girls sitting nearby were talking about how cool we looked and how they were going to go out and find themselves a Black man. Just past their table, an elderly couple kept staring at us, not saying a word; just shaking their heads to show they were disappointed in us."

Job discrimination is another serious issue for many Blacks, though culture and race are again hard to separate. Thirty-five percent of respondents said that people like themselves frequently cannot get a job because they are not bilingual. Another 27 percent said it occasionally happens.

For Alexia Williams, however, job discrimination was deeper than language ability. She is a graduate of Howard University and came to the Valley to care for her ailing mother. In spite of her education, and though she speaks Spanish well enough to get by in most situations, it was next to impossible to get a job. "I applied for jobs from Brownsville to McAllen," she says, "yet no one would give me a job. I heard about a federal job in McAllen. Although it was not what I was looking for, I needed the work, so I decided to go for it. They took all the applicants into a conference room and explained the rules of federal employment. Pointing directly toward me, the supervisor said federal employees cannot have criminal records. I reacted as anyone would and told her that I did not appreciate the way she was treating me. I also threatened to report her. I knew that wouldn't help my chances, but I don't think we should let things like that pass.

"After the orientation, she said that she would get in contact with us. But after two weeks, I had heard nothing, so I went to talk to her. She was surprised to see me again. I asked why no one had called, and she said they had lost my application. Well, I wasn't going to accept that and demanded my rights until I got the job."

Forms of Black Adjustment

As with Anglo newcomers, Blacks who move to the Valley have a wide range of reactions to their situation. Gary Anthony loves it here. "I never have any real problems," he says. "People here just seem to like me. Sure, there's always going be someone who doesn't like you. But hey, that's not my problem. It's theirs."

For some, being one of a handful of Blacks is a plus. "Because we're so small in numbers here," says one Black doctor, "the Hispanics do not see us as a threat, like Whites do. Hispanics tend to be just curious about us, whereas Whites are convinced we're a threat."

Nonetheless, this doctor does have some reservations. "Our children are not exposed to their own culture," he says. "I once asked a Mexican American coworker if he knew where we could find a Santa Claus who was at least a little dark-skinned. My request baffled him, and he asked why. I told him I wanted to take a picture of my son with a non-White Santa, just like we used to do back in Chicago. He told me he had never seen a dark-complected Santa and it had never even occurred to him to look for one. I can't understand why Hispanics here seem to buy into the White image of everything."

Sandra Adams also likes living here, but does admit to occasional problems. "In nursing school," she says, "one little old lady told my supervisor she didn't want me as her nurse because I was Black. That didn't hurt my feelings at all. It meant one less patient I had to deal with. Older people down here can be like that woman, but people my age are not bad. In school I never had any problems with my friends about me being Black. I ate at their houses, played basketball with them, and went out with them in groups. Me being Black didn't matter at all."

Sandra admits, however, that living in a Hispanic environment gets to her at times. "They usually mispronounce my name," she says. "They call me 'Sahndra,' using the Spanish pronunciation. Sometimes I just don't answer. I went to jury duty a few months back and the clerk kept saying the Spanish version of my name. Since I really didn't want to be there, and since I'm very Black, I didn't answer. They almost held me in contempt of court."

Many Blacks just try to fit in, adapting themselves somewhat to local culture and circumstances. Others assimilate into Hispanic culture, learning the language and becoming essentially Black Hispanics. Still others seek out other Blacks and attempt to maintain their identity and culture as Blacks.

LIMITED ASSIMILATION

Mr. Green and his wife have chosen the route of limited assimilation. "We're still Black," he says, "but life in the Valley has changed us in many ways. We've shed many of our own ways and have picked up some Hispanic customs. Once we got over the culture shock, things became easier. When we first arrived here, we encountered food like *barbacoa*, *menudo*, and fajitas, which were almost unheard of in Beaumont. Today we can't imagine life without such foods. Thanks to them, both my wife and I have grown thicker around the waist. We've also come to appreciate local customs. *Quinceañeras* [fifteenth birthday coming-out celebrations], for example, were at first a bit strange. But when we learned they were a young woman's rite of passage from childhood to early adulthood, we found them to be a beautiful custom. In fact, we are preparing for our own daughter's *quinceañera* in December."

ASSIMILATION

Marvin, now a truck driver, came to the Valley when he was thirteen. He had gotten into trouble with gangs and drugs in Chicago, so his grandmother sent him to live with an aunt in South Texas. He grew up with Hispanic friends and learned to speak Spanish with no accent. "Now, when I drive around the country," he says, "I'm OK until I open my mouth to speak. Everyone looks at me funny—Blacks, Whites, and Hispanics. They say I don't speak like a Black person should. Some Blacks even ask if I think I'm better than them. I tell them I am what I am. I don't need to be around other Blacks to be comfortable."

Larry Saenz was only two years old when a couple from Mexico adopted him. They were living in South Texas and took him in when his natural mother left him at the church door. He grew up speaking more Spanish than English. "In school," he says, "I had Hispanic and Anglo friends, like everyone else. In high school, the Hispanic girls found me attractive, and I felt completely at home with everyone. When I went away to college in Austin, though, the problems started. No one wanted me for a roommate. I was an African American who preferred Spanish. In the cafeteria, the Hispanics felt uncomfortable with me sitting with them and the Blacks felt uneasy about my accent. When I went to the Tejano dance clubs, everyone stared at the African American with a Stetson. After four semesters, I gave up and transferred back to UT–Pan American so I could concentrate on my studies."

Sandra Adams also feels assimilated. "Blacks elsewhere think that I'm not Black enough," she says. "I don't drag my words together like my relatives in Houston. If we moved back there, my children would go into culture shock. They would be picked on and maybe even jumped. Most of the people there would try to make them fit their image of what we're supposed to be. This is the best place for us."

SEPARATE IDENTITY AND ACCOMMODATION

In contrast, many Blacks in South Texas do manage to maintain their African American identity. Generally, doing so requires regular association with other Blacks. Kena Johns is twenty-one and has struggled to adjust to the Valley since she came here three years ago. "We all need friends," she says. "I wasn't finding many until I met another Black. Suddenly, I felt accepted; like I belonged. At parties, we didn't try to avoid others, but without thinking, we soon separated ourselves from everyone else. Someone always says we're being unfriendly. One even accused us of being a gang or a band of misfits. We try not to let it bother us because we have each other and we have fun."

Simply being Black, however, is not a sufficient basis for a friendship. Some local Blacks, for example, do not relate to the Black athletes recruited to UT–Pan American. "Some of us Black females raised in South Texas mistrust and shy away from the basketball players," says one young woman. "They're only interested in one thing, and they aren't getting it from me."

Most of the Blacks interviewed seem to have adjusted to the Valley, though most feel it is very important to maintain their culture. Thirty-seven percent of the individuals questioned in the Valley Blacks Survey said Blacks here rarely have their own social gatherings. At the same time, 60 percent said that preserving Black customs and traditions is important to them.

This last percentage is particularly interesting when compared to responses by other ethnic groups to the same question in the Multiethnic Culture Survey (discussed in Chapter 6), in which we compared the cultural orientations of 282 Mexican Americans, 165 Anglos, and 85 Mexican immigrants in the Rio Grande Valley (see Appendix B, no. 10). We asked respondents from each ethnic group, "How important is it for you

Percent

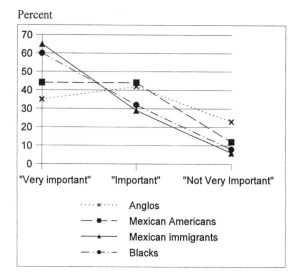

Fig. 8.1. The importance of preserving their customs and traditions to Blacks, Mexican Americans, Anglos, and Mexican Immigrants (Valley Blacks Survey, 1996; Multiethnic Culture Survey, 1996)

to preserve your own religious and ethnic customs and traditions?" Figure 8.1 shows how Blacks in the Valley compare on this item with respondents in the Multiethnic Culture Survey. This figure reveals that preserving one's ethnic heritage appears to be about equally important to Mexican immigrants and to Blacks, less important to Mexican Americans, and least important to Anglos.

Basic Cultural Differences

Though many people say they want to maintain their culture, they are often hard-pressed to explain what that culture is. Culture is deeper than the external manifestations of foods, languages, traditions, or religious customs. If a group wants to preserve its culture, it needs to maintain something almost intangible—the collective ways its members make sense of life and the patterns in the way they interpret things.[5]

Much of culture deals with unspoken assumptions, which are noticed most when contrasted with opposite assumptions. Elva, for example, is a highly educated Hispanic woman. "Right after college," she says, "I started working with IBM in Austin. Two years later I married Bob, who is Anglo. Then my father died and my mother had only my brothers to depend on. They didn't know what to do with her, so I asked her to come to live with me in Austin. She just couldn't. Her whole life was in McAllen, because all of our family was there. After a mental struggle, I decided to leave Austin to come home and sacrifice so that my mother would be happy. My husband freaked out. He was so insensitive, and I know it's because he's Anglo and I'm Mexican American. My boss, also an Anglo, said that my mother's welfare was no excuse to quit my job. I guess Anglos are raised differently. I was raised to be close to my family. To this day, I still worry about my brothers and sisters, whereas my husband hardly even talks to his."

THE FAMILY

Elva's conflict is not just about the relative importance of family in her culture compared to her husband's. It is also about which family is most important: the "family of orientation" (into which we are born) or the "family of procreation" (the one we form when we marry). In many families of Mexican origin, grown children are expected to maintain a strong loyalty to their parents and siblings, even if it causes inconvenience for their spouses.[6] The continued predominance of one's parents is visible in many Mexican households, where grandparents discipline a grandchild even in the presence of the child's own parents.

In the traditional Mexican family, some quasi-family roles exist beyond those formed by blood or marriage. In South Texas, Hispanics take seriously the godparent role found in many Catholic societies. By agreeing to be a *padrina* or *padrino* (godparent), one also becomes a *comadre* or *compadre* (coparent) with the child's parents. This role often bestows not only responsibilities but some expected benefits.

These can be seen in the situation described by Elena, of the day her husband died in an automobile accident. "I was stunned," she says, "to the point that I was unable to make any funeral arrangements. When my *compadre*, the *padrino* of my oldest boy, realized I needed help, he and his wife immediately came to my aid. They made all the funeral arrangements and even found us a permanent place to live. I don't know what I would have done if they had not been there for us."

Anglos are often impressed with the importance Hispanics place on family solidarity, even if they do not understand all the obligations associated with it.[7] One Winter Texan couple, for example, stated: "In Alabama, families really don't go anywhere as much as they do down here. You know. The parents are too busy keeping house and working to even go shopping together. Whenever you need something, you just go in one store and get what you need, then you get out. It's that simple. Here, the malls are constantly packed with families, and you always see them holding hands or hugging each other."

With commitment and family warmth, however, come certain expectations. Were she ever able to do so, for example, Elena would be expected to give special help and consideration to her *compadres* (coparents). One of our Black respondents discovered this from the years he lived among Hispanics in Raymondville. "They discriminate a lot over there," he says. "You have to know somebody or be a very close friend or a family member to get a job. When somebody quits a job, they try to keep the new hire in the family or give it to their *compadres* instead of interviewing to see who's best for the job."

Because many cultural aspects of such roles are unspoken, and even unseen, those unfamiliar with the culture can step into the expectations without realizing it. The Jensens, for example, are a Winter Texan couple who got involved in an Adopt a Family at Christmas program sponsored by their RV park. "They gave us a family from a colonia," says Mrs. Jensen. The father had left them and had gone back to Mexico. The mother had three children, a girl in high school, a toddler, and an infant boy. The toddler had some sort of heart problem.

"When we went there to give them the gifts, the oldest girl had to translate. When we saw how hard off they were, we offered to help with some things for their home. A few days later, we got a phone call from the girl, who was very distressed. She told us that the new shoes we bought her had been ruined when it rained. She asked if we could replace them. I could tell she felt awful about losing those shoes, so we got her another pair.

"About a week later, she called to say that she had been invited to a dance but didn't have anything appropriate to wear and could we help her. A few weeks later, she called again, this time about the baby. He was sick, she told us, and they didn't have a heater in their house. It had been very cold that week, so that evening we bought a heater and took it over to them. A few days later, we stopped in to check on the baby's health. When we found out the heater wasn't in the room with the sleeping baby, but in the daughter's room, we just left. After that, when she called, we just told her we could no longer help."

Although the Jensens ended the relationship because they believed the daughter had inappropriately taken the heater for herself, the repeated requests for assistance equally puzzled them. Quite possibly, they had inadvertently stepped into the role of *padrinos* (godparents) by offering to help the colonia family as they did. The daughter of the family responded much as she would have had they actually been her *padrinos*. In many cultures, such offers imply a deeper relationship—one of benefactor. With the expectation of continued help comes the assumption that the recipient is equally indebted—if not financially, then at least in showing gratitude or deference and "being there" if needed.

Basic Cultural Dimensions as Ideal Types

From the different exploratory interview projects, we recorded many cases of very opposing cultural assumptions. Some of these cultural differences are predicted by sociological theory that compares premodern societies with those that have undergone the processes of industrialization, urbanization, and increasing rationality. Max Weber, for example, distinguished societies that justify their ideas mainly by tradition (where something is right because it has always been done that way) from those that use rational criteria (something is right if it makes sense, as a calculated means to an end).[8] He also used the idea of ideal types to represent the opposite extremes of a particular dimension.

The Life Control Dimension

Tradition serves as a guide when the world is perceived as highly unpredictable and mystical. If life events can neither be explained nor controlled, a person follows ways that have worked, without trying to change, explain, or justify them. On the other hand, in a world dominated by science and rationality, people come to expect things to be calculated, programmed, and efficiently managed. These differences become a part of what we can call deep culture, or those aspects of our culture that we take for granted—just the way things should be.[9] When people question these assumptions, or fail to follow them, we feel disoriented or angry.

At one extreme are people who believe that life gives them little control over what happens to them. One elderly woman born and raised in rural Mexico, for example, told her interviewer of her view of life. "I just hope for the best," she says, "and wait for whatever God has in store for me. We shouldn't try to change things. Yes, I do want a better life for my children, but I want them to realize that their life has already been arranged by God and there is not much they can do about it."[10]

At the opposite extreme is the "can do" attitude that makes us believe that all problems can be solved with enough effort, study, and efficient management. In this idealized (or extreme) view, science and rational organization promote a high expectation for gaining control of life. Individuals with this view want things to be orderly and predictable. Often they seek to promote such order through tight standards, extensive planning, and expecting others to make and keep future commitments. People with this cultural orientation often look for an organized and rationally developed system to control action.[11]

Table 8.1—The Life Control Cultural Dimension

Uncertainty/Flexibility	*Certainty/Programmability*
A. LIFE IS RESPONDING TO EVENTS	A. LIFE IS CONTROLLING EVENTS
"Go with the flow," because life is controlled by forces outside the individual. Standards must be flexible and adaptable to the idiosyncracies of people and unpredictable situations.	"Control the flow," because humans can control social and natural events. Standards must be tight and uniform to control behavior and provide stability.
B. FLEXIBLE ORIENTATION TO TIME	B. RIGID ORIENTATION TO TIME
Time is general and flexible, with little use of deadlines, specific plans, or tight future commitments. A "live for today" attitude is common.	Time is specific and controlling. Specific future commitments, deadlines, and extensive planning are expected. A "sacrifice for tomorrow" attitude is common.

Table 8.1 shows a representation of the two opposite, or ideal-type, cultural orientations related to how much and what type of control we expect in life. Two subdimensions are presented for each extreme. The first deals with whether we should take life as it comes or try to control it. The second is about how much flexibility we should allow in dealing with time and future commitments.

We wanted to see how the cultural differences suggested by these ideal types might represent the cultural orientations of Anglos, Mexican immigrants, and Mexican Americans in South Texas. Anecdotal evidence from the exploratory interviews suggests that Anglos might fall more to the Certainty/Programmability end, Mexicans more to the Uncertainty/ Flexibility end, and Mexican Americans somewhere between, though there would be, of course, many exceptions.

One anecdotal case helps to illustrate this dimension. Paul Martin, an Anglo maquila manager, describes an incident with one of his Mexican engineers. "Juan is one of my best engineers," he says, "but I'm not sure I can keep him. He works hard, but he drives me crazy. Yesterday, for example, I told him to get a pallet of motors ready for shipment by eleven in the morning. I was very specific, telling him that nothing was more important than getting the shipment out on time. When I looked around, though, he was gone—to take a worker to the doctor, someone said. He came back, but soon disappeared again, this time to help fix one of our winding machines. To make a long story short, he missed the shipment because he wasn't thinking long-term. He just responds to things as they come along, with no sense of priority."

Paul is clearly oriented to "controlling the flow," believing that one can plan and even manage the future. Juan, at least in the eyes of his supervisor, takes things more as they come, "going with the flow." If we accept Paul's perception of Juan as accurate, Juan's adaptability may be a realistic response to a background in which life *is* less predictable. Because these orientations are a part of deeply held culture, however, both men will likely interpret the actions of the other as personality flaws.[12]

Societies with a culture that emphasizes a high degree of control often set up laws that govern just about every contingency. Traffic, for example, is highly managed, with systems to keep cars in marked lanes and make drivers obey traffic lights. Countries with a "go with the flow" culture, on the other hand, produce drivers that adapt to each other and the flow of traffic, rather than following lane markers and traffic lights.

Anyone who has driven in Mexico will recognize the "go with the flow" aspect of traffic there. In that context, a good driver knows what nearby drivers are doing and responds accordingly. I have known some very fast-driving taxi drivers in Mexico City, for example, who have driven for twenty or more years without an accident. How do they do it? By watching the flow and knowing the subtle cues by which drivers signal their intentions.

Relationships follow a similar pattern. In "control the flow" societies like the United States, organizational lines of authority and carefully elaborated job descriptions determine patterns of business interaction. In countries with more of a "go with the flow" orientation, people spend more time getting to know each other because you cannot respond to the flow unless you know what it is. In Mexico, knowing the person you are dealing with is as important as knowing his or her position in an organization.

The second part of the Life Control dimension presented in Table 8.1 deals with control of time. One U.S. petroleum engineer who worked in Poza Rica, Veracruz, discovered a different orientation to time there. "I was sent down to work with Mexican engineers, mechanics, and crew," he says. "I was responsible for setting up the equipment and helping them use it. I wanted to get the work done as quick as possible so that I could go home to my wife. I was the only gringo in the entire group. They were supposed to pick me up at my hotel at eight every morning, but never got there until nine o'clock or later. One day, I asked them to hurry so that I could get home. The superintendent told me, 'Señor, you gringos are always in such a hurry. The oil has been in the ground for millions of years. Another day or two won't make that much difference.'"

Many Anglo (and Black) respondents report similar frustrations in dealing with the Hispanic population in South Texas.[13] Brian Boyd, for example, says, "I've noticed that the Valley is much less orderly than what I'm used to. Down here, seven o'clock means seven-thirty or eight. In Michigan, when dinner is at five o'clock, that means be at the table by a quarter of five."

Mark Johnson is a pastor of a local congregation. He finds a slower pace here, even among many Anglos. "As a preacher," he says, "it's considered very important to begin meetings promptly, according to scheduled times. But here I find very little emphasis on the clock. Instead, the norm seems to be arriving a little late. In fact, many of our members are late for everything, including weddings and funerals."

One Mexican American student described a similar attitude regarding the making of future commitments. "Whenever I ask some Mexican people to attend some future event," she says, "they are reluctant to make a commitment. The typical response is 'Si Dios quiere [God willing].' My own grandmother gets angry if we try to pin her down to anything in the future. She believes only God knows what will happen tomorrow. I couldn't even get a firm commitment out of her to participate in my wedding. She said she would be there if she wasn't dead—and she's in perfect health."

In the Multiethnic Culture Survey, we administered a series of Likert-type (agree/disagree) statements to the respondents. We wanted to measure where they stood in relation to both aspects of the Life Control dimension. The responses, shown in Figure 8.2, illustrate how each of the three ethnic groups responded to these items, two of which measure the controlling events aspect and two of which measure orientation to time.

Both of the controlling events items were in the predicted direction, with Mexicans most strongly, then Mexican Americans, and finally Anglos least strongly agreeing that life is subject to little control and seeing the need for greater flexibility.[14] Nevertheless, the differences on the first item were too small to be considered statistically significant.

We found the greatest differences among the three ethnic groups on the third item presented in Figure 8.2. Specifically, it read: "People should be flexible about time and deadlines and should be cautious about making specific plans and future commitments." Mexican immigrants

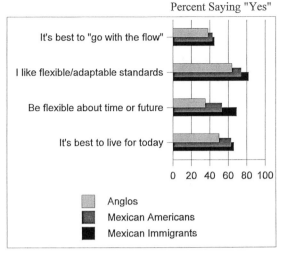

Percent Saying "Yes"

It's best to "go with the flow"

I like flexible/adaptable standards

Be flexible about time or future

It's best to live for today

0   20 40 60 80 100

Anglos
Mexican Americans
Mexican Immigrants

Fig. 8.2. Agreement of Mexican Americans, Anglos, and Mexican Immigrants with statements used to measure low perceived life control (Multiethnic Culture Survey, 1996)

were about twice as likely to agree with this item as were Anglos. Mexican Americans fell about midway between them. The differences on the fourth item were not quite large enough to be statistically significant.

If subsequent research could more firmly establish such differences, it might help explain some cultural misunderstandings often found among the three groups. Indeed, this dimension may explain why some Anglo and Black respondents think Hispanic clerks discriminate against them. More than a few complained that Hispanic clerks often take Spanish-speaking customers ahead of them, out of turn. "Shoe departments are notorious for keeping people waiting," says Linda, "so we sat near the front and tried to make eye contact with all the clerks that were rushing by. But when it was our turn to be waited on, the clerk went right by us and waited on someone who said something to her in Spanish. Not wanting to jump to any conclusions, we walked up to the counter to get someone to help us. Still, they waited on everyone but us. We talked to the manager, but he didn't seem concerned by our complaint. We have shopped there since then, and have received good service, but only when there's no Spanish speaker also waiting."

Though Anglos often attribute such treatment to ethnic discrimination, the Life Control dimension may better explain it. When no system has been set up to keep track of who has been waiting the longest, clerks will unwittingly take someone out of turn. In such situations, customers with a "go with the flow" mentality will know how to use cultural cues to get a clerk's attention. Asking a question, for example, is one way to get a clerk to wait on you. Once the relationship is initiated, it is difficult for the clerk to break it off to wait on another customer. Individuals who know this can get rapid service, while those waiting their turn will often wait longer. If so, this form of "discrimination," to the extent that it exists, may be a form of cultural bias, rather than bigotry (as described in Chapter 4).

The Basis of Legitimacy Dimension

Another potential source of cultural misunderstanding comes from the different foundations upon which any culture legitimizes ideas and actions. In a highly commercial and secular society, for example, products are commonly "legitimized" by invoking science (e.g., "Four out of five dentists surveyed recommend Product X for their patients"). In less secularized societies, in contrast, ancestors, religion, or tradition are often considered the ultimate authority.

Likewise, in less secularized societies, high position often matters more than objective considerations of merit. People in high places should be respected and obeyed, even if their decisions do not make much sense. In contrast, positivistic (objectivity-oriented) culture encourages us to demand proof of almost anything, no matter who says it. Eva, a second-generation Hispanic mother, for example, bemoans how her children demand that she prove her fairness when one child gets something she cannot provide for them all. "When my mother gave one of us something," she recalls, "she never had to justify it. She would just say, 'I did it because I wanted to.' That was the end of it. Not with my kids, though. I constantly have to prove to them I am not treating one of them better than the other."

Respect for authority is very important in many traditional Hispanic homes in South Texas. Tomás Ramos is in his late twenties, married, and the father of one boy. In addition, he is the vice president of a local business firm. Respect for his father is an important tradition. "I started smoking when I was fifteen," he says, "and up to this date I won't smoke in front of my father. It just seems disrespectful, though he doesn't mind that I smoke. I smoke in front of my mom, but when my dad comes around I stop, even if I just lit one up."

Table 8.2 shows a representation of the two opposite cultural orientations related to the major basis of legitimacy. Again, two subdimensions are presented for each extreme. The first relates to whether life's basic explanations come from subjective beliefs and tradition, or whether they are based on pragmatism and objective evidence. The second subdimen-

Table 8.2 — The Basis of Legitimacy Cultural Dimension

Subjectivity/Ascription	*Objectivity/Merit*
A. Subjectivity and Tradition	**A. Objectivity and Pragmatism**
Explanations are legitimized by spiritual or other-worldly knowledge handed down from the past. Faith, religion, customs, and habits guide and legitimize action.	Explanations are legitimized by materialistic and objective knowledge, with the latest seen as the best. Science, reason, and the search for evidence guide and legitimize action.
B. Inherited Position Predominates	**B. Achieved Position Predominates**
One's social position is mainly inherited (ascribed). People with high traditional status must be treated with deference and respect.	One's social position is mainly earned. People must be treated objectively, according to their individual merits (and with little regard to their family background).

sion is related to the source of rank and prestige in social positions — those based on inherited position versus those that are gained through merit and personal achievements.

We did find some anecdotal evidence from the exploratory interviews that those Mexican immigrants who come from a traditional background often fall more to the subjective end of this dimension. Ramón González, for example, has lived here most of his life but still feels that life is controlled by otherworldly forces. "I always go to church," he says, "so that God will protect me. I feel that my favorite team, the Atlanta Braves, lost because I quit going for a while."

Likewise, among very traditional Mexican immigrants, health ailments are often explained in terms of supernatural forces. María Ortega, an immigrant of five years, recently went to a doctor with a very bad stomachache. When she told him that someone had cursed her with the evil eye, however, the doctor became exasperated. "He made me feel stupid," she says. "He said I was too superstitious and that there was no such thing as the evil eye. I felt insulted, so I left the office and went to see another doctor."

Though folk healers (*curanderos*) are much less common in South Texas than some anthropologists have portrayed, beliefs about folk illnesses do persist, especially among poorer Mexicans on both sides of the border. In 1984 I helped conduct a survey of 69 doctors in four border

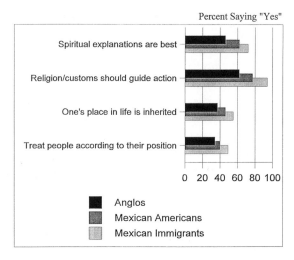

Percent Saying "Yes"

Spiritual explanations are best

Religion/customs should guide action

One's place in life is inherited

Treat people according to their position

0 20 40 60 80 100

■ Anglos
▨ Mexican Americans
☐ Mexican Immigrants

Fig. 8.3. Agreement of Mexican Americans, Anglos, and Mexican Immigrants with items used to measure a traditional basis of legitimacy (Multiethnic Culture Survey, 1996)

cities (two in Mexico and two in the Valley).[15] We found that 57 percent of Mexican American doctors, 49 percent of Mexican doctors, and only 10 percent of Anglo doctors had 10 or more patients a month who reported a folk illness. These included such conditions as *susto* (fright), *mal de ojo* (evil eye), and *mal puesto* (being hexed). Each of these infirmities is believed to be explained by supernatural forces and conditions.

Several questions included in the Multiethnic Culture Survey help us determine the extent to which Mexican immigrants, Mexican Americans, and Anglos follow either subjectivity or objectivity aspects of the Basis of Legitimacy dimension. The results, shown in Figure 8.3, compare the responses on four questions, two for each subdimension.

The results shown in Figure 8.3 show greater differences among the three ethnic categories on the first two items, both of which are related to a preference for otherworldly explanations. The first reads, "The most believable explanations of why things happen are based on spiritual beliefs or knowledge handed down from the past," to which 72 percent of Mexicans, 62 percent of Mexican Americans, and 46 percent of Anglos agreed. The second states: "Faith, religion, customs, and habits are the most important guides to action." Though 32 percent more Mexicans agreed than Anglos, we should note that a majority of all three groups agreed with the item.

Similarly, significantly more Mexicans agreed than Anglos with the third item: "One's place in life in mainly inherited or based on one's family." Still, a majority of all three groups disagreed with the item. Most also disagreed with the fourth statement: "It's important to know a per-

Mexican immigrants and Mexican Americans in South Texas have a strong cultural identification, though much of their culture is distorted in stereotypes (photo courtesy of George C. McLemore).

son's 'place' in life and treat them accordingly." Though the same pattern exists—more Mexicans agreed than did Mexican Americans or Anglos—differences on this item are not statistically significant.

These data provide some support for the proposition that Mexicans might fall more to the Subjectivity/Ascription end of the Basis of Legitimacy dimension than Anglos (with Mexican Americans in between). It would be premature, however, to conclude that Mexican culture is traditional, while Anglo culture is rationalistic. There are several reasons for this. First, though each group generally scored in the predicted direction, the three ethnic categories are closer to each other than they are to the extremes on most items. Second, more work is needed on refining the items and obtaining demonstrably random samples of each ethnic category. Third, even if these differences are substantiated by other studies, they should be viewed more as tendencies than as traits, since many people in each ethnic category scored the opposite of their group's predicted direction. Fourth, we need data on Mexicans in Mexico and on Mexican Americans outside the Valley to see how they might be different from their counterparts in this study.

Besides these methodological concerns, serious questions need to be addressed regarding whether such orientations are really part of each group's culture.[16] One could argue, for example, that they might represent psychological adaptations by individuals to harsh life conditions, rather than culture passed on from one generation to the next. Thus, if more Mexican immigrants than Anglos perceive little control over time and events in their lives, is it because of an orientation learned from culture, or is it a somewhat realistic response to how out of control life really is for people at the bottom?[17]

A related question asks whether differences commonly found among a particular ethnic group are part of their ethnic culture, or whether they might be part of a worldwide "culture of poverty." Oscar Lewis first used this term to describe a culture "common to the poor of all nations which has its own structure and rationale, as a way of life passed down from generation to generation along family lines."[18] Accordingly, Mexican immigrants and Mexican Americans might have a culture that perceives less control of life and supports traditionalism over rationality, but does so because most of its members come from a background of poverty. Lewis recognized that people do respond psychologically to harsh conditions, but he went on to propose that over time this response becomes part of culture that gets passed on from parents to their children.[19]

To examine such questions, we explored the importance of income differences among the three ethnic categories. Not surprisingly, we found that only 25 percent of our Anglo respondents in the Multiethnic Culture Survey claimed an annual family income of less than $26,000, while 60 percent of Mexican Americans and 83 percent of Mexicans were in this low-income category. Nevertheless, when we looked at how income is related to the cultural dimensions of Tables 8.1 and 8.2, we found that only two of the items have a relationship to income that is statistically significant. These are the third item in Figure 8.2 ("Be flexible about time and future commitments") and the second one in Figure 8.3 ("Religion and customs should guide action"). In each case, the lower the income, the more likely respondents were to agree with the items. Nevertheless, though social class may be related to the cultural dimensions described, it appears to have a weaker relation than ethnic status.

In reality, though, ethnic culture and class culture are not necessarily competing explanations. Mexico is a country with considerable poverty. People who can barely survive will likely feel little control over life events. In addition, tradition and religious explanations are frequently all that desperately poor people have to hang on to. But finding an economic basis for cultural beliefs does not rule out the possibility that they also have an ethnic basis. Many foods identified with Mexico, for example, are foods born of economic necessity and developed into something of world-renowned taste. Culture born in deprivation is still culture.

At the crux of this debate is the issue of what needs to change for people of Mexican origin to prosper in the United States. On the cultural side are those who see Mexican culture and the culture of poverty as primary obstacles to "moving up" in U.S. society. Thomas Sowell alleges that such immigrant groups as Mexicans have a culture that discourages political participation, education, and upward mobility.[20] In addition, he believes that such patterns are so ingrained that they persist after many generations.[21] In its extreme version, this position calls for cutting off immigration for such groups because they will not assimilate and their culture will always keep them poor.

A milder version of the cultural argument is advanced by those who allege that Mexican immigrants have some cultural traits that hold them back, but that these can be eliminated through assimilation. Linda Chávez, for example, alleges that "Hispanics can and will prosper in the United States by following the example of the millions before them."[22] In other words—assimilate.

In contrast to these cultural explanations of limited mobility are structural arguments. Essentially, the structural position argues that economics, rather than Mexican or Mexican American culture, produces high levels of intergenerational poverty. Earl Shorris, for example, compares a woman living in a South Texas colonia with a Hispanic woman who sits on the board of regents of the University of California.[23] Though both have experienced prejudice and segregation, he says, the colonia woman has a greatly reduced sense of control. "The poor woman's fatalism," he argues, "is determined by her economic condition."[24]

Advocates of this position blame the structure of limited opportunities for the negative attitudes they find among the poor. Stephen Steinberg, for example, proposes that if "lower-class ethnics seem to live according to a different set of values, this is primarily a cultural manifestation of their being trapped in poverty."[25] In this view, the way out of the colonia and the migrant life of poverty is through true structural changes, not efforts to increase cultural assimilation.

So goes the debate. Conservatives call for abandonment of Hispanic culture through the process of assimilation. They claim this is necessary for poor Mexican Americans to make it out of poverty. Liberals advocate opening the structure of opportunity to low-income Mexican Americans, claiming that their culture has no real impact on their life chances.

Often, this debate misses two important points. First, as Octavio Romano charges, many sociological and anthropological studies exaggerate certain features of traditional Mexican culture.[26] In addition, many of these studies lump together Mexican and Mexican American culture, with little serious investigation of differences between the two.[27]

A second mistake, however, is the opposite assumption, that culture has no relation to an immigrant's life chances. Culture learned in a village or *rancho* (ranch, rural dwelling) in Mexico will create some difficulties for those trying to survive in a highly industrialized and bureaucratized system. Culture is, after all, an adaptive mechanism that enables people to do well in their own culture, but generally not as well in a foreign cultural environment.[28]

Assimilation or Accommodation?

Even more basic are the concerns of how rapidly immigrants and their descendants adapt and how much of their culture they retain. On the one hand are those who claim assimilation is needed to eliminate "undesirable" cultural traits. In addition, they propose that it also reduces the ethnocentrism and cultural bias of the dominant society. Essentially, they're saying to Mexican Americans, "Get rid of your differences because they only hold you back and make Anglos see you as outsiders."

ASSIMILATION

One person we interviewed, Mr. Reese, presents an extreme example of a Mexican American who has internalized this point of view. He is a fifth-generation Mexican American, raised outside the Valley. "We changed the family name from Ruiz," he says, "because Anglos were more likely to accept us. Besides, we're part Anglo because a Texas Ranger got several Ruiz women pregnant. Ever since he came into the family, we have not really thought of ourselves as Mexican Americans. I'm engaged to an Anglo woman, and the tiny bit of Mexican culture still in me will disappear with our children. Being a Mexican doesn't get you anywhere."

Ana Garcia has a similar opinion. Both her parents were raised in McAllen. Her father has often told her stories of his early school years there. "He got in trouble many times for speaking Spanish," she says. "Then, shortly after he married, my dad joined the military and we grew up outside the Valley. When we returned, we weren't the same. We spoke English with an Anglo accent, because our parents raised us that way. My dad said that the service he gave to his country made him a true American. I'm now married to an Anglo, so my two children will not speak nor understand Spanish. But knowing the Anglo way should give them an advantage in life."

With some Mexican Americans, assimilation is a reaction to the harsh discrimination described in Chapter 4. Johnny Martinez, for example, started out as a laborer. "I worked hard all my life," he says, "starting at a very early age. The gringos used to call me 'Elbow Greaser' because I worked so hard. I tried to ignore their comments, but finally decided I wanted to be accepted. I tried to look and act White and started laughing at their jokes and learned to speak English well. I told my parents not to make me *carne guisada* [meat stew] and bean tacos for lunch anymore because I was going to start eating American food. I started reading books about sports and government, so I could talk to them. They started noticing that I was different from the rest and began accepting me. They called me Johnny and, over time, I forgot my culture.

"It felt good being accepted by them. After I got married, I kept this style and passed it on to my children. Now that I've retired, I have a boat, a new car each year, and a house on the lake. The only thing I don't like about the Valley is paying taxes to support Mexicans who only want food stamps and other welfare from the government."

ACCOMMODATION

In contrast to the assimilation argument is the accommodation position. It favors allowing ethnic minorities to maintain much of their cultural identity, proposing that cultural identity is necessary to promote in-group solidarity in the fight for equality. In addition, advocates of accommodation believe that many aspects of ethnic culture are worth keeping because they promote a positive self-concept and have value in and of themselves. Their basic position is "Hang on to your culture because you need to stick together and because it's worth keeping."

Many South Texas Hispanics value their culture because of negative traits they see in Anglo culture. Ascención Torres and his wife, Mercedes Torres, for example, regret not having done more to preserve Mexican family ideals. "We got married with the blessing of our parents," he says. "We wouldn't have done so without it. Whenever we've had problems in our marriage, we've worked it out. Divorce was never an option in our culture. And if I didn't treat my wife right, I'd have a lot of people to answer to. But our daughter was raised here in the U.S. When she got married, it wasn't two months till she was fighting with her husband and spending the night at our house. A year later, she got divorced. We tried to help them work it out, but they said getting a divorce was no big deal. That's what they see here on TV and how their friends look at it."

Antonio López, an older migrant worker, also hates the pressures to lose his culture. "Every time we go up north," he says, "we feel unwelcome. Sometimes, it's our own race. I remember pulling up to a gas station in Colorado. I asked the guy, who was a Mexican American, something in Spanish. He became so angry that he denied us service. I'll never forget that. One of my own blood denied me service because he was insulted that I spoke Spanish to him."

Before considering which of these positions, assimilation or accommodation, is most common in South Texas today, we should note that each process involves cultural and structural manifestations. In the 1960s, Milton Gordon emphasized that we cannot treat assimilation as a single process.[29] Though he identified several subtypes of assimilation (including marital, identification, attitude-receptional, and behavior-receptional), his main contribution was to distinguish between cultural and structural assimilation. Though Gordon's idea of structural assimilation was too limited, including only assimilation into close, personal associations, Dale McLemore has expanded it to include all forms of integration into the structures of society.[30] In this view, structural assimilation would include not only integrating minority groups into cliques and personal relationships but also their full acceptance into the economic, educational, political, and legal systems of society.

The same point needs to be made regarding accommodation. With accommodation, each group maintains elements of its own culture (cultural pluralism). In addition, the group may have separate institutions (churches, schools, etc.). Two extreme forms of structural pluralism would be segregation and separatism. A less extreme form of structural accommodation is minority status for certain ethnic or racial groups. These possibilities are represented in Table 8.3.

Table 8.3 — Types of Accommodation and Assimilation

ELEMENTS OF SOCIETY	Forms of Accommodation	Forms of Assimilation
Culture	1. Cultural pluralism (separate ethnic identity)	2. Cultural Assimilation (similar cultural identity)
Structure	3. Structural pluralism (separate institutions or minority status)	4. Structural assimilation (same institutions and equality of status)

Where to from Here?

Table 8.3 allows us to distinguish various possibilities of interethnic adjustment. More important, it allows us to see some directions ethnic relations have gone in the past and where they may be headed today.[31]

THE SEGREGATION ERA

During the early 1900s, the direction of ethnic relations in South Texas was the "old segregation," or an effort by Anglos to use cultural pluralism to keep Mexican people in Texas in subjugation. Initially, Anglos made few efforts to anglicize Mexican Americans, and social institutions were set up to "keep them in their place." Most cities in South Texas had a "Mexican town" with separate Mexican schools.[32]

Sara Hinojosa remembers what it was like. "We, the Mexican Americans, were the undesirables in town," she says. "We knew what they thought of us. Everyone called our school 'la escuela de los burros' [the donkeys' school]. Our teachers were all Anglos except the principal's helper. Some students who had been held back many times were eighteen years old. I was thirteen then and had many problems with the older boys. They had ideas about sex and things, and I hadn't even had time to think about that."

Following World War II, some things began to change. Though the goal of Anglo society remained largely segregationist (enforced structural pluralism), under the "new segregation," schools and other institutions increasingly tried to force Anglo culture on Mexican Americans. More Mexican Americans began attending Anglo schools, though not as equals. Schools strongly enforced a no-Spanish policy through the 1950s, forcing many Mexican American children to drop Spanish, at least on school property. In addition, teachers often anglicized the names of their Hispanic students.

Frequently, such practices caught students between their parents and the school. Roberto Salinas, for example, wondered why he could not speak Spanish at school. But instead of asking why, he did what they told him, because he knew his parents would punish him harder at home if he got in trouble at school. "My father would always tell me to obey my teachers," he says, "but when I did, he became angry with me. One of my teachers told me to write my name as 'Robert,' because we lived in the United States and not Mexico. When my father saw that I was writing 'Robert' on my school papers, he got mad and made me put an *o* at the end of my name on every school paper."

THE CHICANO ERA

With the coming of the Civil Rights era, Chicano activists rejected segregation and fought for structural assimilation. In addition, they saw cultural pluralism, rather than cultural assimilation, as the way to achieve it. One man interviewed, Juan Antonio Díaz, exemplifies this position. "I once had a friend," he says, "who said, 'In the eyes of an Anglo, you'll always be Mexican. No matter how much money or education you have, you'll still be Mexican.' I didn't like it, but to a certain extent he was right. We might get accepted, but only to a certain extent. But I can live with that. I'm glad my father came from Mexico to give his family a better life. He has a life here he couldn't even dream of in Mexico. Will I ever assimilate? Not me. My culture tells me who I am. I might have been born here, but I'm proud to have Mexican ancestors. Every time I hear my dad tell me about the toys he had to make for himself because he was poor, I get chills up and down my spine."

The basic goal of the Chicano movement was equality (structural assimilation). Cultural pride and cultural pluralism were the primary means of achieving it. Bilingual education and the push for multiculturalism were manifestations of this combination.

THE POST-CHICANO ERA

In recent years, many Chicano activists have moved into the middle class, and the push for cultural nationalism has largely subsided.[33] So marked is this decline that some writers have called the current state of affairs the "Post-Chicano Era."[34] Once Chicanos moved into the middle class, such writers assert, many began to minimize their insistence on cultural pluralism, though they continued strongly advocating structural assimilation. For Mexican Americans several generations removed from the initial immigration experience, both forms of assimilation became increasingly common.

Still, many Mexican Americans resisted full assimilation. "Being a Mexican American," said one of our interviewers, "is like being pulled in a tug-of-war. Losing some of your cultural values is part of the package of being Mexican American. You can't be 'All American' because you sure aren't White; and you can't feel exploding pride when the Mexican national anthem is played because you're not Mexican. It's hard to decide which culture to be loyal to."

Often, the changes are gradual. Angélica Ortiz, for example, still clings to her Mexican culture. She frowns upon Mexican Americans who have adopted Anglo mannerisms and culture. Nevertheless, she now celebrates the U.S. holiday of Thanksgiving (though with Mexican dishes), and her Christmas celebrations have lost many traditions she grew up with in Mexico.

Unlike many Mexican Americans, Angélica uses the Spanish version of her name, although her children no longer use both surnames (paternal and maternal, as is the custom in Mexico). Many of her friends have taken anglicized versions of their first name. Ben, for example, whose real name is Benito, remembers when his name was changed. He was five years old and had just started school in Lubbock, Texas. "The teacher was making name tags for everyone," he says. "She came up to me and asked my name. When I told her, she said that from now on my name would be Ben. After that, I've always been Ben. Even my high school diploma has that name on it."

We asked all the Hispanic respondents in the Multiethnic Culture Survey how important it was to their parents that they used the Spanish version of their first name, rather than the anglicized equivalent. Forty-eight percent of Mexican respondents said "very important," compared to 21 percent of Mexican Americans who gave this response. These figures could support the idea that maintaining the Spanish version of one's name becomes less important with each generation in the United States.[35]

A similar change seems to take place in relation to the importance of maintaining Spanish. Sixty-four percent of Mexicans said it was very important to their parents that they spoke good Spanish, double the 32 percent of Mexican Americans with this response. In fact, a few Mexican American parents said their children should drop Spanish altogether.

Today, in the Post-Chicano era, there are strong strains of both cultural pluralism and cultural assimilation among Mexican Americans in

South Texas. Nevertheless, there is widespread agreement on the need to achieve structural assimilation.

Today Mexican Americans in South Texas are clearly culturally different from Mexican immigrants, though they continue to maintain many similar aspects in their cultural identity. As we saw in Figures 8.2 and 8.3, which present evidence regarding the cultural dimensions, Mexican Americans fall between Mexican immigrants and Anglos in their responses to all the items listed. Though the different social-class position of each group may help explain this, it is also likely that Mexican Americans are in a process of assimilating certain aspects of Anglo culture.

Nonetheless, not all cultural assimilation is caused by the adoption of Anglo culture. As Norma Williams proposes, the increasing similarity of Mexican Americans and Anglos may be due more to the impact on each group of similar societal and global processes.[36] Indeed, this may help explain the substantial drop in parental indifference to education presented in Figure 1.1 (see Chapter 1). Over fifty years, the number of migrant farmworkers reporting the two categories of parental indifference to education dropped from more than 50 percent to less than 5 percent. Most likely, the growing economic pressures for a good education and the facilities provided to attain it account more for this change than does contact with Anglo culture.

Nevertheless, one should not equate without question the changes toward "modernity" with Anglo culture. As we saw in Figure 8.3, for example, even most South Texas Anglos surveyed thought religion and customs should guide action. In addition, more than 60 percent of Anglos preferred flexible and adaptable standards, attitudes more commonly associated with a traditional cultural orientation (see Figure 8.2).

With the combined force of Anglo culture and modernity, however, traditional culture often changes within one or two generations. Janie, for example, is seventeen and lives with both her mother and grandmother. "There are times," she says, "when I just don't agree, especially with my grandmother. She is old and set in her ways. She expects me to be like she was at my age, but my priorities are different. Her world revolves around family and religion. I'm more concerned with school and being with my friends. She doesn't understand that many times I'd rather do something with my friends than family things. I try to avoid arguing with her, though, because I realize that she just wants the best for me. I respect her for that."

Often the pressures for assimilation are more subtle. Some young Hispanics, for example, find the lifestyle of the United States appealing.

Martina, for example, is a Mexican immigrant who came to the United States as a young child. "I've been living here for eight years," she says. "There are many things I miss about Mexico, but I also like many things here. Life here is more organized. I'm very happy now that I speak English. I have a lot of friends and I like most of the customs and rules here."

For most young Hispanics, friends are perhaps the greatest assimilating influence. When Anabel turns fifteen, her aunts want to give her a *quinceañera* (fifteenth birthday party). She has resisted, though, because she feels that none of her Anglo friends will come. "Instead," she says, "I've asked my aunts for a sweet sixteen birthday party. They don't like it, but I think they'll go along with it."

Still, South Texas today also has many factors that favor cultural pluralism, in large part due to its proximity to Mexico and the constant contact with Mexico and with Mexican immigrants and shoppers. As a result, there are counterpressures to maintain certain elements of Mexican culture. David, for example, grew up in Michigan. He moved to the Valley when his father became ill and wanted to return to be near family. "I felt like an outcast here," he says, "since I spoke and understood little Spanish. They often excluded me from conversations, and they called me 'el gringo prieto' [the dark gringo]. I had to learn Spanish, and now I speak it fluently. I wish my mother, a Mexican, had reminded us of our roots and instilled the language when we were younger."

On the other hand, some Anglos are assimilating certain aspects of Hispanic culture. Indeed, as Figure 8.1 shows, they expressed the least desire to preserve their own culture, perhaps making them more open to other cultural forms. Lorrin Smith, for example, speaks Spanish well because he was exposed to it by the family's live-in maid. In high school, he joined Estudiantina, a Hispanic performing group. "In Estudiantina," he says, "I'm the only Anglo, though there have been others in the past. Sometimes I get to do the *gritos* [shouts]." Lorrin likes much of the Hispanic way of life and cannot imagine marrying an Anglo woman because, he says, "they're boring."

Conclusion

Actually, many Anglos and Mexican Americans in South Texas have no problems with a mixed identity. Mexican Americans especially feel deep loyalty to the United States but maintain a cultural identity that is neither Mexican nor Anglo. The people of South Texas have a unique culture with identifiable music forms, an emerging language (Tex-Mex), and identifiable foods and lifestyle. As migrants have taken this culture

*Though Mexican-origin
people of South Texas may
disagree about how much
assimilation should occur,
most are united in their
desire to achieve greater
structural equality*
(photo courtesy of
George C. McLemore).

northward along the migrant trails and up the ladder of mobility, it has
contributed to the Chicano culture of the United States.

South Texas then is a "stirring pot" rather than a melting pot. Many
diverse groups here give, take, and create something new. All partake of
elements of a central culture, while retaining basic elements of their own.
Most of the respondents in our surveys, for example, whether Anglo,
Black, Mexican American, or Mexican, agreed that it is important for
newcomers to learn both English and Spanish. Most respondents from
each group also said that they like the traditions, customs, and lifestyle of
the Valley.

As the Hispanic population increases in the rest of the United States,
observers may find it instructive to look to South Texas as a *frontera*, accepting both "frontier" and "border" as translations of this word. Anglo
culture is enriched, not destroyed, when Hispanics are present in larger
numbers. Despite historical conflicts, people along the border can look

past the discrimination and appreciate the benefits of a multicultural society. In this way, the South Texas border has become a frontier of race and ethnic relations in the United States.

Still, as in the past, the Lower Rio Grande Valley of South Texas continues to be a world apart. Its unique flavor is one of the first things newcomers notice, some with dismay and others with delight. You may love the Valley, or you may count the days until you leave, but you will know you are somewhere very different. As one joke making the rounds puts it, "The Valley is a great place to live—it's so close to the United States."

Appendix A

Student Interviewers Whose Accounts Are Included in the Book

The following students at the University of Texas–Pan American contributed anecdotes that are included in this book. Their names are listed according to the chapter in which their accounts appear. If a student provided more than one story to a chapter, the total number of accounts is placed in parentheses by the student's name.

Preface/Introduction
Alma Alfaro
José Cavazos
Erasmo Escobedo (2)
Yolanda García
Nora Maldonado
Dalinda I. Ramirez
Rogena Robinson
Diana Linda Rodriquez
Kevin Trussel

Chapter 1
Verónica Barrera
Rolando Cano
Angie Cervantez (2)
Maria Contreras
Delfino Manuel Cortez, Jr.
Francisco Cruz
Raquel Enriquez
Donna Garcia
Arculando García
Belinda García
Yolanda Garza
Carlos Garza
Armando O. Gonzalez
Jorge Gonzalez
Maria Imelda Gonzalez
Emmy Guerrero
Eduardo Guzman (2)
Cynthia Huerta
Luis Loera (2)

Nancy Longoria
Maria Lopez
José Lopez
Yolanda Luévano
Lorena Martinez
Carmen Martinez
Iris Mendoza
Guadalupe Palacios, Jr.
Jesse Pantoja
Yvonne Porras
Jaime Ramos
Laura Rendon
Michelle M. Reyna
Debra Rivas
Ruby Rodriquez Salinas
Rosalinda Rosas
Cindi Z. Salinas (2)
Thelma Solis
Pedro Soria
Viana Eliza Torres (2)
Fernando Valdez
Enedelia Vasquez
Norma J. Wirsche (2)
Robert Zamora (4)

Chapter 2
Alma Alfaro (2)
Francisco Cantú (2)
David Castillo (4)
Juanita V. Cox
Eric M. Cruz

Aisa Garza (2)
Diana Y. Garza
Marisa Garza
Teresa Guerrero (3)
Blanca Gutierrez (2)
Aracelia Hernandez
Mariano Hinojosa
Lois Leuders (2)
Nancy Leyva (3)
Floriza Lozano
Gloria Ochoa
Jessie Ramirez (3)
Jenny Robledo (2)
Patricia Robles
Maribel Rodriquez
Crecencio Sanchez, Jr.
Tony Villarreal
Marianilla Villarreal
Meme Wisdom (3)
Amy Wright (2)

Chapter 3
Norma Adams
Norma Alfaro
Julian Almaguer
Vicente Alvarez
Ana Lisa Cavazos (2)
Janie Chapa
James Closner
Laila de Leon
Lisa de los Santos

Sandra Enriquez
Hillary García
Michael D. García
Patricia García
Perfecto Garza
Lilia Garza (2)
Nelda Garza
Cynthia Ann Gonzalez (2)
Josefina A. Gonzalez
Velma Guerrero
Oneida Lopez
Eliga Madrigal
Melissa Martinez
Marina Medina
Severa D. Mejorado (2)
Diana Morán
Ana Catalina Perez (2)
Irene Perez (2)
Victor Ríos III
Celeste Robledo (3)
Ana M. Sanchez
María Sandoval
Gerry Sauceda (4)
Rosa Solis (2)
Donna Stapleton
Theresa Vair (3)
Corina D. Vargas (3)
Dora Vela
Magda Villarreal

Chapter 4
Martha Alcantar
Marta Anta (3)
Delia Isabel Barrera
Raúl Cantú
María Alicia Chapa
Pedro Cisneros, Jr.
Mercy Flores (2)
Sara Alicia Garza
Beatriz Gonzalez
Sandra M. Gonzalez
Yvette Gonzalez (2)
Martha Gutierrez (3)
Yadhira Y. Hernandez
Claudia E. Ibarra (2)
Christi Leal (4)
Verónica Lopez

Audry Martinez
Flor Martinez
Kelly Medina (2)
Katia Molina
Thanya Moreno
María L. Pardo (2)
Vilda Perez
Anne M. Rader
Janie C. Ramirez
José A. Rodriquez (5)
Sandra Rodriquez (4)
Ena Noemi Rojas
Norina Ruiz
Taryna Romero
Pauline Salinas
Beatrice Sánchez
Lilia Varela
Rosario Villegas (2)
Erica Villarreal
Hector Villarreal

Chapter 5
Beth Marie Adame
Nora Barker
Martha J. Cano
Ricardo Castañeda
Linda Catterton
Angie Cervantez (3)
Mike Chavez (2)
Linda Elizabeth Cortez
Diana Flores (2)
Ronald Flores
Melisa Flores
Ruben Flores (2)
Judy Fonseca (2)
San Juanita Fonseca
Fred García (2)
Martha A. García
Maribel Garza
Román Garza, Jr. (2)
Jimmy Gómez
Iliana Hinojosa
Nadine Lopez (2)
Norma Lopez (2)
Yolanda Lumbreras (2)
Michelle L. Marino
Vianey M. Moreno

Ruben Magallan (2)
Norma Maldonado
Laura Medellin
Olga Medrano
Velma Montes
Vianey M. Moreno
Marisol Ornelas
Craig Ownsby
Barbara L. Powell (3)
Crissy Quiroz (2)
Cleo Ramirez
Teresa Ramirez
Jesús Ramos (2)
Evangelina C. Rangel
Patricia Robles
Maribel Salazar
Elizabeth Salinas (2)
Grace Salinas (4)
Arlene G. Silva
Elizabeth F. Soliz
Aimee Trejo
Linda M. Villarreal

Chapter 6
Michelle Anderson
José Arrévalo
Harvie Belshie
Paulina Cárdenas
Esmeralda Casanova (2)
Glenda L. Cantú
Linda Catterton
Sandra Chavez (2)
Eric M. Cruz (2)
Juan Curiel
Rosalinda del Toro
Mercy Flores
Judy Fonseca
Keith Galligan
Jesús García (3)
Judy Garza
Raychel Garza
Melissa Gonzalez
Derley Guajardo
Gus Guajardo
Carolina Guerra
Margarita Guerrero (2)
Laura Marie Hernandez

Jessica A. Jimenez
Carlos Larios (4)
D. Larsen (3)
Jorge Gil Leyva (2)
San Juanita Maldonado
Daniel Milian
Nadia Negrete
Diego Olague
Christopher Perez
Fernando Perez
Gerrie Perez
Tony Perez
José Reyes
Sandra Rocha
Omar I. Rodriquez
Ascensión Rubio
Teresa Salinas (2)
Marina Salazar
Hilda M. Saenz
Dorothy D. Serna
Russel Spoon
Eugenio Torres
Lisette Trad (2)
Gabriela Trejo
Eliza Treviño (2)
Mónica Villarreal
Rosario Villegas

Chapter 7
Cristal L. Alvarado (2)
Ignacio Almaguer
Arlene Andrade
Nora Barker (4)
Karen Birkenmeyer (3)
Beth Kohert Bell
Cesar Blanco (2)
Margaret E. Brooks
Milly Brown
Martha J. Cano
David Joe Cavazos
Tracy Clements
Arturo de Leon
Edgar Espinoza (3)
Janie Flores
Loy Gillis
Juana M. Gonzalez
Iliana Hinojosa

Maria Isabel Hayden (2)
Dolly Hussfield
Ana Ibarra
Taylor Jorgensen
Orlando Lerma
Anita Lloyd
Martina Lopez
Marta Luévano
Aleida Mares (2)
David A. Martinez (2)
José L. Mendoza (2)
Paulina Muriel
Yolanda Narvaez
Tony Perez
Soila G. Perez (2)
Diana L. Rodriquez
Elizabeth Rosales
Rosie Saenz
Jorge L. Salinas
Ruby R. Salinas
Michelle Scherrey (3)
Cari Tanksley (2)
Brent Thrash
Ricardo Torres (4)
Belinda Treviño (3)
Manny Treviño
Nancy Treviño
Catherine Vela (2)
Rosie Villegas
Deborah C. Venecia (3)
Loren B. York

Chapter 8
Beatriz Alanis
Lázaro Alvarez, Jr. (2)
Marco Alvarez (2)
Nora A. Barker
Astrid H. Bonilla
Myrna G. Cantú (4)
Esmeralda Casanova
Roxanne Cepetillo
Suzette D. Chavez (6)
Peggy Eilts
Diana Y. Garza
Lilia Garza
Raúl Gonzalez
Victor Hernandez (2)

Jennifer L. Honn
Marissa Nelly Hinojosa
R. James
James Manuel Layton
Sonya Lopez
David A. Martinez
Victoria L. Martinez
Rita L. Mills
Ascensión Rubio (6)
Rosie Saenz
Belinda Salazar
Joey Salazar (4)
Dolly Saldivar (2)
Derek Sanders (2)
Cynthia Ann Taylor (2)
Belinda Treviño
Kevin Trussel (4)
Stephen D. West (3)

Borderlife Interview Surveys

Appendix B

Demographic variables: The following are data from the ten Borderlife interview surveys examined in this book. The frequency of responses on key variables is provided, as well as the date of each survey and number of respondents (in parentheses). Note that the totals for each item may not equal the total number of respondents due to missing data from some respondents on some of the items.

1. MIGRANT FARMWORKER SURVEY, 1993 (N = 260)

Sex Distribution
Female   142 (55.9%)
Male   112 (44.1%)

Age Distribution
0–24   59 (23.0%)
25–34   56 (21.9%)
35–44   47 (18.4%)
45–54   46 (18.0%)
55 plus   48 (18.8%)

Marital Status
Single   71 (27.5%)
Married   167 (64.7%)
Divorced   10 (03.9%)
Widowed   7 (02.7%)
Separated   3 (01.2%)

Place of Birth
Mexico   84 (32.3%)
Rio Grande Valley   132 (50.8%)
Elsewhere in Texas   25 (09.6%)
Elsewhere in U.S.   19 (07.3%)

Number of Children (Married Respondents Only)
None   13 (07.2%)
1–3   86 (47.5%)
4–6   54 (29.8%)
7 plus   28 (15.4%)

Most Frequent Destination as a Migrant
Western U.S.   54 (21.0%)
North Central U.S.   162 (62.8%)
Eastern U.S.   19 (07.4%)
Southern U.S.   22 (08.6%)

Level of Education (Years of school completed)
0–3 years   35 (13.2%)
4–8 years   63 (23.9%)
9–11 years   51 (19.3%)
12 plus   115 (43.6%)

Father's Level of Education (Years of school completed)
None   98 (37.8%)
1–6 years   113 (43.6%)
7–9 years   28 (10.8%)
10–11 years   13 (05.0%)
High school plus   7 (02.7%)

2. COLONIA RESIDENTS SURVEY, 1994 (N = 545)

Sex distribution
Female   482 (89.4%)
Male   57 (10.6%)

Age distribution
0–24   84 (15.6%)
25–34   182 (33.8%)
35–44   133 (24.7%)
45–54   88 (16.4%)
55 plus   51 (09.5%)

Marital status

Never Married	42 (07.8%)
Married	438 (81.1%)
Widowed/Divorced/	
Separated	59 (10.9%)

Where respondent was raised

Rio Grande Valley	116 (21.4%)
Elsewhere in Texas	13 (02.4%)
Elsewhere in U.S.	10 (01.8%)
Mexico	389 (71.8%)
Other	14 (02.6%)

Level of education (years of school completed)

0–3	128 (23.7%)
4–8	220 (40.7%)
9–11	106 (19.6%)
12 plus	87 (16.1%)

Respondent's number of children

None	45 (08.4%)
1–3	237 (44.2%)
4–6	178 (33.2%)
7–9	45 (08.4%)
10 plus	31 (05.8%)

Annual family income

$0–$5,999	206 (42.9%)
$6,000–$11,999	174 (36.3%)
$12,000–$17,999	67 (13.9%)
$18,000 plus	33 (06.8%)

Number of persons living in respondent's home during past year

1 or 2	49 (09.2%)
3 or 4	148 (27.8%)
5 or 6	214 (40.2%)
7 or 8	75 (14.1%)
9 plus	47 (08.9%)

---

3. UNDOCUMENTED MAIDS SURVEY, 1993 (N = 162)

Age distribution

0–19	26 (16.5%)
20–29	65 (40.6%)
30–39	41 (25.6%)
40 plus	28 (17.5%)

Level of education (years of school completed)

None	21 (13.0%)
1–6	84 (51.8%)
7–9	40 (24.7%)
10 plus	17 (10.5%)

Marital status

Single	85 (53.3%)
Married	51 (31.9%)
Widowed/Divorced/	
Separated	24 (15.0%)

Origin (Where did you live before coming to the U.S.?)

Northern Mexico	92 (58.2%)
Central Mexico	35 (22.2%)
South Mexico/Other	31 (19.6%)

Previous work experience (Main type of work before coming to U.S.)

None	61 (37.9%)
Unskilled	61 (37.9%)
Skilled	21 (13.0%)
Professional/	
Technical/Other	18 (11.2%)

Starting Age (How old were you when you became a maid?)

19 or less	73 (45.3%)
20–29	66 (41.0%)
30 or older	22 (13.7%)

Living Arrangements (Do you live with the family?)

Live-in	122 (75.8%)
Live outside	39 (24.2%)

Work load (How many hours a day are you expected to work?

0–6	14 (10.0%)
7–9	44 (31.4%)
10 plus	82 (58.6%)

Employer's Ethnicity

Anglo	37 (23.6%)
Mexican American	100 (63.7%)
Mexican	20 (12.7%)

4. EMPLOYERS OF UNDOCUMENTED MAIDS SURVEY, 1993 (N = 136)

Place of birth

Rio Grande Valley	52 (39.1%)
Elsewhere in Texas	25 (18.8%)
Elsewhere in U.S.	19 (14.3%)
Mexico	36 (27.1%)

Level of education (Years of school completed)

None–9th	18 (14.2%)
10th–12th	25 (18.7%)
Grades 12 plus	91 (67.9%)

Marital status

Single	9 (06.7%)
Married	114 (84.4%)
Widowed/Divorced/ Separated	12 (09.3%)

Spouse's occupation

Unskilled	12 (09.3%)
Skilled labor	14 (10.9%)
Technical/ Professional	52 (40.3%)
Self-employed	39 (30.2%)
Other	12 (09.3%)

Ethnicity

Anglo	37 (27.4%)
Mexican American	67 (49.6%)
Mexican	27 (20.0%)
Other	4 (03.0%)

Fluency in English

Very fluent	73 (54.1%)
Fluent	27 (20.0%)
Somewhat fluent	20 (14.8%)
Very limited/None	15 (11.1%)

Fluency in Spanish

Very fluent	64 (47.1%)
Fluent	21 (15.4%)
Very limited/None	51 (37.5%)

Estimate of maid's immigration status

No papers	55 (40.4%)
Legal, without work permission	45 (33.1%)
Legal resident	8 (05.9%)
Don't know	28 (20.6%)

5. FORMER STUDENTS SURVEY, 1994 (N = 243)

Sex distribution

Female	149 (61.0%)
Male	94 (39.0%)

Age distribution

0–24	50 (21.0%)
25–34	48 (20.0%)
35–44	51 (21.0%)
45–54	50 (20.6%)
55 plus	44 (18.0%)

Level of Education (Years of school completed)

0–3	5 (02.0%)
4–8	24 (10.0%)
9–11	60 (25.0%)
12 plus	151 (63.0%)

Ethnic Status

Mexican American	181 (77.0%)
Mexican	9 (04.0%)
Anglo	28 (12.0%)
Other	16 (07.0%)

Hispanic respondents' ability to speak English before starting first grade

Fluent	57 (26.0%)
Fairly fluent	42 (19.0%)
Some, but limited	46 (21.0%)
Very limited	25 (12.0%)
Not at all	46 (21.0%)

Respondent's place of birth

Mexico	19 (08.0%)
Valley	174 (72.0%)
Elsewhere in Texas	25 (10.0%)
Elsewhere in U.S.	22 (09.0%)

Father's place of birth

Mexico	87 (36.0%)
Valley	98 (41.0%)
Elsewhere in Texas	36 (15.0%)
Elsewhere in U.S.	17 (07.0%)

Mother's place of birth

Mexico	77 (32.0%)
Valley	110 (46.0%)
Elsewhere in Texas	37 (15.0%)
Elsewhere in U.S.	16 (07.0%)

6. MEXICAN IMMIGRANTS SURVEY, 1995 (N = 324)

Sex distribution

Female	177 (54.6%)
Male	146 (45.1%)

Age distribution

0–18	7 (02.2%)
19–30	126 (38.9%)
31–45	98 (30.2%)
46–65	71 (21.9%)
66 plus	22 (06.8%)

Level of education (Years of school completed)

Did not attend	28 (08.6%)
1–6	100 (30.9%)
7–9	45 (13.9%)
10–12	50 (15.4%)
Some college	101 (31.2%)

How fluently respondent can speak English

Very fluent	41 (12.7%)
Fluent	77 (23.8%)
Somewhat fluent	88 (27.2%)
Only basics	87 (26.9%)
Not at all	31 (09.6%)

Annual family income

Under $13,000	137 (42.4%)
$13,000–$26,000	106 (32.8%)
$26,000–$50,000	54 (16.7%)
Over $50,000	26 (08.0%)

Term respondent prefers to describe his or her ethnic status

Mexican	180 (55.7%)
Mexican American	53 (16.4%)
Hispanic	75 (23.2%)
Latino American	11 (03.4%)
Chicano	3 (00.1%)

Part of Mexico in which respondent was born

Southern Mexico	65 (20.2%)
Central Mexico	81 (25.2%)
Northwest Mexico	39 (12.1%)
Northeast Mexico	112 (34.8%)
Other	25 (07.8%)

7. ANGLO NEWCOMERS SURVEY, 1996 (N = 224)

Sex distribution

Male	119 (54.1%)
Female	101 (45.9%)

Age distribution

0–18	6 (02.7%)
19–30	89 (40.5%)
31–45	53 (24.1%)
46–65	57 (25.9%)
66 plus	15 (06.8%)

Level of education (Years of school completed)

0–9	5 (02.3%)
10–12	49 (23.0%)
Some college	45 (21.1%)
College graduate	114 (53.5%)

How fluently respondent can speak Spanish

Very fluent	9 (04.1%)
Fluent	18 (08.2%)
Somewhat fluent	58 (26.4%)
Only basics	79 (35.9%)
Not at all	56 (25.5%)

Annual family income

Under $13,000	6 (02.8%)
$13,000–$26,000	50 (23.5%)
$26,000–$50,000	95 (44.6%)
Over $50,000	61 (28.6%)

Term respondent prefers to describe his or her ethnic status

Anglo	92 (42.2%)
White	95 (44.2%)
Other or no preference	26 (12.1%)

Respondent's place of birth

Other Texas	55 (25.2%)
West/Midwest U.S.	73 (33.5%)
Northeast U.S.	54 (24.8%)
Southeast U.S.	20 (09.2%)
Other	16 (07.3%)

---

8. WINTER TEXANS SURVEY, 1995 (N = 326)

Sex distribution

Female	165 (51.2%)
Male	157 (48.8%)

Age distribution

50–59	32 (10.0%)
60–69	147 (45.9%)
70–79	127 (39.7%)
80 plus	14 (04.4%)

Level of education (Years of school completed)

0–9	11 (03.4%)
10–11	26 (08.1%)
High school graduate	130 (40.6%)
Some college	70 (21.9%)
College graduate plus	83 (25.9%)

Number of years ago respondent started coming to the Valley

First time	18 (05.6%)
2–5	84 (26.1%)
6–10	115 (35.7%)
11–20	84 (26.1%)
20 plus	21 (06.5%)

Type of residence in Valley

Fixed mobile home	137 (42.4%)
Small mobile home	69 (21.4%)
Motorized R.V.	69 (21.4%)
Apartment/Home	32 (09.9%)
Other	15 (04.6%)

Respondent's main reason for coming to the Valley

I like the people	37 (11.9%)
I need the climate	105 (33.7%)
Local attractions	61 (19.6%)
Other winter Texans	28 (09.0%)
Other	78 (25.7%)

How much contact with Hispanics (Before coming to the Valley)

A lot	26 (08.0%)
Quite a bit	50 (15.5%)
Occasional	101 (31.3%)
Little or none	146 (45.2%)

9. VALLEY BLACKS SURVEY, 1996 (N = 37)

Sex distribution
Female   19 (51.4%)
Male   18 (48.6%)

Age distribution
0–18   1 (02.7%)
19–30   17 (45.9%)
31–45   12 (32.4%)
46–65   3 (08.1%)
66 plus 4 (10.8%)

Level of education (Years of school completed)
0–9   3 (08.1%)
10–12   11 (29.7%)
Some college   14 (37.8%)
College graduate 9 (24.3%)

How many years ago respondent came to the Valley
Within 1 year 4 (10.8%)
2–3   14 (37.8%)
4–5   8 (21.6%)
6–10   2 (05.4%)
11 plus   9 (24.3%)

How fluently respondent can speak Spanish
Very fluent   3 (08.1%)
Fluent   1 (02.7%)
Somewhat fluent   8 (21.6%)
Only basics   11 (29.7%)
Not at all   14 (37.8%)

Annual family income
Under $13,000   5 (16.1%)
$13,000–$26,000   10 (32.3%)
$26,000–$50,000   9 (29.0%)
Over $50,000   7 (22.6%)

Term respondent prefers to describe his or her ethnic status
Black   23 (62.2%)
African American   10 (27.0%)
Other or no preference   4 (10.8%)

Respondent's place of birth
Other Texas   16 (43.2%)
West/Midwest U.S.   9 (24.3%)
Northeast U.S.   5 (13.5%)
Southeast U.S.   2 (05.0%)
Other   5 (13.5%)

10. MULTIETHNIC CULTURE SURVEY, 1996 (N = 532)

Sex distribution
Female   276 (51.9%)
Male   256 (48.1%)

Age distribution
0–18   38 (07.1%)
19–30   279 (52.4%)
31–45   121 (22.7%)
46–65   80 (15.0%)
66 plus 14 (02.6%)

Ethnicity
Mexican American   262 (49.4%)
Anglo   164 (30.9%)
Mexican (raised in Mexico)   83 (15.7%)
Other   20 (03.8%)

Estimated annual family income
Under $13,000   118 (22.2%)
$13,000–$26,000   164 (30.8%)
$26,000–$50,000   152 (28.6%)
Over $50,000   96 (18.0%)

Respondent's ability to speak English on starting school
Not at all   114 (21.5%)
Very little   71 (13.4%)
Moderately well   44 (8.3%)
Quite well   68 (12.8%)
Very well   234 (44.1%)

Term Anglo respondents prefer to designate their ethnic or racial status

Anglo	96 (58.5%)
White	68 (41.5%)

Term Mexican-origin respondents prefer to describe their ethnic status

Chicano	4 (01.2%)
Latino	3 (09.0%)
Mexican/Mexicano	83 (24.1%)
Mexican American	139 (40.3%)
Hispanic	116 (33.6%)

Respondent's place of birth

Rio Grande Valley	226 (42.5%)
Other Texas	91 (17.1%)
Other U.S.	87 (16.4%)
Mexico	124 (23.3%)

Notes

Preface

1. Martínez, of course, uses this term differently, to describe a type of person residing in the border area (core borderlander) who is largely binational and bicultural.

Introduction

1. These figures were extracted from the 1990 data in Table 2-1 of John R. Weeks and Roberto Ham-Chande, eds., *Demographic Dynamics of the U.S.-Mexico Border* (El Paso: Texas Western Press, 1992).

2. Any correspondence of the names used throughout the text to actual persons is purely coincidental.

3. Wayne A. Cornelius compares the relative value of random sampling (with its inevitably low response rate) and "snowball" sampling (getting interviewees to identify others like themselves). He concludes, as we have, that an interviewer can have more confidence in snowball sampling when people want to remain hidden. See his *Interviewing Undocumented Immigrants: Methodological Reflections Based on Fieldwork in Mexico and the U.S.*, Working Papers in U S -Mexican Studies, no. 2 (La Jolla, Calif.: Program in United States–Mexican Studies, University of California at San Diego, 1982), 10.

4. Unless otherwise noted, the material for this brief history of the Lower Rio Grande borderlands is based on Mario L. Sánchez, ed., *A Shared Experience: The History, Architecture, and Historic Designations of the Lower Rio Grande Heritage Corridor*, 2d ed. (Austin: Los Caminos del Río Heritage Project, Texas Historical Commission, 1994; available from http://www.rice.edu/armadillo/Past/Book; Internet). Accessed online 25 and 31 March 1997, 1 and 30 April 1997, and 31 July 1997.

5. The Rio Grande was often confused with Río Soto la Marina, 120 miles south of the Rio Grande.

6. This account is based on Martín Salinas, *Indians of the Rio Grande Delta: Their Role in the History of Southern Texas and Northeastern Mexico*, Texas Archaeology and Ethnohistory Series (Austin: University of Texas Press, 1990), 14–27, and Sánchez, ed., *A Shared Experience*.

7. Helen Simons and Cathryn A. Hoyt cite the route proposed by Alex D. Krieger in 1961 as the one "most widely accepted today." It crosses the Rio Grande in the general vicinity of Hidalgo County. See Helen Simons and Cathryn A. Hoyt, eds., *Hispanic Texas: A Historical Guide* (Austin: University of Texas Press, 1992), 381. For a more detailed discussion of the lively debate over which route Cabeza de Vaca took, see Donald E. Chipman, "In Search of Cabeza de Vaca's Route across Texas," *Southwestern Historical Quarterly* 91 (October 1987).

8. For an excellent discussion of the Coahuiltecans, see Martín Salinas, *Indians of the Rio Grande Delta*, 14–27.

9. Lawrence Francis Hill's *José de Escandón and the Founding of Nuevo Santander: A Study in Spanish Colonization*, Profmex Monograph Series (1926; reprint, Columbus: Ohio State University Press, 1990) remains one of the best descriptions of the colonization era.

10. This conflict is well described in Oscar J. Martínez, *Troublesome Border* (Tucson: University of Arizona Press, 1988).

11. According to Harold U. Faulkner, Lincoln believed the war was unnecessary and unconstitutional. See Harold U. Faulkner, *American Political and Social History* (New York: Appleton-Century-Crofts, 1948), 325.

12. For a good description of this and other episodes associated with Cortina, see Jerry D. Thompson, *Juan Cortina and the Texas-Mexico Frontier* (El Paso: Texas Western Press, 1994).

13. For a good description of conflict and accommodation in South Texas during the nineteenth and twentieth centuries, see David Montejano, *Anglos and Mexicans in the Making of Texas, 1836–1986* (Austin: University of Texas Press, 1987).

14. Montejano, *Anglos and Mexicans*.

15. Montejano attributes this to four events: World War II, the mechanization of labor-intensive agriculture, the emergence of urban-based political power, and pressure from below and outside (or the civil rights struggle of the 1960s). See his *Anglos and Mexicans*, 264.

16. See Ellwyn R. Stoddard and John Hedderson, *Patterns of Poverty along the US-Mexico Border*, Borderlands Research Monograph Series, no. 3 (Las Cruces: Joint Border Research Institute, New Mexico State University, 1989), and Rogelio Saenz and Marie Ballejos, "Industrial Development and Persistent Poverty in the Lower Rio Grande Valley," in *Forgotten Places: Uneven Development in Rural America*, ed. Thomas A. Lyson and William W. Falk (Lawrence: University Press of Kansas, 1993).

17. James W. Russell uses survey evidence to show that "the term 'Chicano' may be becoming rapidly obsolete. . . . [B]y the 1990s few people of Mexican descent in the United States identified themselves as Chicanos." *After the Fifth Sun: Class and Race in North America* (Englewood Cliffs, N. J.: Prentice Hall, 1994), 232.

18. See, for example, William J. Wilson, *The Declining Significance of Race: Blacks and Changing American Institutions*, 2d ed. (Chicago: University of Chicago Press, 1980), and David L. Featherman and Robert M. Hauser, *Opportunity and Change*, Studies in Population Series (New York: Academic Press, 1978).

19. This view, particularly prevalent in the 1960s and 1970s, still survives in academic and educational circles. One recent version is Lawrence E. Harrison, *Who Prospers: How Cultural Values Shape Economic and Political Success* (New York: Basic Books, 1992).

20. Robert E. Park, *Race and Culture* (1926; reprint, New York: Free Press, 1964).

21. S. Dale McLemore, *Racial and Ethnic Relations in America*, 4th ed. (Boston: Allyn and Bacon, 1994).

Chapter 1

1. Richard Baker finds that such stereotypes about farmworkers, even those as contradictory as this one, are fairly common. See his *Los Dos Mundos: Rural Mexican Americans, Another America* (Logan: Utah State University Press, 1995).

2. The danger and hardship of the long trips are discussed by Robert Coles, *Uprooted Children: The Early Life of Migrant Farm Workers* (New York: Harper and Row, 1971).

3. Michael Harrington comments on the invisibility of farmworkers and the tendency of many people to think they are an anachronism. See Michael Harrington, *The Other America: Poverty in the United States* (New York: Macmillan, 1962).

4. Richard Baker finds that the public is poorly informed about the number of farmworkers and the situations they continue to face. See *Los Dos Mundos.*

5. Luis F. B. Plascenia, Miguel Ceballos, and Robert W. Glover, *Texas Farm Worker Enumeration Project* (Austin: Center for the Study of Human Resources, University of Texas at Austin, 1989).

6. University of Texas System, Texas-Mexico Border Health Coordination Office, *Texas-Mexico Border County Demographics and Health Statistics, 1994,* by Rumaldo Z. Juárez et al. TMBHCO Series Report 93–94, no. 2 (Edinburg: University of Texas System, Texas-Mexico Border Health Coordination Office, 1994), 15–25.

7. University of Texas System, *Texas-Mexico Border County Demographics,* 218.

8. National Migrant Health Program, *Atlas of State Profiles Which Estimate Number of Migrant and Seasonal Farm Workers and Members of Their Families* (Rockville, Md.: Bureau of Primary Health Care, U.S. Department of Health and Human Services, 1990).

9. Sonny Lopez, "Chile Pickers Live Meager Life on Streets," *El Paso Herald Post,* 7 November 1994, secs. 1D, 5D; Ronald L. Goldfarb, *Migrant Farm Workers: A Caste of Despair* (Ames: Iowa State University Press, 1981).

10. Maralyn Edid, *Farm Labor Organizing: Trends and Prospects* (Ithaca, N.Y.: ILR Press, 1994).

11. Isabel Valle, *Fields of Toil: A Migrant Family's Journey* (Pullman: Washington State University Press, 1994); testimony by David Duran before the U.S. Commission on Security and Cooperation in Europe, Washington, D.C., October 9, 1992, reported in U.S. Congress, Commission on Security and Cooperation in Europe, *Migrant Farmworkers in the United States* (Washington, D.C.: Commission on Security and Cooperation in Europe, 1993); U.S. Commission on Agricultural Workers, *Report of the Commission on Agricultural Workers,* 4 vols. (Washington, D.C.: Commission on Agricultural Workers, 1993).

12. National Advisory Council on Migrant Health, *1993 Recommendations of the National Advisory Council on Migrant Health* (Rockville, Md.: National Advisory Council on Migrant Health, 1993); Housing Assistance Council, *A Proposal for Addressing the Housing Needs of Farm Workers and Migrant Workers* (Washington, D.C.: U.S. Government Printing Office, 1992).

13. Edid, *Farm Labor Organizing.*

14. U.S. Commission on Agricultural Workers, *Report.*

15. Valle, *Fields of Toil.*

16. Specific patterns of abuse are outlined in Herbert O. Mason, Andrew J. Alvarado, and Gray L. Riley, "The Citrus Industry in California and Yuma County, Arizona," in *Case Studies and Research Reports Prepared for the Commission on Agricultural Workers, 1989–1993,* vol. 2 of *Report of the Commission on Agricultural Workers* (Washington, D.C.: U.S. Government Printing Office, 1993); Goldfarb, *Migrant Farm Workers;* and Edward Kissam and Anna García, "The Changing Composition of Southwest Michigan's Farm Labor Force: Indirect Impacts of IRCA," in *Case Studies and Research Reports Prepared for the Commission on Agricultural Workers, 1989–1993,* vol. 2 of *Report of the Commission on Agricultural Workers* (Washington, D.C.: U.S. Government Printing Office, 1993).

17. Goldfarb, *Migrant Farm Workers;* Kissam and García, "Southwest Michigan's Farm Labor Force."

18. Exposure to hazardous chemicals constitutes the most common occupational hazard for migrant farmworkers. See U.S. General Accounting Office, *Hired Farm Workers: Health and Well-Being at Risk: Report to Congressional Requesters* (Washington, D.C.: U.S. General Accounting Office, 1992), and Leticia Maravilla, "Migrant Farmworker Children," U.S. Congress, Commission on Security and Cooperation in Europe, *Migrant Farmworkers*. According to the Environmental Protection Agency, over half the nation's 4.4 million farmworkers are exposed to pesticides in the course of their work. The EPA estimates that 313,000 farmworkers experience pesticide-related illnesses each year. See U.S. Environmental Protection Agency, Office of Pesticides and Toxic Substances, *EPA's Pesticide Programs* (Washington, D.C.: U.S. Environmental Protection Agency, 1992).

19. Texas Network for Environmental and Economic Justice, *Toxics in Texas and Their Impact on Communities of Color* (Austin: Texas Center for Policy Studies, 1993).

20. Baker, *Los Dos Mundos*.

21. Valle, *Fields of Toil*.

22. Rogelio Saenz, "The Demography of Mexicans in the Midwest," in *Immigration and Ethnic Communities: A Focus on Latinos* (East Lansing: Julian Samora Research Institute, Michigan State University, 1996); Dennis Nodín Valdés, "Historical Foundations of Latino Immigration and Community Formation in Twentieth-Century Michigan and the Midwest," in *Immigration and Ethnic Communities: A Focus on Latinos*, ed. Refugio I. Rochin (East Lansing: Julian Samora Research Institute, Michigan State University, 1996).

Chapter 2

1. Some of the data reported in this chapter appeared in "Building Strengths from Within: *Colonias* of the Rio Grande Valley," published in *Journal of Borderlands Studies* 11, no. 2 (fall 1996).

2. U S. Congress, House Select Committee on Hunger, *Colonias: A Third World within Our Borders: Hearings*, 101st Cong., 1st sess., 1990.

3. Lyndon B. Johnson School of Public Affairs, *Colonias in the Lower Rio Grande Valley of South Texas: A Summary Report*, Policy Research Project Reports, no. 18 (Austin: University of Texas at Austin, 1977).

4. Texas Water Development Board, *Water and Wastewater Needs of Texas Colonias, 1995 Update* (Austin, Texas Water Development Board, 1995).

5. Texas Department of Human Services, *The Colonias Fact Book: A Survey of Living Conditions in Rural Areas of South Texas and West Texas Border Counties*, by Exiquio Salinas (Austin: Texas Department of Human Services, 1988), p. 6–3.

6. United States Department of Commerce, Economics, and Statistical Administration, Bureau of the Census, *Statistical Abstract of the United States, 1994*, 114th ed., Table 708 (Washington, D.C.: U.S. Government Printing Office, 1995).

7. Texas Department of Human Services, *Colonias Factbook*, p. 2–3.

8. Texas Attorney General's Office, *Socioeconomic Characteristics of Colonia Areas in Hidalgo County: What the 1990 Census Shows* (Austin: Texas Attorney General's Office, 1993), 5.

9. Lyndon B. Johnson School of Public Affairs, *Colonia Housing and Infrastructure: Current Population and Housing Characteristics, Future Growth, and Housing, Water, and Wastewater Needs* (Austin: University of Texas at Austin, 1996), 31.

10. Lyndon B. Johnson School of Public Affairs, *Colonias in the Lower Rio Grande Valley*, 9.

11. This figure is an approximation for an average-sized colonia family. Federal guidelines require an income 25 percent above the poverty line for granting resident alien status to a spouse. See *Immigration Reform and Immigrant Responsibility Act of 1996*.

12. As of this writing, the State Department plans to issue these cards only at U.S. consulates, making it more difficult for border residents who live far away from the few consular offices in northeastern Mexico.

13. Texas Department of Human Services, *Colonias Factbook*, p. 2–5.

14. Oscar Martinez, *Border People: Life and Society in the U.S.-Mexico Borderlands* (Tucson: University of Arizona Press, 1994).

15. Martinez, *Border People*, 314.

16. Texas Water Development Board, *Water and Wastewater Needs of Texas Colonias*.

17. Texas Water Development Board, *Water and Wastewater Needs of Texas Colonias*.

18. Texas Department of Human Services, *Colonias Factbook*, p. 3–4.

19. Dianne C. Betts and Daniel J. Slottje, *Crisis on the Rio Grande: Poverty, Unemployment, and Economic Development on the Texas-Mexico Border* (Boulder: Westview Press, 1994), 75-77.

20. Texas Department of Human Services, Office of Strategic Management, Research and Development, *Partnership for Self-Sufficiency: Public and Private Initiatives: 1989 Report and Recommendations*, by Penny Tisdale (Austin: Texas Department of Human Services, 1989), 37.

21. Texas Department of Human Services, *Colonias Factbook*, p. 5–3.

22. This figure is very close to the one obtained by the Texas Department of Human Services survey that showed 46 percent of employed Rio Grande Valley colonia residents involved in field work. Texas Department of Human Services, *Colonias Factbook*, p. 5–4.

23. Ellwyn R. Stoddard, *Patterns of Poverty along the U.S.-Mexico Border* (El Paso: Center for Inter-American Studies, University of Texas at El Paso and Organization of U S. Border Cities and Counties, 1978).

24. Durkheim called the bond based on similarity of situation and occupation "mechanical solidarity."

Chapter 3

1. This is a recurrent theme in many studies of domestic servants. See Mary Romero, *Maid in the U.S.A.* (New York: Routledge, 1992), and Alice Childress, *Like One of the Family: Conversations from a Domestic's Life* (New York: Independence, 1956).

2. Mary García Castro, "What Is Bought and Sold in Domestic Service? The Case of Bogotá: A Critical Review," in *Muchachas No More: Household Workers in Latin America and the Caribbean*, ed. Elsa M. Chaney and Mary García Castro (Philadelphia: Temple University Press, 1989), 122.

3. Judith Rollins sees immigrant women as particularly vulnerable to such exploitation, which she calls "occupational ghettoization." See Judith Rollins, *Between Women: Domestics and Their Employers* (Philadelphia: Temple University Press, 1985).

4. Childress, *Like One of the Family*.

5. For more discussion of this general proposition, see Robert A. Baron and Don Byrne, *Social Psychology: Understanding Human Interaction*, 4th ed. (Boston: Allyn and Bacon, 1987), 188-189, and George C. Homans, *The Human Group* (New York: Harcourt, 1950), 111. Specific reference to its applicability in the case of domestic servants can be found in Mónica Gogna, "Domestic Workers in Buenos Aires," in *Muchachas No More: Household Workers in Latin America and the Caribbean*, ed. Elsa M. Chaney and Mary García Castro (Philadelphia: Temple University Press, 1989).

6. Romero, *Maid in the U.S.A.*; Evelyn Nakano Glenn, *Issei, Nesei, War Bride: Three Generations of Japanese American Women in Domestic Service* (Philadelphia: Temple University Press, 1986).

7. A discussion of related factors in the literature can be found in Pierrette Hondagneu-Sotelo, *Gendered Transitions: Mexican Experiences of Immigration* (Berkeley: University of California Press, 1994).

8. Luis Alberto Urrea, *Across the Wire: Life and Hard Times on the Mexican Border* (New York: Doubleday, Anchor Books, 1993); Hondagneu-Sotelo, *Gendered Transitions*.

9. Ted Connover, *Coyotes: A Journey through the Secret World of America's Illegal Aliens* (New York: Vintage Books, 1987).

10. Hondagneu-Sotelo, *Gendered Transitions*; Romero, *Maid in the U.S.A.*; Glenn, *Issei, Nesei, War Bride*.

11. Hondagneu-Sotelo, *Gendered Transitions*; Gogna, "Domestic Workers"; Romero, *Maid in the U.S.A.*.

12. Mary Goldsmith, "Politics and Programs of Domestic Workers' Organizations in Mexico," in *Muchachas No More: Household Workers in Latin America and the Caribbean*, ed. Elsa M. Chaney and Mary García Castro (Philadelphia: Temple University Press, 1989); Glenn, *Issei, Nesei, War Bride*.

13. Goldsmith, "Domestic Workers' Organizations."

14. Elizabeth Kuznesof, "A History of Domestic Service in Spanish America, 1492–1890," in *Muchachas No More: Household Workers in Latin America and the Caribbean*, ed. Elsa M. Chaney and Mary García Castro (Philadelphia: Temple University Press, 1989).

15. This, according to Shellee Cohen, is a common contradiction inherent in the employer-employee relationship. At issue is the lack of respect and trust afforded domestic workers. See Shellee Cohen, "Just a Little Respect: West Indian Domestic Workers in New York City," in *Muchachas No More: Household Workers in Latin America and the Caribbean*, ed. Elsa M. Chaney and Mary García Castro (Philadelphia: Temple University Press, 1989).

16. Cohen, "Just a Little Respect."

17. García Castro, "Domestic Service"; Gogna, "Domestic Workers in Buenos Aires."

18. Glenn also discusses duties frequently assigned to maids. See Glenn, *Issei, Nesei, War Bride*.

19. Many maids must even indefinitely "suspend" their roles as wives and mothers because it is inconvenient to their employer. See Kuzsnesof, "Domestic Service in Spanish America," and Glenn, *Issei, Nesei, War Bride*.

20. Romero, *Maid in the U.S.A.*

21. Glenn, *Issei, Nesei, War Bride*; Romero, *Maid in the U.S.A.*

22. Sherrie A. Kossoudji and Susan I. Ranney, "The Labor Market Experience of Female Migrants: The Case of Temporary Mexican Migration to the United States," *International Migration Review* 18 (1984); Hondagneu-Sotelo, *Gendered Transitions.*

23. Though most of the undocumented maids interviewed get room and board, the fact that they have to be available twenty-four hours a day minimizes any benefit of such "extras."

24. Sandra Lauderdale Graham, *House and Street: The Domestic World of Servants and Masters in Nineteenth-Century Rio de Janeiro* (Austin: University of Texas Press, 1988).

25. Romero, *Maid in the U.S.A.*

26. Patricia Mohammed, "Domestic Workers in the Caribbean," In *Muchachas No More: Household Workers in Latin America and the Caribbean,* ed. Elsa M. Chaney and Mary García Castro (Philadelphia: Temple University Press, 1989).

27. Cohen, "Just a Little Respect"; Romero, *Maid in the U.S.A.*

28. Thea Schellekens and Anja van der Schoot, "Household Workers in Peru: The Difficult Road to Organization," in *Muchachas No More: Household Workers in Latin Ameica and the Caribbean,* ed. Elsa M. Chaney and Mary García Castro (Philadelphia: Temple University Press, 1989).

29. Romero, *Maid in the U.S.A.*; Glenn, *Issei, Nesei, War Bride.*

30. Lauderdale Graham, *House and Street*; Glenn, *Issei, Nesei, War Bride.*

31. Lauderdale Graham, *House and Street*; Goldsmith, "Domestic Workers' Organizations"; Thelma Gálvez and Rosalba Todaro, "Housework for Pay in Chile: Not Just Another Job," in *Muchachas No More: Household Workers in Latin America and the Caribbean,* ed. Elsa M. Chaney and Mary García Castro (Philadelphia: Temple University Press, 1989).

32. Cohen discusses some of these inherent contradictions in the role of a domestic servant living in the employer's home. See Cohen, "Just a Little Respect."

33. Cohen, "Just a Little Respect."

34. Glenn, *Issei, Nesei, War Bride*; Lauderdale Graham, *House and Street.*

35. There has been considerable debate about whether immigrants intend to be only sojourners or seek permanent residence. See Alejandro Portes and Ruben G. Rumbaut, *Immigrant America* (Berkeley: University of California Press, 1990); Jorge Bustamante, "La política de inmigración de Estados Unidos: Un análisis de sus contradicciones," *Estudios Sociológicos* 1 (1983); and Michael Piore, *Birds of Passage: Migrant Labor and Industrial Societies* (Cambridge: Cambridge University Press, 1979).

36. Cohen describes how the role of domestic service helps the domestic worker to "assimilate" the different values and fulfill the expectations of the host society. See Cohen, "Just a Little Respect."

Chapter 4

1. Patrick Oster has a chapter entitled "The Junior" about wealthy (and often snobbish) Mexican children in his book *The Mexicans: A Personal Portrait of a People* (New York: W. Morrow, 1989).

2. Ellwyn Stoddard, *Maquila: Assembly Plants in Northern Mexico* (El Paso: Texas Western Press, 1987).

3. Stoddard, *Maquila.*

4. Based on figures from UNICEF and Mexican government agencies cited in

Gerardo Albarrán de Alba, "En el Distrito Federal la infancia no es prioridad: Se multiplican la producción de niños que viven, crecen y mueren en las calles," *Proceso* (Mexico) (17 June 1996).

5. This rapid increase is most likely due to the economic crisis in Mexico at this time, which hit particularly hard at the poorest segment of Mexican society.

6. Albarrán de Alba reports that 88 percent of street children in Mexico City can read and write, although most have dropped out of school, either because of economic necessity or family problems. See his "En el Distrito Federal."

7. Using studies by UNICEF and others, Albarrán de Alba estimates that 44 percent of children living on the streets of Mexico City have left their families because of abuse. See Albarrán de Alba, "En el Distrito Federal."

8. In Mexico City, Albarrán de Alba estimates, 12 percent of street children are involved in begging. See his "En el Distrito Federal."

9. Albarrán de Alba reports that 62 percent of Mexico City's street children claim to have been detained by police officials, with 35 percent of these reporting physical or verbal abuse at the hands of police. See his "En el Distrito Federal."

10. *Wall Street Journal*, 30 March 1994; McAllen Chamber of Commerce, *McAllen: A Market Profile, 1995–96* (McAllen, Tex.: McAllen Chamber of Commerce, 1995), p. 26.

11. John Kenneth Galbraith, *American Capitalism: The Concept of Countervailing Power* (Boston: Houghton Mifflin, 1952).

12. George J. Borjas, *Friends or Strangers: The Impact of Immigrants on the U.S. Economy* (New York: Basic Books, 1990).

13. "Compensation Overview," *Twin Plant News*, May 1990, 34.

14. Pierre Bourdieu presents an insightful analysis of the ways that culture becomes "capital," ensuring the advantages of the elites of society and blocking opportunities for groups at the bottom. See his *Outline of a Theory of Practice* (Cambridge University Press, 1977).

15. Stoddard, *Maquila.*

16. One of the most forceful arguments that maquilas are exploiters is made by Augusta Dwyer, *On the Line: Life on the U.S.-Mexican Border* (London: Latin American Bureau, 1994).

17. See Ellwyn R. Stoddard, "Texas Higher Education and Border Funding Inequities: Implication for Border Universities and Transborder Cooperation." *Río Bravo: A Journal of Research and Issues* 2, no. 1 (1992).

18. Joe R. Feagin and Clairece Booher Feagin also present a typology of discrimination that distinguishes intentional from unintentional harm. They identify four types: Type A, isolate discrimination; Type B, small-group discrimination; Type C, direct institutionalized discrimination; and Type D, indirect institutionalized discrimination. See their *Racial and Ethnic Relations* (Upper Saddle River, N.J.: Prentice-Hall, 1996).

19. Oscar Martínez describes a similar situation in other border cities, though he states that empirical evidence of pressure to enter such relationships is unavailable. See Martínez, *Border People*, 327.

Chapter 5

1. Some of the data described in this chapter was published in Chad Richardson, María Olivia Villarreal-Solano, and Cruz C. Torres, "Anglo-Hispanic Rela-

tions in South Texas Schools from 1945 to 1993: A Triangulated Profile," *Río Bravo* 3, no. 2 (spring 1994).

2. Martínez, *Troublesome Border*.

3. Montejano, *Anglos and Mexicans*.

4. According to Rodolfo Acuña, Anglos believed in the supremacy of the English language and culture. Their basic argument was simple: Spanish-speaking people lived in the United States, and they had the burden of learning English; teachers had no such duty to learn Spanish. See Rodolfo Acuña, *Occupied America: A History of Chicanos*, 3d ed. (New York: Harper and Row, 1988).

5. Douglas E. Foley makes this the central theme of his ethnographic study of a small South Texas town, showing that the schools there perpetuated inequality by teaching "a materialistic culture that is intensely competitive, individualistic, and unegalitarian." *Learning Capitalist Culture* (Philadelphia: University of Pennsylvania Press, 1990), xv. The social conflict waged in the schools in this century against Mexican Americans is also the theme of Guadalupe San Miguel's *Let All of Them Take Heed: Mexican Americans and the Campaign for Educational Equality in Texas, 1910–1981*, Mexican American Monographs, no. 11 (Austin: University of Texas Press, 1987).

6. Montejano, *Anglos and Mexicans*, 230.

7. Montejano defines four periods of ethnic relations between Anglos and Mexican-origin people in Texas: Incorporation (1836–1900); Reconstruction (1900–1920); Segregation (1920–1940); and Integration (1940–1986). See Montejano, *Anglos and Mexicans*. Rodolfo Alvarez also proposes four historical periods (or "generations") of Mexican Americans in the United States. His "Creation Generation" coincides with Montejano's "Incorporation" period. Alvarez' second period, the "Migrant Generation," lasted until about 1940. His third period, the "Mexican-American Generation," lasted until about 1960, when the "Chicano Generation" emerged.

8. Earl Shorris, *Latinos: A Biography of the People* (New York: W. W. Norton, 1992).

9. Matt S. Meier and Feliciano Rivera, *The Chicanos: A History of Mexican Americans* (New York: Hill and Wang, 1972), 221.

10. McLemore, *Racial and Ethnic Relations in America*, 257.

11. Meier and Rivera, *The Chicanos*, 250.

12. Ignacio M. García, *United We Win: The Rise and Fall of La Raza Unida Party* (Tucson: MASRC, University of Arizona, 1989), 10.

13. Linda Chavez, *Out of the Barrio: Toward a New Politics of Hispanic Assimilation* (New York: Basic Books, 1991), 29.

14. As compiled by Betts and Slottje, *Crisis on the Rio Grande*, Table 1.1.

15. High schools included are those in McAllen, Mission, Pharr–San Juan–Alamo, Edinburg, Donna, Weslaco, Harlingen, Lyford, Raymondville, and Port Isabel.

16. The student population by 1990 had a higher Hispanic percentage than the overall Valley population because of a higher birthrate among Hispanics, which yields more Hispanics in the school-age population.

17. Region One Education Service Center, *Disaggregation of PEIMS Student Data* (Edinburg, Tex.: Region One Education Service Center, 1995).

18. Region One includes the four counties of the Valley, plus Jim Hogg, Zapata, and Webb counties.

19. University of Texas System, Texas-Mexico Border Health Coordination Office, *Texas-Mexico Border County Demographics and Health Statistics, 1994,* by Rumaldo Z. Juárez et al., TMBHCO Series Report 93–94, no. 2 (Edinburg, Tex.: Texas-Mexico Border Health Coordination Office, University of Texas System, 1994), Table 1.3.

20. Region One Education Service Center, *Texas Assessment of Academic Skills: Demographic Performance Summary* (Edinburg, Tex.: Region One Education Service Center, 1996).

Chapter 6

1. This process of assimilation, or of transforming the identity of foreign immigrants to "American," is often referred to in the popular press and in scholarly discourse as a "three-generation process" because it is thought to take that long to assimilate. Still, it has been observed that in many instances the third generation (or grandchildren of immigrants) recognize that they have lost something and begin to seek in some ways to reestablish elements of their ethnic identity. See McLemore, *Racial and Ethnic Relations in America,* 5.

2. For a review of some specific differences, see Margarita Hidalgo, "Español mexicano y español chicano: Problemas y propuestas fundamentales," in *Language Problems and Language Planning* 2 (1987).

3. Research on this issue is rather limited. Nevertheless, one excellent source of articles is Harley L. Browning and Rodolfo O. De la Garza, eds., *Mexican Immigrants and Mexican Americans: An Evolving Relation* (Austin: Center for Mexican American Studies, University of Texas at Austin, 1986). For a good discussion of how the relationship between Mexican immigrants and Mexican Americans has changed over time, see David G. Gutiérrez, *Walls and Mirrors: Mexican Americans, Mexican Immigrants, and the Politics of Ethnicity* (Berkeley: University of California Press, 1995). Finally, Rodolfo O. De la Garza and Claudio Vargas provide an excellent review of the changing relations between Chicano activists and the Mexican government in "The Mexican-Origin Population of the United States as a Political Force in the Borderlands: From Paisanos to Pochos to Potential Political Allies," in *Changing Boundaries in the Americas,* ed. Lawrence A. Herzog (San Diego: Center for U.S.-Mexican Studies, University of California at San Diego, 1992).

4. Tom Barry, Harry Browne, and Beth Sims state that until the 1980s, most Mexican immigrants were sojourners, not permanent settlers. Though large percentages of Mexican immigrants do still come and go as migrants, the majority now clearly seek to become permanent residents. See Tom Barry, Harry Browne, and Beth Sims, *Crossing the Line: Immigrants, Economic Integration, and Drug Enforcement on the U.S.-Mexico Border* (Albuquerque: Resource Center Press, 1994), 36. See also Leo Chávez, Esteban Flores, and María López-Garza, "Migrants and Settlers: Comparison of Undocumented Mexicans and Central Americans in the United States," *Frontera Norte* (El Colegio de la Frontera Norte, Tijuana, Baja Calif.) 1, no. 1 (1989).

5. David M. Heer reviews some of the important factors related to the decision to migrate. See his *Undocumented Mexicans in the United States* (New York: Cambridge University Press, 1990), 8–11. See also Ellwyn Stoddard, "A Conceptual Analysis of the Alien Invasion: Institutionalized Support of Illegal Mexican Aliens in the United States," *International Migration Review* 10 (1976), and Theo-

dore E. Downing, "Explaining Migration in Mexico and Elsewhere," in *Migration across Frontiers: Mexico and the United States*, ed. Fernando Camara and Robert Van Kemper, Latin American Anthropology Group, vol. 3 (Albany: Institute for Meso-american Studies, State University of New York at Albany, 1979).

6. It is likely that the low number of high-income respondents found for the survey is due to their low representation in the overall population of Mexican immigrants. Rogelio Saenz, for example, reports that only 3.5 percent of Mexican immigrants in the Southwest are in managerial or professional occupations, with another 10 percent in technical, sales, and administrative occupations. See Rogelio Saenz, "The Demography of Mexicans in the Midwest," in *Immigration and Ethnic Communities: A Focus on Latinos* (East Lansing: Julian Samora Research Institute, Michigan State University, 1996), 27.

7. Chad Richardson and Joe Feagin, "The Dynamics of Legalization: Undocumented Mexican Immigrants in the United States," *Research in Political Sociology* 3 (1987).

8. Heer, *Undocumented Mexicans*, reports a wide range of responses among undocumented Mexicans in the United States concerning whether they wanted to remain in the United States or return to Mexico. In a study by Wayne Cornelius, only 19 percent claimed they wanted to remain in the United States. See Cornelius, *Mexican Migration*. In another study, by Sheldon L. Maram, approximately 70 percent claimed they had never returned to Mexico after entering the United States. See Sheldon L. Maram, *Hispanic Workers in the Garment and Restaurant Industries in Los Angeles County: A Social and Economic Profile*, Working Papers in U.S.-Mexican Studies, no. 12 (La Jolla: Program in United States–Mexican Studies, University of California at San Diego, 1980).

9. Heer, *Undocumented Mexicans*, 199. According to Jorge G. Castañeda, the total number of Mexicans who legalized their status through the amnesty provisions of the Immigration Act of 1986 was 1,322,000. See Jorge G. Castañeda, "The Fear of Americanization," in *Limits to Friendship: The United States and Mexico*, ed. Robert A. Pastor and Jorge G. Castañeda (New York: Random House, 1988), 318.

10. De la Garza and Vargas, "Mexican-Origin Population," 92.

11. As Rodolfo O. De la Garza and Claudio Vargas point out, this negative image is based not only on widespread reports of corruption and poverty but on stereotyped images in the media and movies. See "Mexican-Origin Population," 108.

12. Jorge Castañeda proposes that the intense desire of Mexicans to hold on to their culture is a major factor limiting greater migration to the United States. "Many more Mexicans might well want to go to the United States," he says, "but on the condition that they 'stay' Mexican, that they be able to come back to the old country, and that their quality of life remain as Mexican as possible." "The Fear of Americanization," 324.

13. Nestor Rodríguez and Rogelio T. Nuñez, who conducted a study of undocumented Mexicans and Chicanos in Austin and San Antonio, Texas, report that they "found various expressions of the mutually critical perceptions of both groups, indicating that lower-working-class Chicanos and indocumentados appraise each other negatively." "An Exploration of Factors That Contribute to Differentiation between Chicanos and Indocumentados," in *Mexican Immigrants and Mexican Americans: An Evolving Relation*, ed. Harley L. Browning and Rodolfo O. De la Garza (Austin: Center for Mexican American Studies, University of Texas, 1986), 140.

Chapter 7

1. According to U.S. census data compiled by Dianne C. Betts and Daniel J. Slottje, the non-Hispanic population of the Valley increased from 101,019 in 1950 to 114,457 in 1970. It dropped sharply to 75,278 in 1980 but then increased to 105,292 in 1980. After that it continued to rise, to 107,595 in 1990. Although the non-Hispanic population has increased in numbers during the past 30 years, its percentage of the Valley population has decreased due to the even greater increases of the Hispanic population. See Betts and Slottje, *Crisis on the Rio Grande*, 8–9.

2. According to data compiled by the Texas-Mexico Border Health Coordination Office, University of Texas System, in the Rio Grande Valley 51 percent of Spanish-speaking young people ages 5 to 17 speak English "very well." Some 47 percent of Spanish-speaking Valley adults from 18 to 64 years of age speak English very well, while only 22 percent of Spanish-speaking Valley adults over 65 speak English very well. See University of Texas System, Texas-Mexico Border Health Coordination Office, *Lower Rio Grande Valley Demographics and Health Statistics, 1994*, by Rumaldo Z. Juárez et al. (Edinburg, Tex.: Texas-Mexico Border Health Coordination Office, University of Texas System, 1994), 19.

3. Lillian B. Rubin finds that many working-class whites feel especially threatened by the new immigrants. "It's not surprising, therefore," she states, "that working-class women and men speak so angrily about the recent influx of immigrants. They not only see their jobs and their way of life threatened, they feel bruised and assaulted by an environment that seems suddenly to have turned color and in which they feel like strangers in their own land." *Families on the Fault Line: America's Working Class Speaks about the Family, the Economy, Race, and Ethnicity* (New York: Harper Perennial, 1994), 184.

4. Though some investigators (e.g., Oscar Martínez, *Border People*) prefer to limit the distinction of "newcomer" to individuals who have lived in the border area for a specific length of time, we chose to include all who have moved to the Valley as adults, in order to distinguish them from those raised in the Valley. We did, however, include a question on how long they had lived in the Valley. Even newcomers with the longest residence in the Valley scored lower than the Anglos raised in the Valley on each item listed in Figure 7.1.

5. Rubin points out that the presence of immigrants has a decidedly different impact on Anglos of different social classes. "For people who use immigrant labor, legal or illegal," she says, " there's a payoff for the inconvenience—a payoff that doesn't exist for the [working class] families in this study but that sometimes costs them dearly. For while it may be true that American workers aren't eager for many of the jobs immigrants are willing to take, it's also true that the presence of a large immigrant population—especially those who come from developing countries where living standards are far below our own—helps to make these jobs undesirable by keeping wages depressed well below what most American workers are willing to accept." *Families on the Fault Line*, 183–184.

6. For an excellent historical description of some of the harsh attitudes of South Texas farmers toward Mexican workers and their exploitation of these workers during the mid-twentieth-century years, see Carrol Norquest, *Rio Grande Wetbacks: Mexican Migrant Workers* (Albuquerque: University of New Mexico Press, 1972).

7. Katherine O. See and William J. Wilson analyzed many studies of this hypothesis and concluded that such work appears to "provide qualified support for the

view that equal-status contact reduces prejudice." "Race and Ethnicity," in *Handbook of Sociology*, ed. Neil J. Smelser (Newbury Park, Calif.: Sage Publications, 1988), 228.

8. Lea Ybarra has demonstrated that the degree of male domination, or *machismo*, is related more to social class than to Mexican background. See Lea Ybarra, "Empirical and Theoretical Developments in the Study of the Chicano Family," in *The State of Chicano Research on Family, Labor, and Migration*, ed. Armando Valdez, Albert Carrillo, and Tomás Almaguer (Stanford: Stanford Center for Chicano Research, 1983).

9. See C. Lyn Larson, *Headin' South: The Texas Snowbirds* (Austin: Hogg Foundation for Mental Health, 1986), and Vern Vincent, Nader Asgary, Gilberto de los Santos, and Victor Dávila, *1994–95 Winter Visitor Survey* (Edinburg: College of Business Administration, University of Texas–Pan American, 1996).

10. Vincent et al., *1994–95 Winter Visitor Survey*.

Chapter 8

1. The struggle for Black identity was well expressed by Ralph Ellison, renowned Black author of *The Invisible Man* and other works, who said, "When I discover who I am, I'll be free."

2. Much of the historical information on Blacks in the Valley was extracted from Valerie Goerlitz Ramírez, "A Brief History of the African-American Community in the Rio Grande Valley" (Rio Grande Valley Historical Collection, University of Texas–Pan American Library, Edinburg, undated manuscript).

3. Mexico, like the Valley, has virtually no Blacks, mainly because they married into the local population. According to James W. Russell, most former slaves intermarried to such an extent that few identifiable Blacks can be found today in Mexico. See Russell, *After the Fifth Sun*. During the slavery era in the United States, Mexico was a haven for escaped slaves and resisted U.S. government efforts to extradite them. Among those who fled were two personal slaves of Texas' first president, Sam Houston, who escaped across the Rio Grande into Matamoros. More information about the underground railway to Mexico can be obtained in Rosalie Schwartz, *Across the Rio to Freedom: U.S. Negroes in Mexico*, Southwestern Studies Monographs, no. 44 (El Paso: Texas Western Press, University of Texas at El Paso, 1975).

4. Barbara Renaud González claims there is a definite bias against Blacks among Latinos. "According to a 1993 census report," she says, "about one-third of Latinos marry whites. . . . Less than 3 percent of Latinos dare to marry into black families. Young Latinas are absolutely—vale más que no—prohibited from dating black men." "The Mexican Dark Secret," Hispanic Link News Service, 22 October 1995.

5. Max Weber, a pioneer in the sociology of culture, defined culture as "the endowment of a finite segment of the meaningless infinity of events in the world with meaning and significance from the standpoint of human beings." Max Weber, *Max Weber on the Methodology of the Social Sciences* (1922; reprint, Glencoe, Ill.: Free Press, 1949), 81. Another sociological definition of culture, posed by Edward Sapir, is that it embraces the general values, attitudes, beliefs, and views of life. Sapir further proposed that it defines the significance of action and thought of a whole group of people across lifetimes, signifying value for them. See Edward Sapir, "Culture, Genuine and Spurious," *American Journal of Sociology* 29, no. 4 (1924).

Perhaps the most widely accepted anthropological definition of culture was proposed by Alfred L. Kroeber and Clyde Kluckhohn, who said, "Culture consists of patterns, explicit and implicit, of and for behavior acquired and transmitted by symbols, constituting the distinctive achievement of human groups, including their embodiment in artifacts." *Culture: A Critical Review of Concepts and Definitions,* Papers of the Peabody Museum, vol. 47 (Cambridge: Harvard University, 1952), 181.

6. Susan E. Keefe and Amado M. Padilla found that the extended family ties of Mexican Americans were stronger than the extended family ties not only of Anglos but also of first-generation Mexican immigrants. See their *Chicano Ethnicity* (Albuquerque: University of New Mexico Press, 1987).

7. Norma Williams conducted a study of changes in Mexican American families in three cities, of which two—Corpus Christi and Harlingen—were in South Texas. She contrasted "traditional" families with those that were more "current." She found that in recent decades the levels of cohesiveness and male dominance among Mexican Americans have become more similar to the levels found among Anglos. She concludes, however, that the convergence is due less to Anglo conformity than to global social processes that are changing all families. See Norma Williams, *The Mexican American Family: Tradition and Change* (Dix Hills, N.Y.: General Hall, 1990).

8. Max Weber, *The Protestant Ethic and the Spirit of Capitalism* (1905; reprint, New York: Scribner's Sons, 1958).

9. Jules Henry is one of the strongest advocates of the concept that culture is so deeply embedded that it not only becomes invisible but begins to impose itself on us. See his *Culture against Man* (New York: Random House, 1963). Ralph Linton likewise maintained that culture may so dominate our thinking that we fail to recognize its influence. See Ralph Linton, *The Study of Man,* Century Science Series (New York: Appleton-Century-Crofts, 1936).

10. This deterministic attitude was fairly rare among the people we interviewed. Indeed, it was a source of conflict in some homes where immigrant grandparents had such an outlook on life. None of the younger Mexican Americans we interviewed shared such fatalistic conceptualizations of the world.

11. Much of this cultural orientation was described by Max Weber and is clearly summarized in Ralph Schroeder, *Max Weber and the Sociology of Culture,* Theory, Culture, and Society Series (London: Sage Publications, 1992).

12. Eva S. Kras presents an interesting example of this by contrasting letters written by a U.S. manager and his Mexican counterpart. Both fail to see the behavior of the other as a response to culture, and blame the behavior on personality flaws. See Eva S. Kras, *Management in Two Cultures* (Yarmouth, Maine: Intercultural Press, 1989).

13. Though we suspect that many of the Anglo perceptions were influenced by stereotypes, sufficient evidence exists to establish some differences in the time orientation of Mexican-origin people in South Texas. Earl Shorris attributes time-related differences to structural factors (like poverty). "The unique sense of time common to Latinos," he proposes, "is not presentness, but uncertainty." *Latinos,* 116. For the same reason, the orientation to time dimension is included here in the Life Control dimension because we see it as a form of uncertainty or a lack of perceived control of time.

14. The wording for these items is as follows: "In life, people have to learn to

'go with the flow' because what happens to us is often outside the control of the individual" and "Standards must be flexible and adaptable because people are different and have different situations."

15. Reported in Harry Martin et al., "Folk Illnesses Reported to Physicians in the Lower Rio Grande Valley: A Binational Comparison," *Ethnology* 24, no. 3 (July 1985).

16. Indeed, William Madsen's failure to interpret his findings in light of such cautions is largely responsible for much of the criticism of his rather stereotypical portrait of South Texas Mexican Americans. See William Madsen, *Mexican Americans of South Texas*, Case Studies in Cultural Anthropology (New York: Holt, Rinehart and Winston, 1964).

17. Earl Shorris says, for example, "Latinos . . . know exactly what time it is, but they are so aware of the rules of fate that action often eludes them." *Latinos*, 116.

18. Oscar Lewis, *La Vida: A Puerto Rican Family in the Culture of Poverty—San Juan and New York* (New York: Random House, 1966), xliii.

19. Though the culture of poverty argument proposed by Lewis acknowledges the impact of class position, it is often lumped with other "cultural deprivation" suppositions and attacked for "blaming the victim." See, for example, William Ryan, *Blaming the Victim* (New York: Vintage Books, 1971).

20. Thomas Sowell, *Ethnic America: A History* (New York: Basic Books, 1981); Thomas Sowell, *Economics and Politics of Race: An International Perspective* (New York: Quill, 1983).

21. A more shrill version of Sowell's position is advocated by Peter Brimelow, *Alien Nation: Common Sense about America's Immigration Disaster* (New York: Random House, 1995).

22. Linda Chavez, *Out of the Barrio: Toward a New Politics of Hispanic Assimilation* (New York: Basic Books, 1991), 171.

23. Shorris, *Latinos*, 114–117.

24. Recently, Susan Meyer tested the assumption that low income is responsible for the lack of mobility among the poor. She compared the impact of a dollar from welfare with a dollar from wages. She then compared welfare recipients in states with high benefits with those in states with low benefits. Finally, she examined whether national income trends were matched by improvements in the achievements of children. In each of these examinations, she found that income gains had a rather small effect on other social and educational gains by children, which suggests that low income may not be as significant as some structural advocates have alleged. Nevertheless, the structural argument includes low income as only one structural impediment to social mobility among the poor. See Susan Meyer, *What Money Can't Buy: Family Income and Children's Life Chances* (Cambridge: Harvard University Press, 1997).

25. Stephen Steinberg, *The Ethnic Myth: Race, Ethnicity, and Class in America* (Boston: Beacon Press, 1989), 127.

26. Octavio Ignacio Romano-V., "The Anthropology and Sociology of the Mexican-Americans: The Distortion of Mexican-American History," in *Voices: Readings from El Grito, a Journal of Contemporary Mexican Thought, 1967–1971*, rev. ed., ed. Octavio Ignacio Romano-V. (Berkeley: Quinto Sol Publications, 1973).

27. Our finding that Mexican immigrants had a somewhat different sense of control over time and life events, for example, should not be seen as a sign of apa-

thy or inability to take collective action. Indeed, it could be argued that the higher measures of responsiveness we found among Mexican immigrants (and some Mexican Americans in South Texas) might make it *more* likely that they would take collective action against oppression, as they did during the Starr County strike of 1967 and the Edcouch-Elsa school walkout of 1968.

28. For a view that gives importance to both cultural and structural factors, see Cornel West, *Race Matters* (Boston: Beacon Press, 1993). Indeed, West claims these factors are so tightly intertwined that it makes no sense to argue for either as an independent factor.

29. Milton Myron Gordon, *Assimilation in American Life: The Role of Race, Religion, and National Origins* (New York: Oxford University Press, 1964).

30. McLemore, *Racial and Ethnic Relations in America.*

31. These are, of course, idealized types. During each of the eras in question, a variety of forms of accommodation and assimilation were involved in the adjustment of Anglos and Mexicanos to each other in South Texas.

32. Montejano, *Anglos and Mexicans,* 262.

33. Montejano says, "Cultural nationalism, an attractive philosophy during the mobilization against the Anglos, provided no strategy or instructions once 'los they' had been overcome." *Anglos and Mexicans,* 290.

34. Mario García uses the term "Post Chicano Generation" to describe this era. See Mario García, *Mexican Americans: Leadership, Ideology, and Identity* (New Haven: Yale University Press, 1989).

35. We found it much more common, however, for Mexican Americans in the Valley to maintain the Spanish pronunciation of their last name.

36. Norma Williams, *The Mexican American Family: Tradition and Change* (Dix Hills, N.Y.: General Hall, 1993), 145.

Bibliography

Acuña, Rodolfo. *Occupied America*. San Francisco: Canfield Press, 1972; New York: Harper and Row, 1988.

Albarrán de Alba, Gerardo. "En el Distrito Federal la infancia no es prioridad: Se multiplican la producción de niños que viven, crecen y mueren en las calles." *Proceso* (Mexico) (17 June 1996): 16–23.

Alvarez, Rodolfo. "The Psycho-historical and Socioeconomic Development of the Chicano Community in the United States." In *The Mexican American Experience: An Interdisciplinary Anthology*, edited by Rodolfo O. De la Garza, Frank D. Bean, Charles M. Bonjean, Ricardo Romo, and Rodolfo Alvarez, 33–56. Austin: University of Texas Press, 1985.

Baker, Richard. *Los Dos Mundos: Rural Mexican Americans, Another America*. Logan: Utah State University Press, 1995.

Baron, Robert A., and Donn Byrne. *Social Psychology: Understanding Human Interaction*. 4th ed. Boston: Allyn and Bacon, 1987.

Barry, Tom, Harry Browne, and Beth Sims. *Crossing the Line: Immigrants, Economic Integration, and Drug Enforcement on the U.S.-Mexico Border*. Albuquerque: Resource Center Press, 1994.

Betts, Dianne C., and Daniel J. Slottje. *Crisis on the Rio Grande: Poverty, Unemployment, and Economic Development on the Texas-Mexico Border*. Boulder: Westview Press, 1994.

Borjas, George J. *Friends or Strangers: The Impact of Immigrants on the U.S. Economy*. New York: Basic Books, 1990.

Bourdieu, Pierre. *Outline of a Theory of Practice*. Translated by Richard Nice. Cambridge Studies in Social Anthropology, no. 16. Cambridge: Cambridge University Press, 1977.

Brimelow, Peter. 1995. *Alien Nation: Common Sense about America's Immigration Disaster*. New York: Random House, 1995.

Browning, Harley L., and Rodolfo O. De la Garza, eds. *Mexican Immigrants and Mexican Americans: An Evolving Relation*. Austin: Center for Mexican American Studies, University of Texas at Austin, 1986.

Bustamante, Jorge. "La política de inmigración de Estados Unidos: Un análisis de sus contradicciones." *Estudios Sociológicos* 1 (1983): 93–119.

Castañeda, Jorge G. "The Fear of Americanization." In *Limits to Friendship: The United States and Mexico*, edited by Robert A. Pastor and Jorge G. Castañeda, 314–341. New York: Random House, 1988.

Chávez, Leo, Esteban Flores, and María López-Garza. "Migrants and Settlers: Comparison of Undocumented Mexicans and Central Americans in the United States." *Frontera Norte* (El Colegio de la Frontera Norte, Tijuana, Baja Calif.) 1, no. 1 (1989): 35–51.

Chávez, Linda. *Out of the Barrio: Toward a New Politics of Hispanic Assimilation*. New York: Basic Books, 1991.

Childress, Alice. *Like One of the Family: Conversations from a Domestic's Life*. New York: Independence, 1956.

Chipman, Donald E. "In Search of Cabeza de Vaca's Route across Texas." *Southwestern Historical Quarterly* 91 (October 1987): 127–148.

COHEN, SHELLEE. "Just a Little Respect: West Indian Domestic Workers in New York City." In *Muchachas No More: Household Workers in Latin America and the Caribbean*, edited by Elsa M. Chaney and Mary García Castro, 171–194. Philadelphia: Temple University Press, 1989.

COLES, ROBERT. *Uprooted Children: The Early Life of Migrant Farm Workers.* New York: Harper and Row, Perennial Library, 1971.

"Compensation Overview." *Twin Plant News* (El Paso, Texas), May 1990, 34.

CONNOVER, TED. *Coyotes: A Journey through the Secret World of America's Illegal Aliens.* New York: Vintage Books, 1987.

CORNELIUS, WAYNE A. *Interviewing Undocumented Immigrants: Methodological Reflections Based on Fieldwork in Mexico and the U.S.* Working Papers in U.S.-Mexican Studies, no. 2. La Jolla, Calif.: Program in United States–Mexican Studies, University of California at San Diego, 1982.

———. *Mexican Migration to the United States: Causes, Consequences, and U.S. Responses.* Cambridge: Center for International Studies, Massachusetts Institute of Technology, 1978.

DE LA GARZA, RODOLFO O., AND CLAUDIO VARGAS. "The Mexican-Origin Population of the United States as a Political Force in the Borderlands: From Paisanos to Pochos to Potential Political Allies." In *Changing Boundaries in the Americas*, edited by Lawrence A. Herzog, 89–111. San Diego: Center for U.S.-Mexican Studies, University of California at San Diego, 1992.

DOWNING, THEODORE E. "Explaining Migration in Mexico and Elsewhere." In *Migration across Frontiers: Mexico and the United States*, edited by Fernando Camara and Robert Van Kemper, 87–106. Latin American Anthropology Group, vol. 3. Albany: Institute for Mesoamerican Studies, State University of New York at Albany, 1979.

DWYER, AUGUSTA. *On the Line: Life on the U.S.-Mexico Border.* London: Latin American Bureau, 1994.

EDID, MARALYN. *Farm Labor Organizing: Trends and Prospects.* Ithaca, N.Y.: ILR Press, 1994.

ELLISON, RALPH. *The Invisible Man.* New York: Vintage Books, 1972.

FAULKNER, HAROLD U. *American Political and Social History.* New York: Appleton-Century-Crofts, 1948.

FEAGIN, JOE R., AND CLAIRECE BOOHER FEAGIN. *Racial and Ethnic Relations.* Upper Saddle River, N.J.: Prentice-Hall, 1996.

FEATHERMAN, DAVID L., AND ROBERT M. HAUSER. *Opportunity and Change.* Studies in Population Series. New York: Academic Press, 1978.

FOLEY, DOUGLAS F. *Learning Capitalist Culture: Deep in the Heart of Tejas.* Contemporary Ethnography Series. Philadelphia: University of Pennsylvania Press, 1990.

GALBRAITH, JOHN KENNETH. *American Capitalism: The Concept of Countervailing Power.* Boston: Houghton Mifflin, 1952.

GÁLVEZ, THELMA, AND ROSALBA TODARO. "Housework for Pay in Chile: Not Just Another Job." In *Muchachas No More: Household Workers in Latin America and the Caribbean*, edited by Elsa M. Chaney and Mary García Castro, 307–351. Philadelphia: Temple University Press, 1989.

GARCÍA, IGNACIO M. *United We Win: The Rise and Fall of La Raza Unida Party.* Tucson: MASRC, University of Arizona, 1989.

GARCÍA, MARIO T. *Mexican Americans: Leadership, Ideology, and Identity.* New Haven: Yale University Press, 1989.

GARCÍA CASTRO, MARY. "What Is Bought and Sold in Domestic Service? The Case of Bogotá: A Critical Review." In *Muchachas No More: Household Workers in Latin America and the Caribbean,* edited by Elsa M. Chaney and Mary García Castro, 105–116. Philadelphia: Temple University Press, 1989.

GLENN, EVELYN NAKANO. *Issei, Nesei, War Bride: Three Generations of Japanese American Women in Domestic Service.* Philadelphia: Temple University Press, 1986.

GOGNA, MÓNICA. "Domestic Workers in Buenos Aires." In *Muchachas No More: Household Workers in Latin America and the Caribbean,* edited by Elsa M. Chaney and Mary García Castro, 83–104. Philadelphia: Temple University Press, 1989.

GOLDFARB, RONALD L. *Migrant Farm Workers: A Caste of Despair.* Ames: Iowa State University Press, 1981.

GOLDSMITH, MARY. "Politics and Programs of Domestic Workers' Organizations in Mexico." In *Muchachas No More: Household Workers in Latin America and the Caribbean,* edited by Elsa M. Chaney and Mary García Castro, 221–243. Philadelphia: Temple University Press, 1989.

GONZÁLEZ, BARBARA RENAUD. "The Mexican Dark Secret." Hispanic Link News Service, 22 October 1995.

GORDON, MILTON MYRON. *Assimilation in American Life: The Role of Race, Religion, and National Origins.* New York: Oxford University Press, 1964.

GUTIÉRREZ, DAVID G. *Walls and Mirrors: Mexican Americans, Mexican Immigrants, and the Politics of Ethnicity.* Berkeley: University of California Press, 1995.

HARRINGTON, MICHAEL. *The Other America: Poverty in the United States.* New York: Macmillan, 1962.

HARRISON, LAWRENCE E. *Who Prospers? How Cultural Values Shape Economic and Political Success.* New York: Basic Books, 1992.

HEER, DAVID M. *Undocumented Mexicans in the United States.* New York: Cambridge University Press, 1990.

HENRY, JULES. *Culture against Man.* New York: Random House, 1963.

HIDALGO, MARGARITA. "Español mexicano y español chicano: Problemas y propuestas fundamentales." In *Language Problems and Language Planning* (University of Texas Press) 2 (1987): 166–193.

HILL, LAWRENCE FRANCIS. *José de Escandón and the Founding of Nuevo Santander: A Study in Spanish Colonization.* Profmex Monograph Series. 1926. Reprint, Columbus: Ohio State University Press, 1990.

HOMANS, GEORGE C. *The Human Group.* New York: Harcourt, 1950.

HONDAGNEU-SOTELO, PIERRETTE. *Gendered Transitions: Mexican Experiences of Immigration.* Berkeley: University of California Press, 1994.

HOUSING ASSISTANCE COUNCIL. *A Proposal for Addressing the Housing Needs of Farm Workers and Migrant Workers.* Washington, D.C.: U.S. Government Printing Office, 1992.

Immigration Reform and Immigrant Responsibility Act of 1996. U.S. Statutes 110 (1996): 3009–3546.

JUÁREZ, RUMALDO Z., ET AL. See University of Texas System.

KEEFE, SUSAN E., AND AMADO M. PADILLA. *Chicano Ethnicity.* Albuquerque: University of New Mexico Press, 1987.

KISSAM, EDWARD, AND ANNA GARCÍA. "The Changing Composition of Southwest Michigan's Farm Labor Force: Indirect Impacts of IRCA." In *Case Studies and Research Reports Prepared for the Commission on Agricultural Workers, 1989–1993,* 196–218. Vol. 2 of *Report of the Commission on Agricultural Workers,* by U.S. Commission on Agricultural Workers. Washington, D.C.: U.S. Government Printing Office, 1993.

KOSSOUDJI, SHERRIE A., AND SUSAN I. RANNEY. "The Labor Market Experience of Female Migrants: The Case of Temporary Mexican Migration to the United States." *International Migration Review* 18 (1984): 1120–1143.

KRAS, EVA S. *Management in Two Cultures.* Yarmouth, Maine: Intercultural Press, 1989.

KROEBER, ALFRED L., AND CLYDE KLUCKHOHN. *Culture: A Critical Review of Concepts and Definitions.* Papers of the Peabody Museum, vol. 47. Cambridge: Harvard University, 1952.

KUZNESOF, ELIZABETH. "A History of Domestic Service in Spanish America, 1492–1890." In *Muchachas No More: Household Workers in Latin America and the Caribbean,* edited by Elsa M. Chaney and Mary García Castro, 17–36. Philadelphia: Temple University Press, 1989.

LARSON, C. LYN. *Headin' South: The Texas Snowbirds.* Austin: Hogg Foundation for Mental Health, 1986.

LAUDERDALE GRAHAM, SANDRA. *House and Street: The Domestic World of Servants and Masters in Nineteenth-Century Rio de Janeiro.* Austin: University of Texas Press, 1988.

LEWIS, OSCAR. *La Vida: A Puerto Rican Family in the Culture of Poverty—San Juan and New York.* New York: Random House, 1966.

LINTON, RALPH. *The Study of Man.* Century Science Series. New York: Appleton-Century-Crofts, 1936.

LYNDON B. JOHNSON SCHOOL OF PUBLIC AFFAIRS. *Colonia Housing and Infrastructure: Current Population and Housing Characteristics, Future Growth, and Housing, Water, and Wastewater Needs.* Austin: University of Texas at Austin, 1996.

LYNDON B. JOHNSON SCHOOL OF PUBLIC AFFAIRS, LOWER RIO GRANDE VALLEY RESEARCH PROJECT. *Colonias in the Lower Rio Grande Valley of South Texas: A Summary Report.* Policy Research Project Reports, no. 18. Austin: University of Texas at Austin, 1977.

MADSEN, WILLIAM. *Mexican Americans of South Texas.* Case Studies in Cultural Anthropology. New York: Holt, Rinehart and Winston, 1964.

MARAM, SHELDON L. *Hispanic Workers in the Garment and Restaurant Industries in Los Angeles County: A Social and Economic Profile.* Working Papers in U.S.-Mexican Studies, no. 12. La Jolla: Program in United States–Mexican Studies, University of California at San Diego, 1980.

MARAVILLA, LETICIA. "Migrant Farmworker Children." In *Migrant Farmworkers in the United States: Briefings of the Commission on Security and Cooperation in Europe,* by U.S. Congress, Commission on Security and Cooperation in Europe. Washington, D.C.: Commission on Security and Cooperation in Europe, 1993.

MARTIN, HARRY, CERVANDO MARTÍNEZ, ROBERT LEON, CHAD RICHARDSON, AND VICTOR REYES ACOSTA. "Folk Illnesses Reported to Physicians in the Lower Rio Grande Valley: A Binational Comparison." *Ethnology* 24, no. 3 (July 1985): 229–236.

Martínez, Oscar J. *Border People: Life and Society in the U.S.-Mexico Borderlands.* Tucson: University of Arizona Press, 1994.

———. *Troublesome Border.* Tucson: University of Arizona Press, 1988.

Mason, Herbert O., Andrew J. Alvarado, and Gray L. Riley. "The Citrus Industry in California and Yuma County, Arizona." In *Case Studies and Research Reports Prepared for the Commission on Agricultural Workers, 1989–1993.* Vol. 2 of *Report of the Commission on Agricultural Workers,* by U.S. Commission on Agricultural Workers. Washington, D.C.: U.S. Government Printing Office, 1993.

McAllen Chamber of Commerce. *McAllen: A Market Profile, 1995–96.* McAllen, Tex.: McAllen Chamber of Commerce, 1995.

McLemore, S. Dale. *Racial and Ethnic Relations in America,* 4th ed. Boston: Allyn and Bacon, 1994.

Meier, Matt S., and Feliciano Rivera. *The Chicanos: A History of Mexican Americans.* American Century Series. New York: Hill and Wang, 1972.

Meyer, Susan. *What Money Can't Buy: Family Income and Children's Life Chances.* Cambridge: Harvard University Press, 1997.

Mohammed, Patricia. "Domestic Workers in the Caribbean." In *Muchachas No More: Household Workers in Latin America and the Caribbean,* edited by Elsa M. Chaney and Mary García Castro, 161–169. Philadelphia: Temple University Press, 1989.

Montejano, David. *Anglos and Mexicans in the Making of Texas, 1836–1986.* Austin: University of Texas Press, 1987.

National Advisory Council on Migrant Health. *1993 Recommendations of the National Advisory Council on Migrant Health.* Rockville, Md.: National Advisory Council on Migrant Health, 1993.

National Migrant Health Program. *Atlas of State Profiles Which Estimate Number of Migrant and Seasonal Farmworkers and Members of Their Families.* Rockville, Md.: Bureau of Primary Health Care, U.S. Department of Health and Human Services, 1990.

Norquest, Carrol. *Rio Grande Wetbacks: Mexican Migrant Workers.* Albuquerque: University of New Mexico Press, 1972.

Oster, Patrick. "The Junior." In *The Mexicans: A Personal Portrait of a People,* 36–45. New York: W. Morrow, 1989.

Park, Robert E. *Race and Culture.* 1926. Reprint, New York: Free Press, 1964.

Piore, Michael. *Birds of Passage: Migrant Labor and Industrial Societies.* Cambridge: Cambridge University Press, 1979.

Plascenia, Luis F. B., Miguel Ceballos, and Robert W. Glover. *Texas Farm Worker Enumeration Project.* Austin: Center for the Study of Human Resources, University of Texas at Austin, 1989.

Portes, Alejandro, and Robert L. Bach. *Latin Journey: Cuban and Mexican Immigrants in the United States.* Berkeley: University of California Press, 1985.

Portes, Alejandro, and Ruben G. Rumbaut. *Immigrant America.* Berkeley: University of California Press, 1990.

Ramírez, Valerie Goerlitz. "A Brief History of the African-American Community in the Rio Grande Valley." Rio Grande Valley Historical Collection, University of Texas–Pan American Library, Edinburg. Undated manuscript.

Region One Education Service Center. *Disaggregation of PEIMS Student Data.* Edinburg, Tex.: Region One Education Service Center, 1995.

———. *Texas Assessment of Academic Skills: Demographic Performance Summary.* Edinburg, Tex.: Region One Education Service Center, 1996.

RICHARDSON, CHAD. "Building Strengths from Within: Colonias of the Rio Grande Valley." *Journal of Borderlands Studies* 11, no. 2 (fall 1996): 51–68.

RICHARDSON, CHAD, AND JOE FEAGIN. "The Dynamics of Legalization: Undocumented Mexican Immigrants in the United States." *Research in Political Sociology* 3 (1987): 179–201.

RICHARDSON, CHAD, MARÍA OLIVIA VILLARREAL-SOLANO, AND CRUZ C. TORRES. "Anglo-Hispanic Relations in South Texas from 1945 to 1993: A Triangulated Profile." *Río Bravo: A Journal of Research and Issues* 3, no. 2 (spring 1994): 114–134.

RODRÍGUEZ, NESTOR, AND ROGELIO T. NUÑEZ. "An Exploration of Factors That Contribute to Differentiation between Chicanos and Indocumentados." In *Mexican Immigrants and Mexican Americans: An Evolving Relation,* edited by Harley L. Browning and Rodolfo O. De la Garza, 138–156. Austin: Center for Mexican American Studies, University of Texas, 1986.

ROLLINS, JUDITH. *Between Women: Domestics and Their Employers.* Philadelphia: Temple University Press, 1985.

ROMANO-V., OCTAVIO IGNACIO. "The Anthropology and Sociology of the Mexican-Americans: The Distortion of Mexican-American History." In *Voices: Readings from El Grito, a Journal of Contemporary Mexican Thought, 1967–1971,* rev. ed., edited by Octavio Ignacio Romano-V., 43–56. Berkeley, Calif.: Quinto Sol Publications, 1973.

ROMERO, MARY. *Maid in the U.S.A.* New York: Routledge, 1992.

RUBIN, LILLIAN B. *Families on the Fault Line: America's Working Class Speaks about the Family, the Economy, Race, and Ethnicity.* New York: Harper Perennial, 1994.

RUSSELL, JAMES W. *After the Fifth Sun: Class and Race in North America.* Englewood Cliffs, N.J.: Prentice Hall, 1994.

RYAN, WILLIAM. *Blaming the Victim.* New York: Vintage Books, 1971.

SAENZ, ROGELIO. "The Demography of Mexicans in the Midwest." In *Immigration and Ethnic Communities: A Focus on Latinos,* 23–29. East Lansing: Julian Samora Research Institute, Michigan State University, 1996.

SAENZ, ROGELIO, AND MARIE BALLEJOS. "Industrial Development and Persistent Poverty in the Lower Rio Grande Valley." In *Forgotten Places: Uneven Development in Rural America,* edited by Thomas A. Lyson and William W. Falk, 102–124. Lawrence: University Press of Kansas, 1993.

SALINAS, EXIQUIO. *See* Texas Department of Human Services.

SALINAS, MARTÍN. *Indians of the Rio Grande Delta: Their Role in the History of Southern Texas and Northeastern Mexico.* Texas Archaeology and Ethnohistory Series. Austin: University of Texas Press, 1990.

SÁNCHEZ, MARIO L., ed. *A Shared Experience: The History, Architecture, and Historical Designations of the Lower Rio Grande Heritage Corridor.* 2d ed. With a foreword by T. R. Fehrenbach and Juan Fidel Zorilla. Austin: Los Caminos del Río Heritage Project, Texas Historical Commission, 1994. Book online; available from http://www.rice.edu/armadillo/Past/Book; Internet.

SAN MIGUEL, GUADALUPE. *Let All of Them Take Heed: Mexican Americans and the Campaign for Educational Equality in Texas, 1910–1981.* Mexican American Monographs, no. 11. Austin: University of Texas Press, 1987.

SAPIR, EDWARD. "Culture, Genuine and Spurious." *American Journal of Sociology* 29, no. 4 (1924): 401–429.

SCHELLEKENS, THEA, AND ANJA VAN DER SCHOOT. "Household Workers in Peru: The Difficult Road to Organization." In *Muchachas No More: Household Workers in Latin America and the Caribbean*, edited by Elsa M. Chaney and Mary García Castro, 291–306. Philadelphia: Temple University Press, 1989.

SCHROEDER, RALPH. *Max Weber and the Sociology of Culture*. Theory, Culture, and Society Series. London: Sage Publications, 1992.

SCHWARTZ, ROSALIE. *Across the Rio to Freedom: U.S. Negroes in Mexico*. Southwestern Studies Monographs, no. 44. El Paso: Texas Western Press, University of Texas at El Paso, 1975.

SEE, KATHERINE O'SULLIVAN, AND WILLIAM J. WILSON. "Race and Ethnicity." In *Handbook of Sociology*, edited by Neil J. Smelser, 223–242. Newbury Park, Calif.: Sage Publications, 1988.

SHORRIS, EARL. *Latinos: A Biography of the People*. New York: W. W. Norton, 1992.

SIMONS, HELEN, AND CATHRYN A. HOYT, eds. *Hispanic Texas: A Historical Guide*. Austin: University of Texas Press, 1992.

SOWELL, THOMAS. *The Economics and Politics of Race: An International Perspective*. New York: Quill, 1983.

———. *Ethnic America: A History*. New York: Basic Books, 1981.

STEINBERG, STEPHEN. *The Ethnic Myth: Race, Ethnicity, and Class in America*. Boston: Beacon Press, 1989.

STODDARD, ELLWYN R. "A Conceptual Analysis of the Alien Invasion: Institutionalized Support of Illegal Mexican Aliens in the United States." *International Migration Review* 10 (1976): 157–190.

———. *Maquila: Assembly Plants in Northern Mexico*. El Paso: Texas Western Press, 1987.

———. *Patterns of Poverty along the U.S.-Mexico Border*. El Paso: Center for Inter-American Studies, University of Texas at El Paso and Organization of U.S. Border Cities and Counties, 1978.

———. "Texas Higher Education and Border Funding Inequities: Implication for Border Universities and Transborder Cooperation." *Río Bravo: A Journal of Research and Issues* 2, no. 1 (1992): 54–75.

STODDARD, ELLWYN R., AND JOHN HEDDERSON. *Patterns of Poverty along the U.S.-Mexico Border*. Borderlands Research Monograph Series, no. 3. Las Cruces: Joint Border Research Institute, New Mexico State University, 1989.

TEXAS ATTORNEY GENERAL'S OFFICE. *Socioeconomic Characteristics of Colonia Areas in Hidalgo County: What the 1990 Census Shows*. Austin: Texas Attorney General's Office, 1993.

TEXAS DEPARTMENT OF HUMAN SERVICES. Office of Strategic Management, Research and Development. *Partnership for Self-Sufficiency: Public and Private Initiatives: 1989 Report and Recommendations*, by Penny H. Tisdale. Austin: Texas Department of Human Services, 1989.

———. *The Colonias Factbook: A Survey of Living Conditions in Rural Areas of South Texas and West Texas Border Counties*, by Exiquio Salinas. Austin: Texas Department of Human Services, 1988.

TEXAS NETWORK FOR ENVIRONMENTAL AND ECONOMIC JUSTICE. *Toxics in Texas and*

Their Impact on Communities of Color. Austin: Texas Center for Policy Studies, 1993.

TEXAS WATER DEVELOPMENT BOARD. *Water and Wastewater Needs of Texas Colonias, 1995 Update.* Austin: Texas Water Development Board, 1995.

THOMPSON, JERRY D. *Juan Cortina and the Texas-Mexico Frontier.* El Paso: Texas Western Press, 1994.

TISDALE, PENNY H. *See* Texas Department of Human Services.

UNIVERSITY OF TEXAS SYSTEM. TEXAS-MEXICO BORDER HEALTH COORDINATION OFFICE. *Texas-Mexico Border County Demographics and Health Statistics, 1994,* by Rumaldo Z. Juárez, Rubén E. Saenz, Armando López, Doreen D. Garza, Karen D. Fossom, and Alicia López-González. TMBHCO Series Report 93–94, no. 2. Edinburg, Tex.: Texas-Mexico Border Health Coordination Office, University of Texas System, 1994.

——. *Lower Rio Grande Valley Demographics and Health Statistics, 1994,* by Rumaldo Z. Juárez, Rubén E. Saenz, Armando López, Doreen D. Garza, Karen D. Fossom, and Alicia López-González. Edinburg, Tex.: Texas-Mexico Border Health Coordination Office, University of Texas System, 1994.

URREA, LUIS ALBERTO. *Across the Wire: Life and Hard Times on the Mexican Border.* New York: Doubleday, Anchor Books, 1993.

U.S. COMMISSION ON AGRICULTURAL WORKERS. *Report of the Commission on Agricultural Workers.* 4 vols. Washington, D.C.: Commission on Agricultural Workers, 1993.

U.S. CONGRESS. COMMISSION ON SECURITY AND COOPERATION IN EUROPE. *Migrant Farmworkers in the United States: Briefings of the Commission on Security and Cooperation in Europe.* Washington, D.C.: U.S. Commission on Security and Cooperation in Europe, 1993.

——. House. Select Committee on Hunger. *Colonias: A Third World within Our Borders: Hearing before the Select Committee on Hunger.* Hearing held in Eagle Pass, Tex., 15 May 1989. 101st Cong., 1st sess., 1990.

U.S. DEPARTMENT OF COMMERCE, ECONOMICS, AND STATISTICAL ADMINISTRATION. Bureau of the Census. *Statistical Abstract of the United States: 1994,* 114th ed. Product Profile, no. 13. Washington, D.C.: U.S. Government Printing Office, 1995.

U.S. ENVIRONMENTAL PROTECTION AGENCY. Office of Pesticides and Toxic Substances. *EPA's Pesticide Programs.* Washington, D.C.: U.S. Environmental Protection Agency, 1992.

——. Office of Policy, Planning, and Evaluation. *Environmental Equity: Reducing Risk for All Communities.* Washington, D.C.: U.S. Environmental Protection Agency, 1992.

U.S. GENERAL ACCOUNTING OFFICE. *Hired Farm Workers: Health and Well-Being at Risk: Report to Congressional Requesters.* Washington, D.C.: U.S. General Accounting Office, 1992.

VALDÉS, DENNIS NODÍN. "Historical Foundations of Latino Immigration and Community Formation in Twentieth-Century Michigan and the Midwest." In *Immigration and Ethnic Communities: A Focus on Latinos,* edited by Refugio I. Rochin, 30–38. East Lansing: Julian Samora Research Institute, Michigan State University, 1996.

VALLE, ISABEL. *Fields of Toil: A Migrant Family's Journey.* Pullman: Washington State University Press, 1994.

VINCENT, VERN, NADER ASGARY, GILBERTO DE LOS SANTOS, AND VICTOR DÁVILA. *1994–95 Winter Visitor Survey.* Edinburg: College of Business Administration, University of Texas–Pan American, 1996.

WEBER, MAX. *Max Weber on the Methodology of the Social Sciences.* 1922. Reprint, Glencoe, Ill.: Free Press, 1949.

———. *The Protestant Ethic and the Spirit of Capitalism.* Translated by Talcott Parsons. With a foreword by R. H. Tawney. 1905. Reprint, New York: Scribner's Sons, 1958.

WEEKS, JOHN R., AND ROBERTO HAM-CHANDE, eds. *Demographic Dynamics of the U.S.-Mexico Border.* El Paso: Texas Western Press, 1992.

WEST, CORNEL. *Race Matters.* Boston: Beacon Press, 1993.

WILLIAMS, NORMA. *The Mexican American Family: Tradition and Change.* Dix Hills, N.Y.: General Hall, 1993.

WILSON, WILLIAM J. *The Declining Significance of Race: Blacks and Changing American Institutions,* 2d ed. Chicago: University of Chicago Press, 1980.

WORLD BANK. *World Development Report.* New York: Oxford University Press, 1988.

YBARRA, LEA. "Empirical and Theoretical Developments in the Study of the Chicano Family." In *The State of Chicano Research on Family, Labor, and Migration,* edited by Armando Valdéz, Albert Carrillo, and Tomás Almaguer, 214–238. Stanford: Stanford Center for Chicano Research, 1983.

Index

accommodation: compared to assimilation, 236–239; defined, 237; an explanation of minority adjustment, 16

achieved status, 230–236

Acuña, Rodolfo, 267n.4

African Americans: bias against by Latinos, 271n.4; desires for inclusion/assimilation, 211–212; desires for separate identity, 211, 212; experiences with bigotry, 214–215; factors related to small population size in South Texas and Mexico, 213, 271n.3; history in the Rio Grande Valley, 212–213; identity, 27; importance of maintaining culture among, 219, 221–222; isolation in South Texas, 215–219; perceptions of Hispanic culture, 215; pressures to assimilate Hispanic culture, 220–222; problems with Spanish, 218; relations with Hispanics in South Texas, 213–222; stereotypes, 214–216;

alien smugglers, 73–74, 161

Alvarez, Rodolfo, 267n.7

Anglo Newcomer Exploratory Interviews, 184–185

Anglo Newcomer Survey, 185, 187–188, 200

Anglo newcomers, definition of, 270n.4

Anglo settlers, violence against Mexican Americans, 9

Anglos in South Texas: adjustment process, 183–189; assimilation, 184–196; bigotry among, 189; bilingual, 189–193; comparisons of newcomers with Valley natives, 187–189, 201; discrimination perceptions among, 184–201; ethnocentrism and bigotry, 177, 178–181; exclusion by Valley Hispanics, 199–201; forms of interaction with Hispanics, 185–201; lower perceptions of discrimination among bilingual Anglos, 189–193; as a

minority, xiii–xiv; monolingualism among, 186–189; perceptions of Hispanic culture, 193–196; preferential treatment by some Hispanics, 197–198; relations with Mexican Americans in South Texas schools, 123–152; resentment of use of Spanish in South Texas, 184–191; stereotypes among Hispanics, 197–198; stereotypes of Mexico, 178–179

ascribed status, 230–236

assimilation: as an adaptive mode among some Mexican Americans, 236–238; Anglicized names as a form of, 241, 242; defined, 236; different for Mexicans than for other nationalities, 163; as an explanation of minority adjustment, 16; factors related to, 242–243; importance of frequent visits to Mexico, 163; importance of proximity to Mexico for, 243; as a multigeneration process, 153; problems for Blacks caused by, 220–221; subtypes of, 238; as a three-generation process, 268n.1

BARCA. *See* Border Association for Refugees and Colonia Advocacy

batos, defined, xv

battlefields in Rio Grande Valley, 1

bigotry: among Anglos in Valley, 189; among Hispanics in Valley, 198–199; defined, 115; examples of, 116; a form of racism, 217, 219; internalization, 137

bilingual Anglos, lower perceptions of discrimination among, 189–193.

bilingual education, 130–131; as a form of tracking, 131; as a means of assimilation, 130

bilingualism, advantages of in South Texas, 185–196.

Blacks. *See* African Americans

bolillos, defined, xv, 183